UTB **2526**

W0172769

Eine Arbeitsgemeinschaft der Verlage

Beltz Verlag Weinheim · Basel
Böhlau Verlag Köln · Weimar · Wien
Verlag Barbara Budrich Opladen · Farmington Hills
facultas.wuv Wien
Wilhelm Fink München
A. Francke Verlag Tübingen und Basel
Haupt Verlag Bern · Stuttgart · Wien
Julius Klinkhardt Verlagsbuchhandlung Bad Heilbrunn
Lucius & Lucius Verlagsgesellschaft Stuttgart
Mohr Siebeck Tübingen
C. F. Müller Verlag Heidelberg
Orell Füssli Verlag Zürich
Verlag Recht und Wirtschaft Frankfurt am Main
Ernst Reinhardt Verlag München · Basel
Ferdinand Schöningh Paderborn · München · Wien · Zürich
Eugen Ulmer Verlag Stuttgart
UVK Verlagsgesellschaft Konstanz
Vandenhoeck & Ruprecht Göttingen
vdf Hochschulverlag AG an der ETH Zürich

MICHAEL MEYER

English and American Literatures

3., überarbeitete und erweiterte Auflage

UTB basics

A. Francke Verlag Tübingen und Basel

Michael Meyer ist Professor für Anglistik an der Universität Koblenz-Landau.

Umschlagabbildung: Atelier Reichert unter Verwendung eines Fotos von Michael Flaig.

Bibliografische Information der Deutschen Nationalbibliothek

Die Deutsche Nationalbibliothek verzeichnet diese Publikation in der Deutschen National-
bibliografie; detaillierte bibliografische Daten sind im Internet über <http://dnb.d-nb.de> abrufbar.

3., überarbeitete und erweiterte Auflage 2008
2., überarbeitete Auflage 2005
1. Auflage 2004

© 2008 · Narr Francke Attempto Verlag GmbH + Co. KG
Dischingerweg 5 · D-72070 Tübingen
ISBN 978-3-7720-8255-9

Internet: http//www.francke.de
E-Mail: info@francke.de

Satz, Layout und Einbandgestaltung: Atelier Reichert, Stuttgart
Druck und Bindung: CPI – Ebner & Spiegel, Ulm
Printed in Germany

ISBN 978-3-8252-2526-1 (UTB-Bestellnummer)

Contents

Prefaces VII

1   Introduction   1
1.1   What is literature?   4
1.2   Literary criticism   10
1.3   Literary history   14
1.4   Bibliography   18

2   Poetry   21
2.1   What are poetic texts and what do we (ab)use them for?   22
2.2   Communication, speaker, situation and topic   26
2.3   Rhetorical form   30
2.4   Poetic form   41
2.4.1 Metre and rhythm   41
2.4.2 Phonological forms, stanzas and types of poems   45
2.5   Postmodern poetry   51
2.6   Guiding questions and exercises   52
2.7   Bibliography   56

3   Narrative   59
3.1   Oral and written narratives   60
3.2   Discourse   63
3.2.1 Narrative situations   63
3.2.2 Voice and focalisation   69
3.2.3 Time   76
3.3   Story   79
3.4   Fiction and metafiction   84
3.5   Guiding questions and exercises   85
3.6   Bibliography   91

4   Drama   95
4.1   Dramatic text and theatrical performance   96
4.2   Verbal communication   99
4.3   Character and action 105
4.4   Place and time 115

4.5   Guiding questions and exercises 120
4.6   Bibliography 126

5   **Literary Theory** 131
5.1   Author 135
5.1.1   Psychoanalysis 137
5.2   Text and code 143
5.2.1   New Criticism 143
5.2.2   Formalism, structuralism and semiotics 145
5.2.3   Deconstructivism, post-structuralism
        and postmodernism 150
5.3   Context 155
5.3.1   Marxism and cultural materialism 155
5.3.2   New Historicism 161
5.3.3   Feminism and gender studies 164
5.3.4   Postcolonialism and multiculturalism 169
5.4   Reader 175
5.5   Bibliography 180

6   **Research papers, presentations and examinations** 185
6.1   Academic standards 186
6.2   Getting organised 186
6.3   Writing a term paper 187
6.3.1   Defining topic, purpose and approach 187
6.3.2   Research for and use of secondary material 190
6.3.3   Writing the first draft 194
6.3.4   Revising the paper 195
6.3.5   Documentation 195
6.4   Presentation 198
6.5   Oral and written examinations 202
6.6   Bibliography 204

7   **Appendix** 225
7.1   Analyses 226
7.2   Index 232
7.3   Acknowledgements 241

Preface

This introduction to analysing literature is intended to bridge the gap between students' needs and academic requirements. It addresses students' difficulties with technical terms and issues in literary studies without oversimplifying matters. Providing helpful tools for reading and research, this book primarily addresses students in the first semesters but is designed to be also helpful for preparing final examinations. The text

▶ concentrates on the major literary genres,
▶ provides many examples from various historical periods,
▶ explains how and why to use approaches and technical terms,
▶ presents a set of guiding questions for the analysis of texts,
▶ offers exercises to practise analysis and interpretation,
▶ comments on and recommends further reading,
▶ gives comprehensive checklists to enable students to cope with papers, presentations and examinations,
▶ concludes with an index of technical terms, authors and titles.

The text highlights key terms in **bold letters** at their first appearance and central statements in *italics*. Wherever the German term differs markedly in spelling, it is provided (*in parentheses*). This book cannot sketch the histories of literatures in English around the world but gives a first overview of the generic and historical variety of literary texts mainly from Great Britain and the United States. The selection of examples follows that of major anthologies and literary histories. The nationality and biographical dates of authors as well as the year of publication are given where available. At the end of each chapter, the lists of works mark titles strongly recommended for further reading with an asterisk*.

The chapters subsequent to the introduction can be read in any order. The structure of the book follows systematic and pragmatic considerations for teaching and studying literature and literary theory. Beginning with the basic analysis of texts from each genre allows you to see how additional approaches provide new questions about and insights into these texts. The initial interpretation of poetry has the advantage of dealing with short texts at the beginning of the semester and of introducing terms of rhetorics, which are helpful for understanding texts from other genres as well. An additional reading of a few short stories and a drama would perfectly complement the texts discussed here.

This introduction is dedicated to my students, whose questions made me repeatedly search for better explanations and examples. My warm thanks go to my students, colleagues and friends Kerstin Eichler, Andreas Eul, Karin Lange, Elin Meek, Anja Müller-Muth, Mary Reid, Monika Reif, Christoph Reinfandt, Isabella Rotsch, Alexander Stützer and Kenneth Wynne, whose comments on various chapters helped me to reconsider and rewrite them. I also thank the editor Stephan Dietrich for his great patience and support. Of course, all remaining mistakes are entirely my fault.

If you have any comments, questions or suggestions, feel free to write to mimeyer@uni-koblenz.de.

Preface to the third edition

The third edition defines more subgenres and adds examples in order to provide a better insight into the historical development of the genres and to offer more texts for discussion. The section on literary theory has been expanded to accommodate more concepts and present a more comprehensive, but still concise, overview of major contemporary approaches to literature. The introduction of basic questions and concepts for a close analysis of texts does not advocate New Critical readings but is meant to provide a basic understanding of specific features of genres. A sophisticated and up-to-date interpretation would combine the perspective of a contemporary approach with particular questions on the genre of the text under discussion, such as an analysis of the gendered composition of a narrative.

Many thanks go to colleagues and students who provided me with feedback on the third edition, such as Sandra Bornstedt, Christoph Houswitschka and Paul Schmuecker, to Karoline Oeser and the editor Kathrin Heyng for their help, my wife Stephanie and my daughter Sarah for their patience.

M. M.

Introduction |1

Contents

1.1	What is literature?	4
1.2	Literary criticism	10
1.3	Literary history	14
1.4	Bibliography	18

Abstract

This chapter gives a brief sketch of the scope of English and American literatures and of the basic disciplines that define literary studies, theory, criticism and history, all of which are interrelated.

Studies serve for delight, for ornament, and for ability. Their chief use for delight is in privateness and retiring; for ornament, is in discourse; and for ability, is in the judgement and disposition of business.
Francis Bacon, "Of Studies" (1625).

Studying English and American literatures gives you access to a wealth of numerous cultures around the world. Besides the obvious suspects of English nationality, "English" literatures include literature written in English by Welsh, Scottish, Anglo-Irish and "Black British" authors, an awkward umbrella term for non-white immigrants or residents in England. *Anglistik* also covers the huge variety of New English Literatures or postcolonial literatures in English written by authors from former colonies. Besides literature written by white authors in (American) English, American literature also comprises "ethnic" (and sometimes multilingual) literatures written within the United States, such as African American, Asian American, Chicano, Indian and Jewish. For historical, political, cultural and geographical reasons, Caribbean and Canadian literatures in English are contested territories between *Anglistik* and *Amerikanistik*. It is impossible to read everything. Take a look at the *Studienordnung* and the *Prüfungsordnung* in order to get an overview of the requirements and your options, and take the opportunity to broaden your horizon beyond the traditional canon of books by "dead white men".

Literary studies: theory, criticism, history

The literary representation of experience allows the reader to share imaginatively others' interpretations of different worlds. Studying literature expands the understanding of (fictional) texts by systematic reflections on what literature is, how it relates to history and culture, and how we can read it in order to arrive at interesting and well-founded insights. (In general terms, studying English and American literatures expands our knowledge of vocabulary and fosters the skills of reading, speaking, writing and intercultural communication in English). **Literary Studies** (roughly: *Literaturwissenschaft*) are defined by three disciplines, which are interrelated: literary theory, criticism and history.

Literary theory (Greek *theorein*: to observe) simply means reflection and poses the questions: what is literature, how does it come into existence, and what does it do for which reasons? The answers to these questions usually imply assumptions about individual identity, society and culture, and suggest a particular **approach** (*Zugang*, *Methode*), a guideline on reading texts.

If you think that you do not need any theory to understand literature, ask yourself why you understand literature the way you do. Literary theory

▶ raises our awareness of what we are doing when we read literature,

▶ provides us with new perspectives and concepts to analyse texts,

▶ helps us to understand secondary material, and

▶ to communicate our own insights to others (Nünning, *Grundkurs* 45).

Literary criticism (*Literaturkritik, Analyse, Interpretation*) describes, analyses, interprets and evaluates literary works in two basic ways: the reader either records his/her more or less subjective impressions of the text or presents an approach that explains its questions and terms of analysis in theoretically informed criticism, which is the aim of literary studies. Its result would be a critique, a serious and profound essay or article.

Literary history (re)constructs the development of literature, taking into account theoretical assumptions, criticism and historical contexts. Literary histories establish and revise a **canon** of works (a list of important texts) and therefore influence what is mainly read at schools and universities. All disciplines are subject to change, and so is literary history. Feminist theory and criticism, for example, boosted the re-reading of "forgotten" women's texts and the rewriting of literary histories in order to include the female tradition.

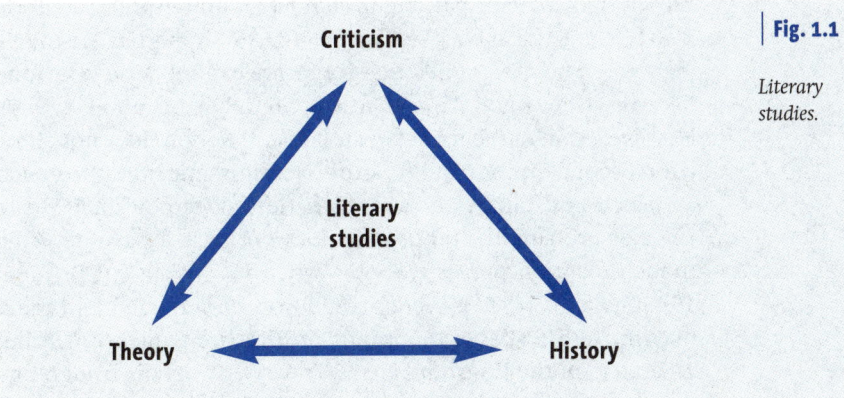

Fig. 1.1

Literary studies.

1.1 | **What is literature?**

It is easier to say why we read literature than to define what literature is. However, our motivation to read literature implies fundamental ideas about what it is, which are in turn closely related to how we read it. Readers are often interested in (1) the world that literature reveals, (2) the entertainment and/or instruction it provides, (3) the author's experience or view of life expressed in it, or (4) the artistic quality of the text itself. We use **extrinsic** information to study the mimetic image of reality, the pragmatic effect upon readers and the expressive origin within the writer. **Intrinsic** readings focus on the text itself (Abrams 6-7). All of these motives have figured for centuries in debates about the nature and function of literature. These discussions show that *literature does not own essential qualities but is rather defined by writers' and readers' negotiations of literary conventions*. Here, I will simply introduce some implications of the various interests, preparing the ground for the presentation of major modern theories in chapter 5.

Aristotle: mimesis

1 Aristotle (384-322 BC) defined **mimesis**, *the imitation of reality*, as a major function of literature in response to Plato (429-347 BC), who denigrated literature as a lie because it represented "appearance rather than truth" (Abrams 9). Aristotle conceded that literature does not give us the factual truth of history but probable truth, something that might have happened as against what did happen. However, he considered literature superior to history because it deals with general and fundamental truth rather than that of particular characters and events (Aristotle 29-31). The English poet Sidney (1554-1586) supported Aristotle's view when he maintained that literature cannot deceive anyone because it does not claim that it is literally true (NAEL 1: 947). However, the boundary between fact and fiction does not allow a foolproof definition of literature. Non-mimetic literature, such as fairy tales, fantasy or science-fiction, does not stick to the rules of probability and usually does not pass for reality. A famous exception proves the rule: when H.G. Wells's (GB, 1866-1946) novel *War of the Worlds* (1898) was broadcasted as a radio play in the US (1938), thousands of listeners panicked, fearing an attack on the US from Mars. – Travel writing, historiography and the essay may cross the border into fictional territory, shap-

ing characters and events according to aesthetic criteria, whereas novels and plays sometimes cannibalise reality for their characters, stories and settings, even if the fictional frame changes their function. – How can we understand the ways in which literature imitates reality? Literature transforms *conceptions* of reality with the help of aesthetic means, such as particular images, constructions of characters, sequences of action, etc. Literature creates possible worlds that can serve as a comment about the "real" world.

2 The Roman writer Horace (65-68 BC) claimed that literature serves the readers' need for **pleasure and/or profit** (Latin *aut delectare aut prodesse*). To define literary pleasure in more modern terms: literature provides an **aesthetic experience** (Greek *aisthesis:* perception; *ästhetische Erfahrung*). This experience can be described as an emotional and imaginative involvement in literature, which often takes the form of sympathy, delight in beauty, amusement, suspense, terror, horror, often accompanied by an intellectual stimulation to reflect on the language, order and meaning of art. "People mutht be amuthed. They can't always be a'learning and a'working", says the lisping director of the circus in Charles Dickens's novel *Hard Times* (1854: 308). Dickens's novel, which resembles contemporary soap operas, is not only sentimental and entertaining but appeals to the reader's **moral and political judgement**. *Hard Times* criticises the heartless and greedy employer and the furious and manipulative unionist alike, opting for a mutually respectful and humane cooperation between capitalists and workers: literature, the school of the nation? Some genres often carry explicit moral messages: fables, didactic poetry, satires or Christian literature, such as John Bunyan's (England, 1628-88) *Pilgrim's Progress* (1678/84), which shows the model way to resist temptation in order to enter heaven. In reverse, Puritans have argued that plays and novels corrupt people because they present examples of immoral behaviour. Even recently, *Harry Potter* came under Christian fire for allegedly leading children astray by promoting interest in magic, occult and evil forces. However, literature does not claim to serve as a guidebook to practical life. The famous Spanish author Cervantes (1547-1616) ridiculed Don Quixote (1605/15), who sees the early modern world according to medieval romances and mistakes himself for a knight in shining armour in heroic strug-

Horace: pleasure and profit

gle against giants, which are nothing other than windmills. The fictional character Joe Savage, whose values of love, manners and dignity are based upon Shakespeare's plays, cannot cope with the futurist *Brave New World* (1932) by Aldous Huxley (GB, 1894-1963) and would be lost in today's permissive and consumerist society. – Books or films may influence what people think about but do not determine how they think about it. We can hardly claim that "readers of literature do it better", that they are *per se* superior human beings and citizens or that literature presents universal values. Contemporary western female readers would not accept the gendered norms of *Hard Times*, which idealises very gentle, submissive and selfless women. Due to historical and cultural changes in taste and in values, contemporary readers may find neither delight nor instruction in literary works which were bestsellers in their time. Thus, *the provision of entertainment and learning is not a steadfast criterion of literature itself but subject to changing attributions*. While the mimetic model of literature stresses its function as a mirror of reality and the pragmatic model its effect upon the reader, the expressive model emphasises the role of the author as the origin of art (Abrams 26).

Wordsworth: expression

3 The English Romantic William Wordsworth (1770-1850) regarded literature primarily as the **author's subjective expression** of his/her emotions and imagination, and in turn read literature as an image of the author's personality (NAEL 2: 250). If the spontaneous and true expression of the inner self was the goal, the perception of external reality, the conventional literary rules and the traditional expectations of the audience were rather in the way. The individual genius created poetic rules of his/her own and was his/her own best reader. The poet ignored or tried to shape the taste of the reader, who could appreciate the text and share the subjective experience in an imaginative response. *While all literature is expressive in the restricted sense that it must have been experienced in the author's mind before it is written down on paper, the question is whether the search for the author's expression finds or rather constructs the personality that is assumed to be behind the text.* Apart from the three extrinsic models mentioned above, the intrinsic one deals with the text itself.

Poe: art for art's sake

4 The American Edgar Allan Poe (1809-49) proclaimed that literature is a purely **aesthetic object** with no reference to reality: it is art

for art's sake. Poe's "Poetic Principle" (1848) rejects the mimetic and moral functions as criteria of literary value: "this poem which is a poem and nothing more – this poem [is] written solely for the poem's sake" (NAAL 1: 1470). Poe stressed the musical language and "*The Rhythmical Creation of Beauty*" (NAAL 1: 1472) in poetry. The English poet and critic Matthew Arnold (1822-88) underlined the "synthesis and exposition" of ideas in "beautiful works" (NAEL 2: 1516). In turn, the critic's task was simply "to see the object as in itself it really is" (NAEL 2: 1514) and to contemplate the ideas revealed in great literature in a disinterested way. While Arnold said that we read poetry "to interpret our life for us, to console us, to sustain us" (NAEL 2: 1535), to form and to cultivate us, he maintained that we should not draw any conclusions that concern practical behaviour in the material world. His assumption that unique works of genius embody universal values corresponds to his demand to leave personal likings and historical preferences out of "objective" literary judgements (NAEL 2: 1536).

In sum, the four traditional perspectives on literature as aesthetic imitation, effect, production and object hardly reveal any self-evident essence of literature but contradictory as well as complementary attributions of its nature, function and value. – As an aesthetic object, every literary text is bound to a genre and to a medium.

Genres *form a system of groups or families of texts defined by sets of conventions, which guide both the writing and reading of texts.* Genres are often distinguished by the form of communication (e.g. narrative, drama), mood or attitude (elegy, satire), content (crime, science-fiction), the relation to reality (mimetic vs. non-mimetic) and aesthetic effect (comedy, horror) or a combination of these criteria. For example, besides content and aesthetic effect, Aristotle used the form of communication in order to distinguish between three basic literary genres: in poetry, only the poet speaks; in drama, actors/characters act and speak, and in epic narrative, the author reports other characters' actions. *A genre is a useful if fuzzy model of a text, which is distinguished by differences from other genres of its time, but which also changes over time.* Contemporary poetry, for example, often ignores metre and rhyme, which have been hallmarks of the genre for centuries. Individual texts follow a genre or deviate from models by combining genres (e.g. verse novel, epic drama) or by intro-

Literary genres

ducing new elements to a genre (physical love, three quartets and a couplet in English Renaissance sonnets in contrast to the Petrarchan model of idealised love, two quartets and two tercets; see 2.4.2, 48-49).

Medium: oral literature

The function of the **medium** cannot be reduced to the mere material form of literature because it is closely related to the ways of communication. Orality (*Mündlichkeit*) is based on contact, participation and community. Oral literature or orature takes place in face-to-face interaction and therefore includes voice, facial expression, gesture and movement to support understanding. Oral presentations of poems or stories take into account the kind, situation and response of the audience, a fact that results in unique performances, which vary the topic, length and complexity of the texts. Orature has existed since time immemorial and is still of great importance in many cultures in Africa, Australia, New Zealand and among Canadian and American Indians. In Anglo-American cultures, radio plays use one-way oral communication at a distance. Poetry slams revive the communal experience of the oral tradition.

Medium: written literature

In comparison to oral texts, the texts of written literature in print (versus manuscript versions) are much more stable. The rise of literature is related to a market of literate customers served by publishers. Print allows the distribution of a text among a large circle of readers even beyond its contemporary culture and history, which considerably increases not only an author's potential readership but also his/her distance from it. In turn, individual readers often need considerable aesthetic knowledge in order to relate to the position of the potential addressee of a text and may want additional cultural and historical knowledge in order to understand it.

Medium: audiovisual literature

Literature is transformed into an audiovisual spectacle in the theatre and the cinema. In contrast to the individual reader of a written text, who can determine the pace of his/her own reception, the communal audience is subject to the rhythm and duration of the performance. The relatively short duration of a show demands the reduction of content and complexity in comparison to a novel. The interplay of verbal and visual signs makes high demands on the spectator. Films combine the audiovisual quality of the theatre with the telling of a story. In addition to setting, lighting, sound, actors and performance, films mediate visual information by (1) camera work, its distance, angle and movement relative to the object, determining the point-of-view, and (2) editing, i.e. the structuring of the cuts, sequence and rhythm of shots. Modern videorecorders and DVD-players allow the spectator to individualise his/her reception of a film as if he/she was reading a book, winding backwards and forwards, slowing down or speeding up the film. Finally, hypertext literature can integrate voice, text, image and film, and create various options for the user to listen to, read, view or even co-author the multimedia text.

The following diagram of literary communication adds the element of the codes (rules, conventions) to the four traditional perspectives. The previous discussion revealed that the aesthetic quality of literature is hardly an inherent essence of the text but results from the historical negotiation of conventions that prescribe how to write and read literature of various genres in various media and cultures.

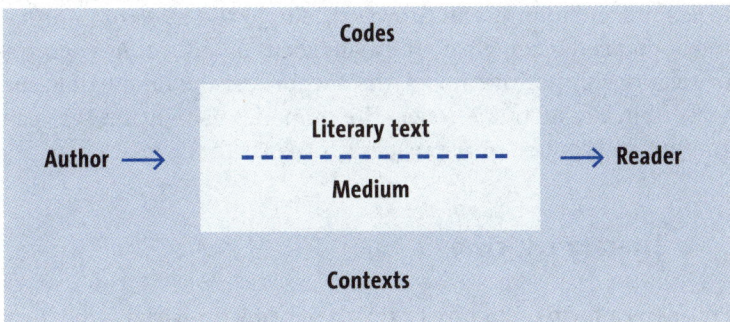

Codes

Literary text

Author ⟶ - - - - - - - - - - - - - - - ⟶ **Reader**

Medium

Contexts

Fig. 1.2

Literary communication (compare Korte 79 and Nünning, Grundkurs 12).

This model reduces literary communication to the author and the reader, ignoring for the sake of clarity publishers, critics, teachers and booksellers, who convey books to buyers and therefore enable literary communication. Usually, *literary communication is asymmetric, excluding a dialogue between reader and author, and non-pragmatic, ignoring immediately practical information*, such as how to repair a bicycle or to prepare mulligatawny soup. In contrast to the precise factual information of a good newspaper article, which should leave no doubt about its meaning, *literature offers ambiguous (vieldeutige) aesthetic information, which is open to different interpretations*. The codes mean the rules of language and aesthetic conventions of genres, which are closely related to cultural norms. The

Codes and contexts

contexts are formed by cultural circumstances in a wide sense. In a novel about contemporary life, the author, the text and the first generation of readers share the social, economic and political contexts. If we want to understand historical literature written before our time, it is useful to relate the context of its writing to the historical era referred to in the text: the play *The Crucible* (1953) about the witch-hunt in 17th century Puritan Salem by the American Arthur Miller (US, 1915-2005) can be read as a scathing comment on Senator McCarthy's persecution of left-winged Americans in the 1950s. The production of the text, as we have noticed, is not only based on the author's subjective imagination but also on aesthetic conventions or codes, the medium and the historical context. In turn, the reader needs to activate his/her everyday knowledge and literary competence in order to understand the text in its particular medium, assuming the role of a listener, reader, spectator or co-author as need be. Depending upon the expressive or mimetic function of the text, the reader would consider biographical or historical information useful. However, due to the mass of information a detailed reading would usually focus on one of the concepts or relationships of the model, the author and the production, the text itself, the aesthetic codes, the mimetic relationship between content and context or the reader's response to the text.

1.2 | Literary criticism

Editing is a form of literary criticism of prime importance because it precedes our reading of books. A reliable text is fundamental to literary criticism. Careful editors compare different versions of a text, often in manuscript, in order to establish a **critical edition** of the text that comes close to the author's last intentions. Recently, editors have also returned to print the early versions of the text in order to come close to the original intention. A critical edition often records various versions of the text and the editor's emendations in a critical apparatus. An **annotated edition** (*kommentierte Ausgabe*), which explains particular uses of words, references and allusions to the historical context, supports an adequate historical understanding of a text.

Literary scholars often make a difference between **hermeneutical interpretation**, which tries to understand *what a text means* in terms of its content and concepts, and the **analysis of poetics**, which tries to describe and explain *how a text creates meaning* by its structure or composition (Culler 58). This difference in focus does not imply that hermeneutics does without rhetoric and aesthetics because it deals with expression in language (Gadamer 28). Art criticism may serve as a vivid example of the difference between interpretation and analysis.

Task

▶ Look at the content and at the composition of Van Gogh's picture and draw your conclusions of what the picture means and how it creates meaning.

Fig.1.3

Vincent van Gogh (1853-1890), Field, 1888 (Collection J. W. Böhler, Lucerne).

We can look at the content and at the artistic form of representation in alternation but hardly at the same time. If you look at the content of Van Gogh's drawing, you can almost see the wind sending ripples across the field on a cloudless summer day and assume that the grain in the foreground has been flattened by a thunderstorm, which disturbed the rural idyll and ruined a part of the harvest. The hermeneutic critic could interpret the picture as an expression of the bouts of madness, from which the painter and his productivity suffered, or generalise the meaning as the intrusion of chaos in peace or as the containment of disorder, given the "right" visual, temporal or cognitive distance towards events.

Looking at the composition, you can see the hand of the artist in the vivid strokes of his pen. Broad, circular and irregular lines in the foreground create movement and perspective in combination with more regular, parallel lines and small, seemingly random dots in the middle ground. The dynamic design of the foreground and the centre of the picture is framed by parallel, closely set lines in the left and right of the picture, which end in a ridge of vertical lines, contained by a double horizontal line (the ridge of hills), which is occasionally pierced by irregular, spiralling strokes. It is a perfect composition that creates harmony of strong opposites (*concordia discors*), in the extreme between the blank, nearly untouched space of the sky in the background and the strongly, almost violently marked foreground. The composition could be read as self-referential in the sense that a wide panorama and far distance towards objects suggest a sense of order and control, which is lost if things are too close at hand.

The aesthetic analysis is less interested in the representation of a field in a rural landscape, which is an ordinary topic, than in its particular artistic shape, which is rather interesting. The hermeneutic interpretation given above draws on experience, historical and cultural knowledge, but is also based on the reading of the aesthetic signs of the drawing: you have to know what the lines represent in order to talk about their meaning. Reading a text, you also have to make sense of the words, the syntax and the imagery to understand characters, actions and circumstances, and vice versa. *The strategies of reading this picture can be transferred to a text, taking external circumstances as an expression of an internal state of mind (landscape – Van Gogh), the literal meaning as a basis of the metaphorical one, and the particular as an instance of general significance (danger of disorder in peace; control by distance).*

Hermeneutics

Hermeneutic understanding works according to a *circular model of the whole and the part: our experience and presuppositions (Vorwissen) form the basis of comprehending new information, which, in turn, adds to and alters our previous knowledge.* Contextual knowledge is as important to understanding as intertextual knowledge, i.e. the relationship between the text in question and others. A general knowledge of literary conventions is a prerequisite to reading a novel as fiction and not as history. In turn a particular novel may expand our conception of aesthetic rules. On a smaller scale, a complete sentence or poem makes sense due to the selection and combination of its words, and the meaning of each word is related to its context in the sentence or the poem. If presuppositions shape our understanding, we run the risk of limiting our experience because we may only see what we know. In order to diminish the danger of merely reasserting our own opinion, it is useful to reconsider what we know of a particular subject and genre at the beginning of an interpretation. If interpretation means entering into a **dialogue** with a text (Gadamer 30), the text must not be reduced to giving answers to our questions, which would mistake literature of the more or less remote past as a solution to contemporary problems of making sense of life. An open dialogue with a text includes the option that the text might question our identity, knowledge or values. If the *process of reading alternates between an involvement in aesthetic experience and a detachment from it,* we can become aware of how our presuppositions influence our understanding of the text and how the text changes our assumptions. Therefore, the hermeneutic circle also refers to the interrelationship between the reader's understanding of him/herself and of a text or an other. For example, in Bram Stoker's (Ireland, 1847-1911) novel *Dracula* (1897), the characters' personal records reveal as much about the vampire as about the characters' desires and fears because they "read" Dracula as a powerful and evil sexual danger.

The circular nature of understanding implies that reading is an unending process and only arrives at preliminary interpretations. An adult re-reading of children's books, especially highly ambiguous ones, such as A. A. Milne's (GB, 1882-1956) *Winnie the Pooh* (1926) or Lewis Carroll's (GB, 1832-98) *Alice's Adventures in Wonderland* (1865), would certainly result in utterly different interpretations from those of childhood times. (For more information on hermeneutics, please see 5.1 and 5.4).

Whether scholarly literary criticism emphasises the question of composition or content, it is required to proceed with awareness of its theoretical assumptions, using well-defined concepts in a systematic and comprehensible way. The subsequent chapters on analysing poetry, narrative and drama, as well as the chapter on theory will suggest useful approaches.

1.3 | Literary history

Literary history (re)constructs literary traditions in particular contexts and periods, posing these questions: why should certain texts and genres be included in or excluded from the canon of "important" texts? How and why did certain texts and genres come into existence? How does a text derive from and depart from specific genres? Which non-literary contexts are relevant to a text? What is the function of literature in its cultural context? The answers to these questions are themselves subject to history and depend upon changing contemporary perspectives on literatures and cultures.

Canon

The selection of "important" authors, genres and texts is related to a canon of established writers and works. Even if some literary histories cover thousands of titles, the great majority of all the texts that have ever been written has been discarded or forgotten. What is important? Innovative texts and/or popular books have a claim to fame. For example, Horace Walpole's (England, 1717-97) *The Castle of Otranto* (1765) initiated the rise of the Gothic novel but probably amuses rather than terrifies readers today. Literature which used to be popular may no longer find favour with readers now, but it can still provide insight into the cultural mentality of the past. Recently, the canon of writers and works has been expanded due to the reconsideration of race, gender, additional genres and subgenres. Thus, Hans Ulrich Seeber's *Englische Literaturgeschichte* devotes its last section to the English literatures from Africa, Australia, Canada, the Caribbean, New Zealand and India. Hubert Zapf's *Amerikanische Literaturgeschichte* also includes a chapter on Canadian literature. Both volumes include extra chapters on women's literature and multicultural literatures written by immigrants to GB and the US because these texts reveal different topics, perspectives or forms. Childrens' literature, crime fiction or science-fiction are now deemed worthy of attention. While poetry, drama and narrative still form the main focus of literary histories, the number of texts included from other genres has expanded, such as autobiography, biography, the essay, historiography and literary theory.

Contexts

The same problem of selection and combination applies to the contexts of literature, economics, society, politics, education, philosophy, the arts, etc. It is difficult to represent the contexts in a

comprehensive way or to select merely one because different contexts are relevant to literature at different times.

Finally, *literary history requires the formation of concepts of periods, of*   Periods
boundaries and transitions between them. Particular events, texts and
contexts, shared assumptions and values are used to define a period. However, an era is often marked by characteristic contradictions and conflicts, and it is difficult to say where one ends and another begins.

It is of no use to deliver a fast-forward overview of literary histo-   A comparison of
ries, which must be simplistic and therefore false, and to drop   literary histories
dozens of names, titles and dates. Instead, a brief comparison of
two versions of British literary history between the end of the 18th
and the beginning of the 20th century reveals two major developments in the recent historiography of literature: *literature is no*
longer considered as a mirror of reality but part of an ongoing cultural ne-
gotiation of values, identities and truths; culture is no longer regarded as a
coherent unity but a process of different forces and ideas in rivalry with
each other. As a result, these literary histories have reassessed mar-
ginalised issues (gender, race), writers (women, "ethnic" writers)
and genres (conduct books, scientific treatises, etc.). The guiding
principle of Hans Ulrich Seeber's *Englische Literaturgeschichte* (1991)
is modernisation, which means secularisation, rationalisation, the
formation of national identities and nation states, the industrial
revolution, the development of democracy, individualisation, etc.
(ix). Ina Schabert's *Englische Literaturgeschichte. Eine neue Darstellung*
aus der Sicht der Geschlechterforschung (1997) concentrates on gender
as a cultural construct in contrast to the biological concept of sex.
Schabert analyses the literary negotiation of gender in connection
with social, economic, scientific and ideological contexts. She reverses the traditional bias that privileged men over women as authors, literary characters and readers. The following juxtaposition
of Seeber's and Schabert's table of contents of two periods represents the major headlines only, which clearly reveal the differences
in guiding principles and the construction of periods.

In Seeber's history, the Pre-Romantic period between 1760 and   Seeber's periodisation
1800 is part of the previous development. Pre-Romanticism reveals
a turn from "objective", timeless and rational neoclassical views of
nature and society towards subjective, time-bound and sentimental (*empfindsam, sentimental*) Romantic views. Seeber combines Romanticism and the Victorian Age under the key concept of mod-

Fig. 1.4

Selections from table of contents of Seeber's and Schabert's literary histories.

Hans Ulrich Seeber,
Englische Literaturgeschichte (1991):

ROMANTIK UND
VIKTORIANISCHE ZEIT
Modernisierung und Literatur im
19. Jahrhundert
Die Literatur der Romantik
Der Roman des 19. Jahrhunderts
Fortschrittsglaube und
Kulturkritik. Zur Prosa der
Viktorianer
Die Lyrik der Viktorianer
VORMODERNE UND MODERNE
Die Krise des Liberalismus und der
Modernisierung
Die Literatur der Übergangszeit
um 1900
Keltische Renaissance und irische
Literatur
Shaw und die Erneuerung des
britischen Dramas
Die modernistische Revolution
um 1910
Wirtschaftskrise, politische
Radikalisierung und Literatur in
den dreißiger Jahren

Ina Schabert,
*Englische Literaturgeschichte.
Eine neue Darstellung aus der Sicht
der Geschlechterforschung*
(1997):

5.   DIE NACHAUFKLÄRERISCHE ZEIT
     (1760-1830)
5.1. Die binäre Geschlechterordnung
     als Anliegen der Erzählliteratur
5.2 Die exklusive Männlichkeit
     der Romantik
5.3 Begehren und Angst: der
     Schauerroman
5.4 Schreibende Paare
5.5 Lyrik von Frauen 1790-1838
6.   DIE VIKTORIANISCHE EPOCHE
     (1830-1900)
6.1 Autorschaft und Geschlechter-
     maskerade
6.2 Geschlechterdifferenz in der Lyrik
6.3 Der Kult des Begehrens im
     Roman
6.4 Masculinities
6.5 Die Frau zwischen weiblicher
     Bestimmung und Selbst-
     gestaltung

ernisation in the 19th century but marks differences in responses to these changes. The French Revolution and the industrial revolution at the end of the 18th century initiated the fall of the old political and economic order and prepared the ground for the rise of capitalism and bourgeois society. For Seeber, highlighting individuality, subjective imagination and nature as a substitute for religion was the male poets' answer to economic and competitive individualism, mechanical rationalisation and metropolitan mass society (222). Whereas the (male) Romantic poets juxtaposed individual needs and social rules, Victorian novelists tried to achieve a compromise between individuals and society in spite of criticising the social and moral problems of modernisation. Seeber also takes into account the female tradition of Victorian novelists, Jane Austen, Anne, Charlotte and Emily Brontë, and George Eliot (male pen-name of Maria Ann Evans) but he mainly presents the canon of male authors, Charles Dickens, William Makepeace Thackeray, Anthony Trollope and George Meredith.

Schabert avoids the term Romanticism as the designation of a whole period because the concept does not adequately represent women's writing in what she calls the Post-Enlightenment Period, 1760-1830. She highlights the development of the binary model of gender between 1760-1830, which establishes a "natural" difference between men and women. The biological difference is linked to differences in sentiment and intellect and justifies the construction of segregated spheres, which reserves the public sphere of economic production for men and relegates women to the private sphere of biological reproduction at home. Whereas most male poets endorse the binary model of gender according to Schabert, women authors are divided over the issue. Schabert stresses that women poets, such as Anna Laetitia Barbauld and Helen Maria Williams, enjoyed popularity in their time, interacted and competed with the male poets William Wordsworth, Samuel Taylor Coleridge, Lord Byron, Percy Bysshe Shelley and John Keats (448-455). In addition to the canonical novelists Ann Radcliffe and Jane Austen, Schabert presents women writers who have been neglected in traditional literary histories, such as Frances Burney, the novelist and poet Charlotte Smith or the poet and playwright Joanna Baillie.

Schabert retains the conventional term Victorian Age (1830-1900), which refers to Queen Victoria's rule between 1837-1901, but redirects attention to the growing participation of women in aesthetic production as against their discriminating segregation. She claims that authors, above all female authors, question the prevalent opposition of gender constructions, combine male and female concepts and promote women's social and political emancipation. Schabert underlines the ambiguity of the Victorian ideal of manliness, which has homoerotic connotations, and gives voice to discontent with the marriage plot as a conservative patriarchal pattern, which subordinates women as wives to husbands. She stresses that the final decades of the 19th century pave the way for the

Schabert's
periodisation

modernist novel of consciousness and innovative female poetry, and dissolve the boundaries between gendered identities: "new" men deviate from heterosexual patriarchal norms and "new" women create autonomous selves. Thus, it seems that Schabert favours a history of women's progress, which overcomes setbacks by the end of the 19th century, whereas Seeber, who combines the late 19th and the early 20th century, stresses a development towards crisis and pessimism. For all the differences between these valuable literary histories, they do not exclude but complement each other. (For further reading, see also 6.6 Bibliography).

1.4 | Bibliography

PRIMARY SOURCES

Abrams, M. H., et al., eds. *The Norton Anthology of English Literature.* 7th ed. 2 vols. New York and London: Norton, 2000. (NAEL 1 and 2).

Baym, Nina, et al., eds. *The Norton Anthology of American Literature.* 3rd ed. 2 vols. New York and London: Norton, 1989. (NAAL 1 and 2).

Bunyan, John. *The Pilgrim's Progress.* With an Introd. and Notes by Roger Sharrock. Repr. London et al.: Penguin, 1987.

Carroll, Lewis. *Alice's Adventures in Wonderland and Through the Looking Glass.* Reissue. New York et al.: Penguin, 2001.

Cervantes Saavedra, Miguel de. *Don Quixote de la Mancha.* Oxford: Oxford University Press, 1998.

Dickens, Charles. *Hard Times: an Authoritative Text; Backgrounds, Sources, and Contemporary Reactions, Criticism.* 2nd ed. Ed. George Ford. New York et al.: Norton, 1990.

Huxley, Aldous. *Brave New World.* New ed. London: Vintage, 2004.

Milne, A. A. *Winnie-the-Pooh.* Illustr. E. H. Shepard. Ed. Barbara Rojahn-Deyk. Stuttgart: Reclam, 1988.

Rowling, Joanne K. *Harry Potter and the Philosopher's Stone.* London: Bloomsbury, 2000.

Stoker, Bram. *Dracula.* Ed. Nina Auerbach and David J. Skal. New York and London: Norton, 1997.

Walpole, Horace. *The Castle of Otranto: a Gothic Story.* Ed. W. S. Lewis. Reissued with New Apparatus. Oxford et al.: Oxford University Press, 1996.

Wells, Herbert G. *War of the Worlds.* London et al.: Penguin, 2005.

SECONDARY SOURCES

Abrams, M. H. *The Mirror and the Lamp: Romantic Theory and the Critical Tradition.* New York: Norton, 1958. (Traditional introduction to literary theories, yet very clear and concise).

Aristoteles. *Poetik. Griechisch/Deutsch.* Stuttgart: Reclam, 1982. (Famous fundamental treatise).

*Beck, Rudolf, Hildegard, and Martin Kuester. *Terminologie der Literaturwissenschaft. Ein Handbuch für das Anglistikstudium.* Ismaning: Hueber, 1998. (Very clear definitions and examples).

*Cuddon, J. A. *A Dictionary of Literary Terms and Literary Theory.* 4th ed. Rev. C. E. Preston. Oxford: Blackwell, 1998. (Concise and helpful explanations).

Culler, Jonathan D. *Literary theory: a very short introduction.* Reissued. Oxford, et al.: Oxford University Press, 2000. (Concise, thoughtful and entertaining).

Gadamer, Hans-Georg. *Wahrheit und Methode. Grundzüge einer philosophischen Hermeneutik.* 2nd ed. Tübingen: Mohr, 1965, quoted in: Kimmich/Renner/Stiegler 28-40.

Hickethier, Knut. *Film- und Fernsehanalyse.* 4th ed. Stuttgart/Weimar: Metzler, 2007. (Very helpful introduction with good examples).

Hügli, Anton. *Philosophielexikon.* 7th ed. Hamburg: Rowohlt, 2007. (Brief and clear characterisations of philosophers and explanations of important theories and concepts).

Kimmich, Dorothee, Rolf Günter Renner, and Bernd Stiegler. *Texte zur Literaturtheorie der Gegenwart.* Stuttgart: Reclam, 1996.

Korte, Barbara, Klaus Peter Müller, and Joseph Schmied. *Einführung in die Anglistik.* 2nd ed. Stuttgart and Weimar: Metzler, 2004. (Comprehensive coverage of studying culture, linguistics, literature and teaching English as a foreign language; very useful, incl. excellent annotated bibliography).

Korte, Helmut. *Einführung in die systematische Filmanalyse.* 3rd ed. Berlin: Schmidt, 2004. (Very clear and helpful guide; includes four comprehensive case studies).

Löffler, Arno, Rudolf Freiburg, Dieter Petzold and Eberhard Späth. *Einführung in das Studium der englischen Literatur.* 7th ed. Tübingen and Basel: Francke, 2006. (Very useful introduction that works with case studies of individual texts; hands-on approach).

Monaco, James. *Film verstehen. Kunst, Technik, Sprache, Geschichte und Theorie des Films.* 6th ed. Reinbeck: Rowohlt, 2005. (Easily accessible, comprehensive and richly illustrated overview).

*Nelmes, Jill, ed. *An Introduction to Film Studies.* 4th ed. New York: Routledge, 2007. (Comprehensive and fascinating overview of institutions of film production, approaches to films, various genres, topics and national film traditions with numerous illustrations).

Nünning, Ansgar, and Vera Nünning. *Grundkurs anglistisch-amerikanistische Literaturwissenschaft.* 6th ed. Stuttgart: Klett, 2007. (Very useful, clear and concise).

Nünning, Ansgar, ed. *Metzler Lexikon Literatur- und Kulturtheorie.* 3rd updated ed. Stuttgart and Weimar: Metzler, 2004. (Comprehensive and sophisticated).

Schabert, Ina. *Englische Literaturgeschichte. Eine neue Darstellung aus der Sicht der Geschlechterforschung.* Stuttgart: Kröner, 1997.

Schabert, Ina. *Englische Literaturgeschichte des 20. Jahrhunderts: eine neue Darstellung aus der Sicht der Geschlechterforschung.* Stuttgart: Kröner, 2006.

*Seeber, Hans Ulrich, ed. *Englische Literaturgeschichte.* 4th ed. Stuttgart and Weimar: Metzler, 2004.

*Zapf, Hubert, ed. *Amerikanische Literaturgeschichte.* 2nd ed. Stuttgart and Weimar: Metzler, 2004.

*Strongly recommended.

Poetry

Contents

2.1	What are poetic texts and what do we (ab)use them for?	22
2.2	Communication, speaker, situation and topic	26
2.3	Rhetorical form	30
2.4	Poetic form	41
2.4.1	Metre and rhythm	41
2.4.2	Phonological forms, stanzas and types of poems	45
2.5	Postmodern poetry	51
2.6	Guiding questions and exercises	52
2.7	Bibliography	56

Abstract

This chapter offers an overview of central concepts for a systematic analysis of poetry, which relates content and form. The author's choice of a speaker in a particular situation is connected to the nature and treatment of the topic. The meanings of a poem result from the interplay between the speaker's situation, the sequence of statements, the rhetorical and poetic forms. Patterns of sound, lines, metre and rhythm create a poetic order that can support or qualify the content.

2.1 | What are poetic texts and what do we (ab)use them for?

Poetry lifts the veil from the hidden beauty of the world, and makes familiar things be as if they were not familiar.
Percy Bysshe Shelley, *A Defence of Poetry*, 1821.

Poetry should be elbowed
out of our working world
to make room for machinery.
Sarah Ellis, 1839.

Poetry seems to be out of step with the rapid pace of modern life dominated by technology and the economy. However, even today poems, would-be poems and texts that use poetic forms are our faithful companions from the cradle to the grave: lullabies, nursery rhymes, proverbs, hymns, advertising slogans, Christmas carols, toasts, pop songs, rap, national anthems, birthday poems and funeral marches. How do you explain the wide gap between the interest in poetic texts outside and inside the classroom? In everyday life, songs and melodious, rhythmic texts are often easily understandable in order to support the act of memorising, to make everyone happily sing along or quickly grasp the message, for example "Max, don't have sex with your ex", "Wave your hands in the air like you just don't care", "An apple a day keeps the doctor away" or "Guinness is good for you" ("*Milch macht müde Männer munter*"). In the classroom, the immediate pleasure in the audible harmony, mood, images of poetic texts and in the communal experience of singing songs together is often displaced by the mechanical analysis of rhyme schemes and the counting of stressed syllables or "worse", by the painful attempt to make sense of the strange uses of words in stranger poems that do not even have rhyme or metre. However, many poems share quite a few features with **nursery rhymes** (*Kinderreime*), which we used to like in our childhood:

> Humpty Dumpty sat on a wall,
> Humpty Dumpty had a great fall,
> All the king's horses and all the king's men
> Couldn't put Humpty together again.

This poem draws attention to its poetic language by the repetition of words, rhymes and rhythmic patterns in **verse** ("verse" designates a single line or poetry in general as opposed to prose; *Vers/zeile*). It poses a riddle: who or rather what is Humpty Dumpty?

The following example of a common nursery rhyme is a little more demanding because the solution of its riddle is not obvious:

> Three blind mice, three blind mice,
> See how they run, see how they run.
> They all ran after the farmer's wife;
> She cut off their tails with a carving knife,
> Did ever you see such a sight in your life
> As three blind mice?
> (anon., Whittaker 169)

As in the first traditional children's song, the speaker remains anonymous. The striking connection of key words by the diphthong /ai/ creates a strong order and harmony in opposition to the gruesome content this chain of words suggests: blind, mice, wife, knife, sight, life. The story it tells is ambiguous and provokes many questions: why are the three mice blind? Why are they running? Why did they run after the farmer's wife? Why did she cut off their tails instead of chasing or killing them? Children might have received or come up with the answers that if the mice had not been blind they would not have come near the woman, or that she was annoyed by the mice and taught them a lesson, which they learned because now they are fleeing from her (for "adult" interpretations see psychoanalytic and structuralist criticism, 137-143, 145-149). The poem stresses the opposition between (in)sight and blindness by the repetitions of "see" and "blind". The nursery rhyme makes us vividly imagine three mice on the run, but what is the lesson? Should children beware of mice or of women except their own mothers? The final question of the poem draws our attention to the fact that art makes us see something new that, in all probability, we never observe in real life.

The American modernist Ezra Pound (1885-1972) also wanted poetry to show new and challenging views at the beginning of the 20th century:

In a Station of the Metro

> The apparition of these faces in the crowd;
> Petals on a wet, black bough.
> (1913, NAAL 2: 1206)

Fig. 2.1

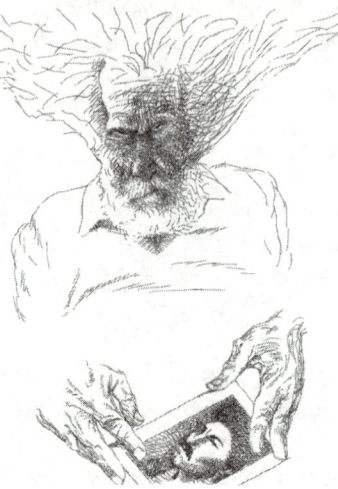

The American poet, critic and editor Ezra Pound (1885-1972) lived mainly in England, France and Italy. He wrote epigrammatic, imagist poems as well as highly elaborate, wide-ranging sequences of poems (e.g. Hugh Selwyn Mauberley, 1920; Cantos, 1915-40) that combine his extensive knowledge of Asian and European culture and history with the criticism of capitalism. He translated poetry from many languages and promoted other writers, such as James Joyce, Ernest Hemingway and T.S. Eliot. His close association with Italian fascism in World War II led to his confinement in an American mental asylum until 1958.

The title of the poem refers to the underground railway in Paris. There is no explicit speaker but rather an anonymous voice. This **imagist poem** presents two sights but leaves the insight up to you: it is a sort of riddle. Regular commuters on the underground railway tend to ignore the familiar hustle and bustle and look inward rather than outward. Here, a vague phenomenon suddenly sparks off an association and acquires beauty in the eye of the beholder: faces set off from the background of the crowd parallel with light petals on a dark bough. The analogy between the images and the fact that the (back)ground is essential to the appearance of visual figures is stressed by the similarity of the dark vowels in "crowd" and "bough". In a unique way, the poem combines two images related by visual parallels and divided by the difference between culture and nature. The *speaker is implicit as a voice, a site of observation and association in order to stress the significance of the images themselves.* The special impact of the poem is less based on the reference to a real underground station or on the subjective expression of innermost feelings but on its own self-referential value due to its particular juxtaposition of two images. This poem generates a new aesthetic experience of beauty and **defamiliarises** (*verfremdet*) our perception of ordinary sights.

Poetry as mirror of reality or expression of subjectivity

These brief examples show that poetry can be anything between **epic**, a story in verse, and **lyric**, a short, subjective, melodious poem (not to be mixed up with lyrics, the words of a song). Differences in poetic modes and forms are related to changing cultural functions of poets and poetry. For example, the neo-classical English author Alexander Pope (1688-1744) saw himself as a representative of society, taste, reason and order. He claimed that poetry should form a mirror of reality and represent general truth in a clear and elevated style: "What oft was thought, but ne'er so well expressed" (*An Essay on Criticism,* 1709/11, NAEL 2: 2515). In opposition, the English Romantic poet William Wordsworth (1770-1850) maintained that "poetry is the spontaneous overflow of powerful feelings: it takes its origin from the emotion recollected in tranquillity" (*Preface to Lyrical Ballads,* 1800/1802, NAEL 2: 250) in a language that resembles the ordinary one but is pleasantly refined by poetic means. He stressed the function of the subjective imagination in visionary poetry, in which "ordinary things should be presented to the mind in an unusual way" (NAEL 1: 241) in order to stimulate and sharpen minds blunted by the monotonous modern life and the flood of sensational information. In turn, modernist poetry takes features from both traditions because it was more interested in impersonality than in soul-searching, but presupposed that individual consciousness is our reality.

Poetry: definition and features

Whatever differences in subjectivity, topic and style, poetry can be primarily defined as
▶ language cast in verse,
  frequently revealing these additional features:
▶ a subjective first-person speaker or voice,
▶ brevity, concentration and reduction,
▶ an unusual use of words and phrases,
▶ suggestive imagery,
▶ rhythm and metre,
▶ repetition of sounds,
▶ lines grouped in stanzas.

2.2 | ## Communication, speaker, situation and topic

Author – speaker – addressee

It would be wrong to identify the explicit **speaker or persona** (*lyrisches Ich* or *Maske*) or the implicit **voice** (*Stimme*) with the real author because every poem defines its speaker by his/her **mood** (*Stimmung*), **tone** (attitude, *Haltung*), questions and statements in a fictional situation, which need not be based on autobiographical experience. Within the text, *a persona or a voice presents his/her present feelings, observations and reflections to an implicit or explicit listener or* fictive **addressee** (*Adressat*). If you merely talk about the content, you ignore the fact that the poem itself is based on literary conventions, which provide a framework for writing and reading. The speaker on the level of the content usually does not know that he/she is in a poem. The author's composition of imagery, verse, rhythm, sound and stanza can support or counteract the persona's utterance to various degrees. The reader has to respect the signals of verse: "Attention! Read slowly and move on in rhythmic steps. Watch the language."

Names and personal pronouns tell us who speaks to whom. The question is in which way the speaker, who assumes the self-reflexive pronoun "I", characterises him/herself directly and indirectly via his/her relationship to the content and the addressee. Therefore, a circular analysis identifies the pronouns and the topic, and then expands the first insight by a close reading of the complete text. The way how the speaker addresses a listener or him/herself, the time and place of the situation, the presentation and unfolding of the topic are of great importance.

Fig. 2.2 |

Poetic communication.

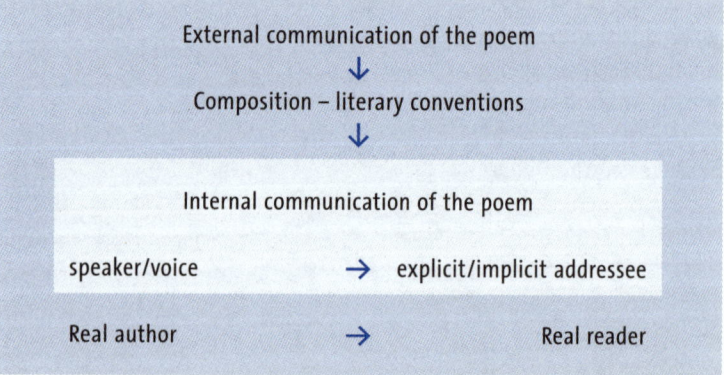

External communication of the poem
↓
Composition – literary conventions
↓

Internal communication of the poem

speaker/voice   →   explicit/implicit addressee

Real author   →   Real reader

The English author Michael Drayton (1563-1631) explores the love between "I" and "you" from the perspective of the first person:

[handwritten annotation: iamb pentameter]

[handwritten annotations in left margin: male voice 2, male voice 2]

a Since there's no help, come, let us kiss and part;
b Nay, I have done, you get no more of me,
a And I am glad, yea, glad with all my heart   *[handwritten: repetition → underlines superficial gladness]*
b That thus so cleanly I myself can free.
c Shake hands for ever, cancel all our vows,
d And when we meet at any time again,
c Be it not seen in either of our brows
d That we one jot of former love retain.
e Now at the last gasp of love's latest breath,   *[handwritten: sonnet abab cdcd efef gg]*
f When, his pulse failing, passion speechless lies,
e When faith is kneeling by his bed of death,
f And innocence is closing up his eyes;
g Now if thou wouldst, when all have given him over,   *[handwritten: couplet]*
g From death to life thou mightst him yet recover.   *[handwritten: sums all up]*
(NAEL 1: 967-68)

[handwritten: eye rhyme]

The speaker wavers between attraction and separation, expressed in the appeal to "kiss and part", and the use of the pronouns "we" and "us" versus "I" and "you". The speaker already apprehends what it will be like after they have broken up but, after having detailed the dying of love, suddenly turns to ask the partner to revive their love. The author's composition of the **English sonnet** (*engl. Sonett*: abab cdcd efef gg) establishes a framework for the development of the argument. In the first quatrain of four lines, the excited speaker expresses relief about the end of the relationship, stressed by short phrases, emphatic expressions ("nay", "yea") and repetitions of "no" and "glad". The second quartet anticipates the future after their separation but ambiguously suggests that the speaker is not as free from love as claimed before by ruling out the possibility of betraying any sign of love in the future. The author's rhymes belie the speaker's denial of love: "vows" – "again" – "brows" – "retain". This tension between the persona and the author is confirmed in the next quartet because the persona delineates the slow death of "love", which the author wraps in an allegory of personifications that is clearly at some remove from the direct expression of emotions. The couplet at the end offers a sudden turn, which is neatly captured in the semantic reversal of the eye rhyme "over" – "recover" (similar spelling but different pronunciation). The speaker, who proposed to break up the relationship, asks his/her partner to save it in the end. After all, the basic opposition between life and death parallels that between being together and apart and undermines the initial happiness about the separation. In a way, Drayton explores subjective emotions that characterise difficult love-relationships in general.

Fig. 2.3

The English poet William Wordsworth (1770-1850) lost both of his parents quite early. He considered childhood as the formative period in life: "The Child is Father of the Man" ("Ode. Intimations of Immortality"). His poetry of loss and memory gave preference to imaginative and visionary experience rather than mere sense perception. The poor and the social outcasts seemed to him subjects worthy of serious poems. He published a seminal collection of Romantic poetry, the Lyrical Ballads, *with Samuel Taylor Coleridge in 1798.*

The Romantic Wordsworth takes care to express unique subjective emotions:

> She dwelt among the untrodden ways
>   Beside the springs of Dove,
> A Maid whom there were none to praise
>   And very few to love:
>
> A violet by a mossy stone
>   Half hidden from the eye!
> — Fair as a star, when only one
>   Is shining in the sky.
>
> She lived unknown, and few could know
>   When Lucy ceased to be;
> But she is in her grave, and, oh,
>   The difference to me!
> (1799/1800, NAEL 2: 252)

The poem does not praise the girl's individual nature as an attractive feature. On the contrary: the speaker undermines his comparison of the girl to a star in an almost ironic way because she is considered beautiful only when no rival is around. The speaker distinguishes himself from others by the particular way he sees and loves Lucy, whom he seems to commemorate less for her sake than for his own. The poem displays an egocentric self because it begins like an epitaph to the unknown girl, putting her down rather than praising her in the middle, and ends with his own elegiac feelings. The poem moves from "She" to "me", and the speaker talks to himself.

Even in poems with an explicit addressee, the "I" and "you" need not take turns as in a real dialogue if the other is addressed in the mind of the persona. Usually, the reader overhears the persona talking to him/herself rather than listening to a conversation. A **dramatic monologue** (*dramatischer Monolog*) implies the presence of a listener and insists on the difference between author and persona, who is given a name that defines the pronoun "I". In T. S. Eliot's (US/GB, 1888-1965) dramatic monologue "The Love Song of J. Alfred Prufrock", the persona asks an addressee to come along:

Monologue versus dialogue

Let us go then, you and I,
When the evening is spread out against the sky
Like a patient etherised upon a table;   *simile, personified*
Let us go, through certain half-deserted streets,
The muttering retreats
Of restless nights in one-night cheap hotels
And sawdust restaurants with oyster-shells:
Streets that follow like a tedious argument
Of insidious intent
To lead you to an overwhelming question . . .
Oh, do not ask 'What is it?'
Let us go and make our visit. [. . .]
(1918/19, NAAL 2: 1268)

It soon becomes obvious that we learn less about the party to be visited than about the melancholy mind of a shy and introspective character: the author's title "Love Song" is ironic and creates a distance towards the persona. The rhyme alludes to the fact that "our visit" contains the answer to "What is it?" because the company of others triggers his tortured self-reflections and sets off his uncertainty and isolation.

Fig. 2.4

The poet, dramatist, critic and editor Thomas Stearns Eliot (1888-1965) emigrated from the US to England. His poems The Waste Land *(1922) and* The Four Quartets *(1935-42) reveal an in-depth knowledge of the European cultural tradition and a sharp, disillusioned perception of contemporary life expressed in versatile poetic form. Andrew Lloyd Webber turned his book of children's verse,* Old Possum's Book of Practical Cats *(1939), into the lyrics of his musical* Cats.

In many poems, we cannot find a speaker or an explicit addressee at all. For example, Ezra Pound's "In a Station of the Metro" (see above, 2.1, 23) foregrounds images of objects. The question is whether and how subjectivity figures in poems without an explicit speaker. In sum, we have to ask *who says what to whom in which way and for which reasons*. The author has numerous options to shape the persona's utterance: figurative speech, sound, metre, rhythm, verse, stanzas and types of poems.

2.3   Rhetorical form

Why don't we say directly what we mean but use **figurative language** (*uneigentliche Sprache*)? What do you mean when you say that someone is "cool"? This individual may be in control of his/her feelings, uninvolved and disinterested or attractive and interesting. Figurative language often helps to describe phenomena by replacing abstract concepts with concrete ones. The traditional definition of "cool" emotions forms the opposite of our images of warm feelings and hot passion. Modern definitions of "cool" vary according to user, reference and situation. The frequent use of images no longer draws attention to its difference from **literal language** (*eigentliche Sprache*). Native speakers are familiar with the expressions "to pull someone's leg", the "leg" (part) of a race, and the legs of a chair, and would not think about the image. Kurt Seligmann's sculpture plays with this image:

Kurt Seligmann:
Das Ultra-Möbelstück,
1938.

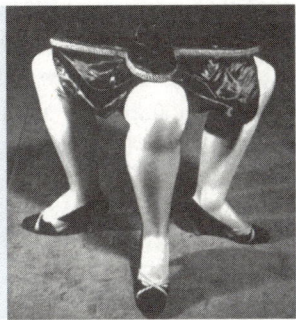

| Fig. 2.5

The term "figurative language" refers to **tropes** (*Wortfiguren*) and **schemes or figures of speech** (*Satzfiguren*). The most common trope is the **simile** (*Vergleich*), which connects two concepts by "like" or "as". If a simile (or a metaphor) links two extremely different concepts in a striking and often complex way, it is called a **conceit** (ital. *concetto*: concept). For example, T. S. Eliot begins "The Love Song of J. Alfred Prufrock" with the lines: "Let us go then, you and I / when the evening is spread out against the sky / like a patient etherised upon a table". The initial harmony in content, rhythm and sound evokes a romantic mood, which is undermined by the strange simile of an anaesthetised patient. The benighted consciousness compares to the dusky sky and comments unfavourably on sentimentality. – The Northern Irish writer Louis MacNeice (1907-63) compares the readers in the "British Museum Reading Room", who flee everyday life and reality, with bats in a cave:

Forms of figurative language

Cranks, hacks, poverty-stricken scholars [...]
Some are too much alive and some are asleep
Hanging like bats in a world of inverted values,
Folded up in themselves in a world which is safe and silent:
This is the British Museum Reading Room. [...]
(Rosengarten/Goldrick-Jones 563)

The **metaphor** (*Metapher*) has been defined as 1) *a shortened or implicit comparison, which substitutes one concept for another*, or 2) as an

Metaphor

interaction between two concepts, which transfers meanings. According to the first understanding, the metaphor presupposes a ground of similarity between the **tenor** (*Gemeintes, Bildempfänger*) and the image or **vehicle** (*Bildspender*). According to the second definition, the metaphor does more because it asks us to see x as y, to regard something in a new light (Bode 94). A metaphor appears in many forms: it combines two nouns ("Jessica, the bird of paradise"), a noun and a verb ("Time flies."), a qualifier and a noun ("stinging pain"), or it takes the shape of a statement ("Edmund is a pig."). Even the common last example shows that a metaphor does more than a simile (e.g.: Edmund *eats like* a pig) because we can rephrase the metaphor in many ways: Edmund is as fat/dirty/greedy/noisy/vulgar as a pig.

Fig. 2.6

Metaphor: transfer of meanings.

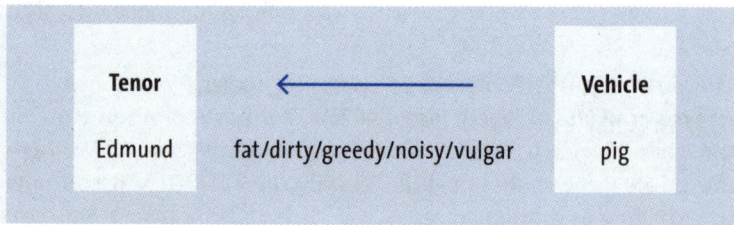

Tenor	←	Vehicle
Edmund	fat/dirty/greedy/noisy/vulgar	pig

Pound's poem "In a Station of the Metro" (see above, 2.1, 23) offers the "Petals on a wet, black bough" as a metaphor for "these faces in the crowd", which sparks off associations and asks us to transfer meanings. If the metaphor suggests the promise of new life in a fresh spring rain, how does that relate to people that might have fled from the rain into the station, waiting in dripping wet coats for the train?

Pun

While simile and metaphor discover similarities in two words that sound differently, the **pun** (*Wortspiel, Paronomasie*) plays with the meanings of two words that are pronounced in the same way. Puns are often used in jokes: Who invented the four-day working week? Robinson: he had all his work done by Friday. – Grandma says: "Men are like linoleum floors: Lay them right and you can walk over them for 30 years."

Metonymy

The **metonymy** (*Metonymie*) replaces a concept by another that is closely related to it. It does not, like the metaphor, explore new meanings but rather varies the focus within the same frame of reference. Typical examples are:

▶ The crown as a sign of status and function replaces the queen.
▶ An abstract noun stands for an institution ("Faith against abortion.").
▶ The name of a place represents its inhabitants ("Manchester welcomes the champions.").
▶ The name of an author signifies his/her work ("Have you read Virginia Woolf?").
▶ The cause replaces the effect or vice versa ("Have you got a light?"; Ecstasy; speed).
▶ The means are used instead of the end ("She spoke her native tongue.").
▶ The container refers to the content ("Have one more glass.").

The **synecdoche** *uses the part for the whole* (**pars pro toto**) *or the whole for the part* (**totum pro parte**) *for reasons of variation or foregrounding* particular aspects or general functions: Synecdoche
▶ A part replaces the whole ("a roof over one's head") or vice versa.
▶ The singular is used instead of the plural ("Man is selfish and cruel.") or vice versa.
▶ The material reduces the object ("the woolly kind": sheep).

Justice.

Fig. 2.7

Allegory

The **allegory** *transforms a general, abstract concept into a concrete image, person or story*. For example, the world is often conceived as a stage and life as a journey. Artists delineate justice as a blindfolded woman with scales and a sword.

Personification

The **personification** *transforms things or abstract concepts into human agents*. Germans tend to be puzzled when someone says that "she broke down", meaning the car, or refers to the sun as "he" and the moon as "she". Without personification, cartoons and animated movies would be half as entertaining.

Fig. 2.8

Uncle Sam has personified the US in cartoons since the 1830s.

The function of tropes

The function of a trope has to be explained in context. Drayton's sonnet (see above, 2.2, 27) personifies love, passion, faith and innocence, who enact a minute play of dying emotions. In "Daffodils", Wordsworth personifies flowers in order to convey the isolated poet's enjoyment of nature as a substitute for alienating society:

> I wandered lonely as a cloud
> That floats on high o'er vales and hills,
> When all at once I saw a crowd,
> A host, of golden daffodils;
> Beside the lake, beneath the trees,
> Fluttering and dancing in the breeze.
>
> Continuous as the stars that shine
> And twinkle on the milky way,

They stretched in never-ending line
Along the margin of a bay:
Ten thousand saw I at a glance,
Tossing their heads in sprightly dance.

 The waves beside them danced; but they
Out-did the sparkling waves in glee:
A poet could not but be gay,
In such a jocund company:
I gazed - and gazed - but little thought
What wealth the show to me had brought:

For oft, when on my couch I lie
In vacant or in pensive mood,
They flash upon that inward eye
 Which is the bliss of solitude;
And then my heart with pleasure fills,
And dances with the daffodils.

(1804/1807, NAEL 2: 284-85)

The **symbol** *evokes a concrete phenomenon which points to abstract, often*   Symbol
more general and ambiguous meanings. We consider many things
"symbolic" in a very general sense in everyday life: white symbolises innocence, a red rose love, black clothes mourning, a dove
peace, a flag a nation, broad white stripes on the tar a pedestrian
crossing. Cultural conventions specify the meanings of traditional
symbols. Artists recycle conventional symbols or create new ones,
which challenge the reader to discover new and complex meanings. For example, the American poet Edgar Allan Poe (1809-49) expands the traditional meaning of the bird of ill omen, "The Raven".
A young man, who fell asleep while reading a strange old book
around midnight, envisions a raven, which responds with the single answer "Nevermore" to all of his questions. The young man
asks the raven whether he would relieve him of his painful memory of the dead Lenore or he would meet her again after death, but
then he becomes annoyed with the obscure bird:

"Get thee back into the tempest and the Night's Plutonian shore!
Leave no black plume as a token of that lie thy soul hath spoken!
Leave my loneliness unbroken! – quit the bust above my door!

Take thy beak from out my heart, and take thy form from off my door!"
 Quoth the Raven "Nevermore."
And the Raven, never flitting, still is sitting, still is sitting
[...]
And the lamp-light o'er him streaming throws his shadow on the floor;
And my soul from out that shadow that lies floating on the floor
 Shall be lifted – nevermore!
(1845, NAAL 1: 1372)

Fig. 2.9

The poet, short story writer and critic Edgar Allen Poe (1809-1849) suffered from poverty and alcoholism. He appreciated a sense of mystery and the macabre, the musical quality and aesthetic effect of language. His fascination with passions and madness in his poems and his tales of horror complement his interest in the intelligent analysis of crimes in his tales of ratiocination.

This raven symbolises the powers of frustration, meaninglessness, melancholy, despair and darkness, which haunt the young man. The Irish poet William Butler Yeats (1865-1939) creates the symbol of the "gyre" (*zirkuläre Bewegung*) in "The Second Coming" (1920/21):

Turning and Turning in the widening gyre
The falcon cannot hear the falconer;
Things fall apart; the centre cannot hold;
Mere anarchy is loosed upon the world,
The blood-dimmed tide is loosed, and everywhere
The ceremony of innocence is drowned;
The best lack all conviction, while the worst
Are full of passionate intensity. [...]
(NAEL 2: 2106-07)

The widening circulation, which is calm and graceful to observe in the flight of birds of prey, assumes a general significance as it is connected to a growing spiral of disruption and chaos in an apocalyptic world.

The Anglo-Irish poet, dramatist and prose writer William Butler Yeats (1865-1939) was torn between his commitments to art and to politics. He promoted the Irish folk tradition, wrote poems and plays based on Celtic mythology, served in the new Irish senate, directed the Abbey Theatre in Dublin, and created modernist poetry with accomplished style and powerful symbols based on his own visionary system of ideas.

Fig. 2.10

Other prominent tropes include **emphasis** (*Betonung*), which is often highlighted by an unusual position of a word in the line ("mercy" in the example below), **euphemism** (*Beschönigung*), which embellishes a phenomenon ("the big sleep" for death), exaggeration in **hyperbole** (*Hyperbel*) and understatement in the negation of **litotes** ("The dinner was *not bad*.").

In **verbal irony**, *the opposite of what is said is meant*. In **situational irony**, *the opposite of what is expected occurs*. How do you spot irony? The detection of irony depends upon the frame of reference and the underlying values. In the following text, the ex-slave and first African American poet Phillis Wheatley (ca 1753-84) shows no evidence that denies her embracing of Christianity as a liberating force in spite of its discriminating colour symbolism:

Further forms of tropes

'Twas mercy brought me from my pagan land,
Taught my benighted soul to understand
That there's a God, that there's a Saviour too:
Once I redemption neither sought nor knew.
Some view our sable race with scornful eye,
"Their colour is a diabolic die."
Remember, Christians, Negroes, black as Cain,
May be refin'd, and join th'angelic train.
(1773, NAAL 1: 729)

A secular reader may think that "mercy" was used ironically because the gain of faith could hardly outweigh the loss of freedom by slavery. However, instead of verbal irony we can find situational irony in the fact that temporal slavery initiates the captive into Christianity and therefore helps her to acquire eternal spiritual liberation.

Fig. 2.11

Phillis Wheatley (ca 1753-1784) was kidnapped as a girl in West Africa and sold into slavery in the US. Having learned to read and write, the teenager began to compose poetry, combining traces of Africa with ideas of Western culture in European poetic forms. Her popularity may have contributed to her liberation but did not prevent her from dying in poverty.

Schemes

Schemes (*Satzfiguren*) deviate from ordinary syntax by the special arrangement of words or phrases. The **inversion** of the word order is a favourite means of emphasis in a language that prefers a rather rigid word order of subject + verb + object: "A woman's face with Nature's own hand painted / Hast thou, the master mistress of my passion" (Sonnet 20, 1609, Shakespeare, 1564-1616, NAEL 1: 1031).

Figures of repetition insist on importance and urgency. The use of **anaphora** (*Anapher*) repeats words at the beginning of lines, **epiphora** (*Epipher*) at the ending of lines as compared to the immediate **repetition** (*Geminatio*) of words: "Tyger! Tyger! burning bright / In the forests of the night, [. . .] Did he smile his work to see? / Did he who made the Lamb make thee?" (1789-94, William Blake, GB, 1757-1827, NAEL 2: 54).

Parallelism

Parallelism, the parallel construction of phrases, is varied by **chiasmus**, repetition in inverted order. John Donne (GB, 1572-1631) uses chiasmus in his poem "The Sun Rising" in order to present love as the perfect conjunction of opposites in the chauvinist metaphors of female states that need male rulers. In parallelism, he neatly captures the statement that, in comparison to love, honour is just as inferior as money:

> She is all states, and all princes I,
> Nothing else is.
> Princes do but play us; compar'd to this,
> All honor's mimic, all wealth alchemy. [. . .]
> (1633, NAEL 1: 1239)

trochaic tetrameter, end rhyme

Tyger! Tyger! burning bright
In the forests of the night,
What immortal hand or eye
Could frame thy fearful symmetry?

In what distant deeps or skies
Burnt the fire of thine eyes?
On what wings dare he aspire?
What the hand dare seize the fire?

And what shoulder, & what art
Could twist the sinews of thy heart?
And when thy heart began to beat,
What dread hand? & what dread feet?

What the hammer? What the chain?
In what furnace was thy brain?
What the anvil? What dread grasp
Dare its deadly terrors clasp?

When the stars threw down their spears
And water'd heaven with their tears,
Did he smile his work to see?
Did he who made the Lamb make thee?

Tyger! Tyger! Burning bright
In the forests of the night,
What immortal hand or eye
Dare frame thy fearful symmetry?

(1790-92; NAEL 2: 54)

Fig. 2.12

The English poet and artist Blake (1757-1827) earned his living by illustrating texts, engraving designs and printing books. His Songs of Innocence and Experience (1794) reveal the irreconcilable contradiction between good and evil, an idyllic paradise and a fallen, corrupt world. The provocative and prophetic rebel expressed his radical ideas of sexual, religious and political liberation in visionary and mythical poems.

The **asyndeton** joins words or phrases by commas only, the **polysyndeton** by conjunctions. These forms often serve emphasis or gradation. The American poet Carl Sandburg (1878-1967) stresses the activities and functions of Chicago by using the means of asyndeton at the beginning and the end of his poem on this city:

Asyndeton

Hog Butcher for the World,
Tool Maker, Stacker of Wheat,
Player with Railroads and the Nation's Freight Handler;
Stormy, husky, brawling,
City of the Big Shoulders:
They tell me you are wicked and I believe them, for I have seen your painted
    women under the gas lamps luring the farm boys.
And they tell me you are crooked and I answer: Yes, it is true I have seen the
    gunman kill and go free to kill again.
And they tell me you are brutal and my reply is: On the faces of women and
    children I have seen the marks of wanton hunger.
And having answered so I turn once more to those who sneer at this my city,
    and I give them back the sneer and say to them:
Come and show me another city with lifted head singing so proud to be alive

and coarse and strong and cunning.
Flinging magnetic curses amid the toil of piling job on job, here is a tall bold
slugger set vivid against the little soft cities;
Fierce as a dog with tongue lapping for action, cunning as a savage pitted
against the wilderness,
Bareheaded,
Shoveling,
Wrecking,
Planning,
Building, breaking, rebuilding,
Under the smoke, dust all over his mouth, laughing with white teeth,
Under the terrible burden of destiny laughing as a young man laughs,
Laughing even as an ignorant fighter laughs who has never lost a battle,
Bragging and laughing that under his wrist is the pulse, and under his ribs
the heart of the people,
Laughing!
Laughing the stormy, husky, brawling laughter of Youth, half-naked, sweating,
proud to be Hog Butcher, Tool Maker, Stacker of Wheat, Player with
railroads and Freight Handler to the Nation.
(1914/16, NAAL 2: 1139)

Matthew Arnold (GB, 1822-88) uses polysyndeton to emphasise despair about the world in "Dover Beach":
[…]
Ah, love, let us be true
To one another! for the world, which seems
To lie before us like a land of dreams,
So various, so beautiful, so new,
Hath really neither joy, nor love, nor light,
Nor certitude, nor peace, nor help for pain […]
(1867, NAEL 2: 1492)

Paradox

Oscar Wilde was a master of the epigrammatic **paradox**, which is a statement that seems to be contradictory and true at the same time ("The only way to get rid of a temptation is to yield to it"; "In this world, there are only two tragedies. One is not getting what one wants, and the other is getting it. The last is much the worst."). The **oxymoron** can be seen as a condensed version of the paradox because it combines two contradictory terms, such as the interesting expression "wise fool" and the deceptive phrase "war for peace".

In order to understand figurative language, you need to know the basic literal and metaphorical uses of a word, but above all, ask the question: "What does figurative language do to the meanings of individual words or phrases in this context?"

Poetic form

Metre and rhythm

Generations of intelligent students have despaired over the questions of how to find out about poetic metre and rhythm, and what they mean. To begin at the beginning: each of us has rhythm – at least the rhythm of breathing, heartbeat and the way we walk. If your heart beats with the *metric regularity of a metronome*, your health may be sound but something in your life may go wrong. Life and poetry are interesting if marked by a dynamic tension between the expected regularity and unforeseen irregularity. Our hearts and poems call for particular attention at missing or extra beats, the speeding up and slowing down of rhythm. Oral speech has a dynamic rhythm that is based on the volume of our breath, the word accent, the word order, the syntactic pattern of phrases and the stress of particular words for emphasis. Metre (*Metrum, Versmaß*) is a highly artificial and perfectly regular sequence of stressed and unstressed syllables in lines of verse. A first very slow and mechanical reading of a poem tells whether it has a metre. If you mark the stressed and unstressed syllables of the metre, your second reading for sense will show where you stress other syllables and deviate from the pattern of the metre. Thus the question is less metre *or* rhythm but the tension between them.

The difference between rhythm and metre

In particular, attention is due to 1) the word accent (see dictionary), 2) the maintenance of a harmonic pattern of stressed and unstressed syllables, 3) the emphasis on specific words according to their relevance for the statement, and 4) the relationship between syntax and verse.

Finding out about metre and rhythm

1 Convention determines stress in words. The "record" (/ x) takes a stress on the first syllable, "to record" (x /) on the second.

2 The metre is defined by the kind and number of **feet** (*Versfüße*), a particular sequence of stressed and unstressed syllables:
  ► **iamb** (*Jambus*): unstressed – stressed (x /, "above"),
  ► **trochee** (*Trochäus*): stressed – unstressed (/ x, "falling"),
  ► **spondee** (*Spondäus*): two stressed (/ /, "artwork"),
  ► **dactyl** (*Daktylus*): stressed – two unstressed (/ x x, "damnable", "*Daktylus*"),
  ► **anapaest** (*Anapäst*): two unstressed – stressed (x x /, "marguerite", "*Anapäst*").
  The most frequent numbers of feet are called:
  ► **trimeter** (*Dreiheber*): "That I did always love" (Emily Dickinson, US, 1830-86),
  ► **tetrameter** (*Vierheber*): "Goe, and catche a falling starre" (John Donne, "Song"),
  ► **pentameter** (*Fünfheber*): "When I do count the clock that tells the time" (William Shakespeare, Sonnet 12).

3 We usually emphasise adjectives, verbs and nouns but not articles, prepositions and conjunctions. Stress makes a difference. The question "You did that to him?" (/x /x /) can make various points: a special emphasis on "You" expresses surprise about the character of the agent (/ x x x x), on "that" implies that the action is unusual or incredible (x x / x x), and on the last word that "he" is a person who would not accept anything of the sort (x x x x /).

4 The boundaries of lines and syntactic units influence the tempo and breaks of the rhythm. The **end-stopped line** (*Zeilenstil*) requires a little pause at the end of the line that agrees with a syntactic unit. The **run-on line** (*Zeilensprung, Enjambement*) demands that the reader passes over the end of the line because the sentence moves on into the next verse. A comma, colon or full stop within a line of verse indicates a pause (**caesura**, *Zäsur*). *The rhythmic dynamics of a poem is determined by the tension between the line of verse and the syntactical order* (Bode 41).

Task

Read out and **scan** (to mark the stresses, *skandieren*) the first stanza of Wordsworth's "Daffodils" (see above, 2.3, 34-35), and analyse in which way it supports or qualifies the content.

Your metric reading of the iambic tetrameter would stress "as" in the first line, "-ils" in the fourth and "in" in the sixth. However, the sense of rhythm according to meaning and the conventional stress of "daffodil" (/xx) allows for minor stresses only. The beginning of the sixth line inverts the iamb and adds one syllable: "Fluttering" (/xx). The first line runs on into the second, whereas line four and five are marked by caesuras. The regular metre creates an underlying harmony. The drifting movement is mirrored by the run-on line. The caesuras suggest that the speaker struggles to come to terms with the sudden overwhelming impressions of nature. The rhythmic deviation of "fluttering" performs the irregular movement expressed by this word in contrast with the regular "dancing".

Task

Scan the nursery rhymes "Humpty Dumpty" and "Three blind mice", quoted above (2.1, 22-23).

They do not have one regular metre but are certainly very rhythmic, using a combination of various feet which is called **sprung rhythm**. Whereas "Humpty Dumpty" prefers trochees and dactyls, "Three blind mice" begins and ends with a sequence of single stressed syllables and privileges iambs and anapaests in the middle. Sprung rhythm provides a particularly vivid and dynamic pattern that comes close to emphatic oral speech.

Free verse (*freier Vers*) in verse paragraphs is even more akin to ordinary speech or prose. Metric poetry can be compared to the regular figures of classical ballet, free verse to the variable movements of modern dance, whose patterns are very flexible but nevertheless follow a choreography. T. S. Eliot's poetry wavers between metric patterns and free verse, a form that corresponds to his belief that a good knowledge of poetic tradition is the basis of innovation (see "The Love Song", 2.2, 29). The American poet Walt Whitman (1819-92) celebrated the ordinary man and liberty in democray in a poetic language liberated from the chains of rhyme, metre and traditional stanza. His form of free verse creates rhythm on top of the stress on meaningful words by the repetition of sounds, words and phrases in rather long lines:

Free verse

44   **POETRY**

Walt Whitman, a kosmos, of Manhattan the son,
Turbulent, fleshy, sensual, eating, drinking and breeding,
No sentimentalist, no stander above men and women or apart from them.
No more modest than immodest.

Unscrew the locks from the doors!
Unscrew the doors themselves from their jambs!
Whoever degrades another degrades me,
And whatever is done or said returns at last to me. [. . .]
("Song of Myself" 24, 1855/81; NAAL 1: 1990)

Fig. 2.13

Walt Whitman (1819-1892) worked as a schoolteacher and journalist. He continuously revised and expanded his verse collection Leaves of Grass *(1855ff.), which provoked the public by celebrating the body, himself, the individual and the common people in highly emotional free verse.*

Another form of free verse is given by Ezra Pound's poem about the Metro, in which rather short lines correspond to syntactical units, as opposed to William Carlos Williams's (US, 1883-1963) poems, which cut down the lines considerably, fragment the syntax, stress the individual word and the visual structure of verse paragraphs (Steele 260-64). For example, "The Locust Tree in Flowers" (1935) evokes how the branch of an old tree, which seems to be almost dead, sprouts new flowers in spring:

Among
of
green

stiff
old
bright

broken
branch
come

white
sweet
May

again.
(Link, *Make it New*: 190)

Phonological forms, stanzas and types of poems 2.4.2

Speech sounds create harmony, support memory, connect lines and mark
stanzas (*Strophen*; the Engl. term "strophe" is rare). Poetry is traditionally associated with the use of **rhyme**, *the identity of the last*
stressed vowel and its subsequent letters in two or more words, in its
diverse forms and variations:

Rhyme patterns

▶ **masculine rhyme** (*männlicher Reim*), the similarity of the last syllables stressed in two lines ("man – fan"),
▶ **feminine rhyme** (double rhyme, *weiblicher Reim*), a stressed syllable
followed by an unstressed one ("gender – bender"),
▶ **triple rhyme** parallels three syllables ("treacherous – lecherous"),
▶ **identical rhyme** (*rührender Reim*) includes the consonants before
the vowel ("know – no"),
▶ **eye-rhyme** (*Augenreim*) looks similar but sounds different ("move –
dove"),
▶ **half-rhymes** (impure/slant/oblique rhyme, *Halbreime*) are less "perfect" than pure or true rhymes because they connect two words
by identical consonants (**consonance**, "loads – lids") or identical
vowels only (**assonance**, "foam – moan"),
▶ **alliteration** links words by the initial letter and is a favourite feature of proverbs ("He who laughs last, laughs longest."),
▶ **internal rhyme** (*Binnenreim*: "East, West, home's best."),
▶ **end rhyme** (*Endreim*) in the shape of the
  ▶ **couplet** (*Paarreim*): aabb,

> **alternate rhyme** (*Kreuzreim*): abab,
> **envelope pattern** (*umarmender Reim*): abba,
> **tail rhyme** (*verschränkter Reim/Schweifreim*): abcabc.

Rhyme and metre were dominant poetic features until the middle of the nineteenth century but slowly gave way to free verse, which also abandoned traditional forms of stanzas in favour of verse paragraphs. Stanzas provide order for thought. The Japanese **haiku** "simply" demands the poet to write a poem in three lines of verse with five syllables, seven, and again five, which is a concise form for the presentation of brief images or insights. The first example is a translation from the Chinese by Ezra Pound about the fate of an emperor's courtesan, the second a more prosaic expression of our contemporary experience with computers. Both haikus are about loss:

O fan of white silk,
    clear as frost on the grass-blade,
You also are laid aside.
(Link, *Make it New*: 138)

Your file was so big.
    It might be very useful.
But now it is gone.
(anonymous)

Types of stanzas

English stanzas are often defined by the number of syllables, the rhyme scheme and the metre. **Couplets** (*Zweizeiler*) are two lines linked by an end rhyme, called heroic couplets if written in iambic pentameter, which was frequently used in 17th century drama. The three lines of a **tercet** (triplet, *Terzett*) form a **terza rima** (*Terzine*) if the middle line of one tercet is turned into the envelope pattern of the following (aba bcb cdc, etc.). The **quatrain** (*Quartett*) often comes with an alternate rhyme or in the shape of the **ballad stanza** (*Balladenstrophe*), which rhymes abcb dbeb or defe, etc., and alternates tetrameter and trimeter, providing a very flexible form.

Ballads

    The oral **folk ballad** (*Volksballade*), a popular song from the Middle Ages to the 19th century, combines features from all genres because it tells a story and presents dialogue in poetic stanzas. The folk ballad sings about love and tragic death, the **street ballad** (*Straßenballade*) about crime and politics since the 16th century.

Written **literary ballads** (*Kunstballaden*) have found favour since the 18th century (Bode 126-30). Edgar Allan Poe's ballad "Annabel Lee" embodies his rather morbid idea that the melancholy death "of a beautiful woman is, unquestionably, the most poetical topic in the world—and equally is it beyond doubt that the lips best suited for such topic are those of a bereaved lover" (NAAL 1: 1463):

It was many and many a year ago,
    In a kingdom by the sea,
That a maiden there lived whom you may know
    By the name of ANNABEL LEE;
And this maiden she lived with no other thought
    Than to love and be loved by me.

I *was* a child and *she* was a child,
    In this kingdom by the sea;
But we loved with a love that was more than love—
    I and my ANNABEL LEE—
With a love that the winged seraphs of heaven
    Coveted her and me.

And this was the reason that, long ago,
    In this kingdom by the sea,
A wind blew out of a cloud, chilling
    My beautiful ANNABEL LEE;
So that her high-born kinsman came
    And bore her away from me,
To shut her up in a sepulchre
    In this kingdom by the sea.

The angels, not half so happy in heaven,
Went envying her and me—
Yes!—that was the reason (as all men know,
    In this kingdom by the sea)
That the wind came out of the cloud by night,
    Chilling and killing my ANNABEL LEE.

But our love it was stronger by far than the love
    Of those who were older than we—
    Of many far wiser than we—

And neither the angels in heaven above,
    Nor the demons down under the sea,
Can ever dissever my soul from the soul
    Of the beautiful ANNABEL LEE:

For the moon never beams, without bringing me dreams
    Of the beautiful ANNABEL LEE;
And the stars never rise, but I feel the bright eyes
    Of the beautiful ANNABEL LEE;
And so, all the night-tide, I lie down by the side
Of my darling—my darling—my life and my bride,
    In the sepulchre there by the sea—
    In her tomb by the sounding sea.
(NAAL 1: 1375-76)

Types of sonnets

The **ottava rima** is a stanza of eight lines rhyming abababcc. Wordsworth shortens the pattern to ababcc in the "Daffodils" (see above, 2.3, 34-35).

Two quatrains and two tercets form the **Italian sonnet** (Latin *sonare*: to sound; *Sonett*). The quatrains (abab abab or abba abba) form the **octett**, which precedes the tercets (cde cde or cdc dcd) of the **sestett** (*Sextett*). The English poets Sir Thomas Wyatt (1503-42) and Henry Howard, Earl of Surrey (1517-47) translated Italian sonnets and transformed their structure into the **English sonnet with three quartets and a couplet**. The Italian form suggests a development of the argument in two steps, such as thesis and antithesis or problem and solution. The English version motivates a variation of one thesis or an alternation of positions in three steps, concluding with a summary or a surprising turn (see Drayton above, 2.2, 27). The English Renaissance poets changed the idealising Petrarcan sonnet from the 14th century into poems on friendship and passionate love that did not exclude physical aspects. The metaphysical poets of the 17th century dared to combine bodily desire and spiritual needs in witty poems. At the end of the 18th century, the English Romantic poets no longer indulged in the great rhetorical show of their predecessors but varied its form and widened the range of topics to include subjective reflections on private situations as well as on history, contemporary society and politics (Bode 131-41).

Percy Bysshe Shelley (GB, 1792-1822) reflected on the relation-ship between art and politics in his sonnet about Ozymandias (1817), the Egyptian ruler also known as Ramses II.

> I met a traveller from an antique land,
> Who said – "Two vast and trunkless legs of stone
> Stand in the desart . . . Near them, on the sand,
> Half sunk, a shattered visage lies, whose frown,
> And wrinkled lip, and sneer of cold command,
> Tell that its sculptor well those passions read
> Which yet survive, stamped on these lifeless things,
> The hand that mocked them, and the heart that fed:
> And on the pedestal, these words appear:
> My name is Ozymandias, king of kings:
> Look on my works, ye Mighty, and despair!
> Nothing beside remains. Round the decay
> Of that colossal Wreck, boundless and bare
> The lone and level sands stretch far away."
> (NAEL 2: 725-26)

In his sonnet "The White House", the Jamaican Claude McKay (1889-1948) appropriated the European tradition for political pur-poses and gave vent to his frustration with racism and segregation in the United States, where he had moved in 1912.

> Your door is shut against my tightened face,
> And I am sharp as steel with discontent;
> But I possess the courage and the grace
> To bear my anger proudly and unbent.
> The pavement slabs burn loose beneath my feet,
> A chafing savage, down the decent street;
> And passion rends my vitals as I pass,
> Where boldly shines your shuttered door of glass.
> Oh, I must search for wisdom every hour,
> Deep in my wrathful bosom sore and raw,
> And find in it the superhuman power
> To hold me to the letter of your law!
> Oh, I must keep my heart inviolate
> Against the potent poison of your hate.
> (1925, Burnett 144)

The **ode** is defined by its solemn and often exalted mood and can take the shape of regular or irregular stanzas of various length and number. John Keats (GB, 1795-1821), who suffered from the death of his parents as a boy and from the loss of his brother as a young man, expressed his delight in sensuous experience and his melancholy awareness of the brevity of life in his poem "To Autumn":

1
Season of mists and mellow fruitfulness,
   Close bosom-friend of the maturing sun;
Conspiring with him how to load and bless
   With fruit the vines that round the thatch-eves run;
To bend with apples the moss'd cottage-trees,
   And fill all fruit with ripeness to the core;
    To swell the gourd, and plump the hazel shells
   With a sweet kernel; to set budding more,
And still more, later flowers for the bees,
Until they think warm days will never cease,
    For summer has o'er-brimm'd their clammy cells.

2
Who hath not seen thee oft amid thy store?
   Sometimes whoever seeks abroad may find
Thee sitting careless on a granary floor,
   Thy hair soft-lifted by the winnowing wind;
Or on a half-reap'd furrow sound asleep,
   Drows'd with the fume of poppies, while thy hook
    Spares the next swath and all its twined flowers:
And sometimes like a gleaner thou dost keep
   Steady thy laden head across a brook;
   Or by a cyder-press, with patient look,
    Thou watchest the last oozings hours by hours.

3
   Where are the songs of spring? Ay, where are they?
    Think not of them, thou hast thy music too,—
   While barred clouds bloom the soft-dying day,
    And touch the stubble-plains with rosy hue;
   Then in a wailful choir the small gnats mourn
    Among the river sallows, borne aloft
     Or sinking as the light wind lives or dies;

And full-grown lambs loud bleat from hilly bourn;
Hedge-crickets sing; and now with treble soft
The red-breast whistles from a garden-croft;
And gathering swallows twitter in the skies.
(1819; NAEL 2: 872-73)

Postmodern poetry | 2.5

Beginning in the 1960s and 1970s, postmodern poets have expressed their scepticism about the possibility to find order and meaning in reality, about language as representation of reality and poetry as the expression of subjectivity. Traditional forms of poetry
could not appropriately render the sense of the indeterminacy and
arbitrariness of experience (cp. Link 666-90). An approach that tries
to find a composition that integrates form and content into a coherent and meaningful whole would be inadequate. Instead, it is
interesting to see how postmodern poetry invites a rethinking of
traditional expectations. In his poem "Our Youth", John Ashbery
(US, 1927-) refuses to give an accessible retrospect, which would
explain how the present self builds on the past. Instead, he compi-
les fragments and associations that sometimes verge on surrea-
lism:

Our Youth
Of bricks ... Who built it? Like some crazy balloon
When love leans on us
Its nights ... The velvety pavement sticks to our feet.
The dead puppies turn us back on love. [...]

Do you know it? Hasn't she
Observed you too? Haven't you been observed to her?
My, haven't the flowers been? Is the evil
In't? What window? What did you say there?

He? Eh? Our youth is dead.
From the minute we discover it with eyes closed
Advancing into the mountain light.
Ouch ... You will never have that young boy,

That boy with the monocle
Could have been your father
He is passing by. No, that other one,
Upstairs. He is the one who wanted to see you. [. . .]

Blue hampers . . . Explosions,
Ice . . . The ridiculous
Vases of porphyry. All that our youth
Can't use, that it was created for.

It's true we have not avoided our destiny
By weeding out the old people.
Our faces have filled with smoke. We escape
Down the cloud ladder, but the problem has not been solved.
(Hall 190-91)

Some phrases begin but remain incomplete like fragments of memory. The poem hardly gives any answers. The questions about the heterosexual gaze take an ironic view of adolescence, the question about the flowers ridicules the adult's nostalgia. Instead, the boyhood of the past seems to be as fleeting as the impression of the boy passing by in the present. Present and past seem to merge. The poem takes the paradoxical perspective that we can neither grasp our past nor free ourselves from the traditions that shape our lives.

2.6 | Guiding questions and exercises

Connecting content with composition

Every critic is first and foremost an individual reader, who develops a subjective understanding of a poem on the basis of personal associations related to experience in life and the knowledge of texts. The interpretation of the meaning, why a poem says something, is certainly influenced by how a poem says it: therefore, it is essential to combine the interpretation of the content with an analysis of the formal composition. The *intrinsic analysis* of a poem, which disregards its context, has two basic options: 1) to go through the whole poem under the consideration of one level after another (situation, communication, voice, content, figurative speech, metre and rhythm, phonological forms and stanza), or 2) to connect all levels in a reading that proceeds line by line, stanza by stanza. The first alternative seems to be easier because you can concentrate on one aspect after another, but it requires a subsequent synthesis of the results from each level of analysis. An extrinsic approach may be of particular interest if the poem is autobiographical, refers to other forms of representation or to historical circumstances. The following checklist merely suggests a way of proceeding which can combine questions and/or vary their order (e.g.: B A C D E F, D A B C E F). An up-to-date interpretation would combine an appropriate contemporary approach to literature (see ch. 5) with questions on analysing poetry.

Guiding questions for analysing poetry

A) Communicative situation
- External: what does the title tell us about the poem?
- Internal: who speaks to whom?
  - Persona or voice, implicit or explicit subjectivity and addressee.
- What is the mode? (lyric or epic/narrative)
- What are the mood (melancholic, happy. . .) and the tone (formal, ironic attitude. . .)?

B) Topic
- What are the situation and subject matter?
- How is the topic developed?
  - Impression, reflection, similarity, contrast, variation. . .
- Which concepts structure the meaning?
  - Love – hate, life – death, nature – culture, self – other. . .

C) Rhetorical form
- Which tropes are used and how do they convey meaning?
  - Simile, metaphor, conceit, metonymy, synecdoche, symbol, personification, allegory, hyperbole, litotes, euphemism, irony. . .
- Which schemes are used and how do they convey meanings?
  - Parallelism, chiasmus, inversion, anaphora, epiphora, repetition, ellipsis, antithesis, oxymoron. . .

D) Poetic form
- Does the poet use metre or free verse?
  - Kind and number of feet: iambic: x /, trochaic: / x, ana-

paestic: x x /, dactylic: / x x. . .
► What is the rhythm and how does it relate to the metre, the syntax and the content?
  ► Major and minor stresses, end-stopped lines, run-on lines, caesuras, sprung rhythm. . .
► Which phonological features fulfil which functions?
  ► Internal or external rhyme, masculine or feminine, continuous, alternate, pure or impure, assonance, consonance, alliteration: harmony, order, unity, memory. . .
► Do traditional forms of stanzas order the content?
► Couplet, triplet, terza rima, quatrain, ballad stanza, sestett, octett. . .
► Does the poem follow or transform a traditional type or create a form of its own?
  ► Nursery rhyme, song, ballad, dramatic monologue, sonnet, haiku. . .

E) Where, how and why do the author's rhetorical and poetic forms support or qualify the persona's position and utterance?

F) Extrinsic approach
► How does the text relate to the author's biography or cultural contexts?
  ► Personal, social, political and economic situations . . .
  ► Ideas in religion, philosophy, the arts and science . . .
►In which way does the text interact with other texts/media?
  ► Responses to texts, pictures and/or graphic depiction of still lives and landscapes,
  ► Music as topic and/or musical rhythm of language,
  ► Reflection about theatre and film or use of cinematic techniques, such as short scenes and quick transitions.

Exercise 1

Analyse Henry Wadsworth Longfellow's (US, 1807-82) poem "Nature" (see appendix for a reading).

As a fond mother, when the day is o'er,
  Leads by the hand her little child to bed,

Half willing, half reluctant to be led,
And leave his broken playthings on the floor,
Still gazing at them through the open door,
Nor wholly reassured and comforted
By promises of others in their stead,
Which, though more splendid, may not please him more;
So Nature deals with us, and takes away
Our playthings one by one, and by the hand
Leads us to rest so gently, that we go
Scarce knowing if we wish to go or stay,
Being too full of sleep to understand
How far the unknown transcends the what we know.

(1876, Link, *Amerikanische Lyrik*: 57-58)

Fig. 2.14

Lorna Dee Cervantes (1954-) was born of Mexican American parents in California. The Chicana writes poems that are frequently concerned with gender, race and ethnicity. She currently teaches English at the University of Colorado in Boulder.

Exercise 2

Analyse the poem by the Mexican American Lorna Dee Cervantes (1954-).

"The Body as Braille"

He tells me "Your back
is so beautiful." He traces
my spine with his hand.

I'm burning like the white ring
around the moon. "A witch's moon,"
dijo mi abuela. The schools call it

"a reflection of ice crystals."
It's a storm brewing in the cauldron

of the sky. I'm in love
but won't tell him
if it's omen
or ice.
(1981, NAAL 2: 2795)

Analyses: see pages 226-227.

2.7 | # Bibliography

PRIMARY SOURCES

Abrams, M. H., et al., eds. *The Norton Anthology of English Literature.* 7th ed. 2 vols. New York and London: Norton, 2000. (NAEL 1 and 2).

Baym, Nina, et al., eds. *The Norton Anthology of American Literature.* 3rd ed. 2 vols. New York and London: Norton, 1989. (NAAL 1 and 2).

Burnett, Paula, ed. *The Penguin Book of Caribbean Verse in English.* London: Penguin, 1986.

Erzgräber, Willi, and Ute Knoedgen, eds. *Moderne Englische Lyrik. Englisch und Deutsch.* 3rd ed. Stuttgart: Reclam, 1994.

Ferguson, Margaret, Mary Jo Salter and Jon Stallworthy. *The Norton Anthology of Poetry.* 5th ed. London and New York: Norton, 2005.

Hall, Donald, ed. *Contemporary American Poetry.* 2nd ed. Rev. and expanded. London et al.: Penguin, 1972.

Kemp, Friedhelm, Werner von Koppenfels, Manfred Pfister, et al., eds. *Englische und Amerikanische Dichtung. Zweisprachig.* 4 vols. Munich: Beck, 2000.

Kennelly, Brendan, ed. *The Penguin Book of Irish Verse.* 2nd ed. London: Penguin, 1981.

Link, Franz, ed. *Amerikanische Lyrik. Vom 17. Jahrhundert bis zur Gegenwart. Bilingual.* Trans. Franz and Annemarie Link. 4th ed. Stuttgart: Reclam, 1998.

Löffler, Arno, and Eberhard Späth, eds. *English Poetry. Eine Anthologie für das Studium.* 4th expanded ed. Tübingen and Basel: Francke, 2003.

Representative Poetry Online. Version 3.0. Ed. Combined Departments of English, University of Toronto. 16 October 2002. University of Toronto. Date of access: 29 August 2007. <http://rpo.library.utoronto.ca/display/index.cfm>. (Major anthology of poetry in English from the 16th to the early 20th century; six indexes).

Rosengarten, Herbert, and Amanda Goldrick-Jones, eds. *The Broadview Anthology of Poetry.* Peterborough (CDN), Orchard Parks (USA), and Hadleigh (GB): Broadview, 1993.

Whittaker, Mervyn and Nicola, eds. *100 Songs. Words and Music.* Stuttgart: Reclam, 1998.

SECONDARY SOURCES

*Baldick, Chris. *The Concise Oxford Dictionary of Literary Terms.* 2nd ed. Oxford: Oxford University Press, 2001. (Very helpful definitions of central terms).

*Beck, R, H., and M. Kuester. *Terminologie der Literaturwissenschaft. Ein Handbuch für das Anglistikstudium*. Ismaning: Hueber, 1998. (Very helpful definitions and examples of technical terms).

*Bode, Christoph. *Einführung in die Lyrikanalyse*. Trier: WVT, 2001. (Very readable, clear and entertaining).

Hamilton, Ian, ed. *The Oxford Companion to Twentieth-Century Poetry in English*. Oxford: Oxford University Press, 1994. (Biographical information and lists of publications of poets from the USA, GB and the Commonwealth; concise information on genres and movements).

Hanke, Michael. *Interpretationen: englische Gedichte des 20. Jahrhunderts*. Stuttgart: Reclam, 1997. (Short and readable interpretations).

*Hühn, Peter. *Geschichte der englischen Lyrik*. 2 vols. Tübingen and Basel: Francke, 1995. (Excellent history of poetry in the form of case studies of individual authors and model interpretations of important poems).

Link, Franz. *Make It New. US-Amerikanische Lyrik des 20. Jahrhunderts*. Paderborn: Schöningh, 1996. (Very helpful overview of major poets and movements; brief interpretations of selected poems).

*Ludwig, Hans-Werner. *Arbeitsbuch Lyrikanalyse*. 5th ed. Tübingen: Narr, 2005. (Very good and reader-friendly textbook with basic information on various approaches to poetry and numerous quotes from critics and poets).

McRae, John. *The Language of Poetry*. London and New York: Routledge, 1998. (A poet's hands-on approach to poetry).

Parini, Jan, ed. *The Columbia History of American Poetry*. New York: Columbia University Press, 1993. (30 essays on movements, poets and forms in context).

Preminger, Alex, and T. V. F. Brogan, eds. *The New Princeton Encyclopaedia of Poetry and Poetics*. Princeton: Princeton University Press, 1993. (Comprehensive guide to history, techniques, genres and criticism of poetry).

Riggs, Thomas, ed. *Contemporary Poets*. 7th ed. Detroit: St. James-Gale, 2001. (American, Australian, Canadian and Indian poets' biographies and lists of publications, short critical essays and selective lists of criticism).

Steele, Timothy. *All the Fun's In How You Say a Thing: An Explanation of Meter and Versification*. Athens: Ohio University Press, 1999. (Clear, readable and entertaining).

*Strongly recommended.

Narrative

Contents

3.1	Oral and written narratives	60
3.2	Discourse	63
3.2.1	Narrative situations	63
3.2.2	Voice and focalisation	69
3.2.3	Time	76
3.3	Story	79
3.4	Fiction and metafiction	84
3.5	Guiding questions and exercises	85
3.6	Bibliography	91

Abstract

Narrative texts present ways of seeing the world in the stories they tell. Stories are about characters in a sequence of actions and events in particular circumstances. It is possible to restrict the analysis of a narrative to the level of the content but it is also important to see that the way a story is perceived and told changes its significance.

3.1 | Oral and written narratives

Change the name, and it's about you, that story.
Horace, *Satires*

We live immersed in narrative, recounting and reassessing the meaning of our past actions, anticipating the outcome of our future projects, situating ourselves at the intersection of several stories not yet completed.
Peter Brooks, *Reading for the Plot*, 1984

Every day, we tell stories about our experience to each other. For the better or worse, we also figure in the stories of others. Young children love to be told stories over and over again, and old people love to tell stories over and over again. The fact that even well-behaved and intelligent couples vehemently argue about who is entitled to tell a particular story in which way and what happened in the first place reminds us to pay close attention to both the manner and the matter of story-telling. Stories come in all shapes and sizes, and it is hard to tell whether they reconstruct or construct the past. Psychoanalysis, medicine, trials and historiography could hardly do without them. They serve to inform and entertain, to provide identity and orientation in the world.

Narrative: story and discourse

A **narrative** (*Erzählung*) combines **discourse** (*Diskurs, Erzählweise*), *the form of how something is told by whom to whom*, and **story**, *the content of what is told*.

We know what a good story in the traditional sense is when we hear one, and we can sense that we told a good story if the listener no longer asks "what's next?" and "why?". The novelist E.M. Forster used this insight when he presented *a sequence of two events* as a **story** (*Geschichte*): "'The king died and then the queen died'". He continued that the **plot** (*Handlungsstruktur*) provided the logical connection between the events, adding ". . . of grief" (in Genette 20, German trans. 203). In response, the narratologist Genette said that the simple headline "The king died" (20) already qualifies for a minimal story because "as soon as there is an action or an event, even a single one, there is a story because there is a transformation, a transition from an earlier state to a later and resultant state" (19, Germ. trans. 202).

Oral storytelling

Oral storytelling is the origin of narrative texts (Fludernik). Oral stories distinctly reveal central narrative features. In order to be interesting and meaningful to a listener, a good story needs to be wrapped and presented like a gift. Mark how the narrator presents her experience in Alice Childress's (US, 1920-1994) short story "Health-Card" (1956), which imitates oral storytelling:

Well, Marge, I started an extra job today. . . . Just wait, girl. Don't laugh yet. Just wait till I tell you. . . . The woman seems real nice. . . . Well, you know what I mean. [. . .] Comes the afternoon, I was busy waxin' woodwork when I notice her hoverin' over me kind of timid-like. She passed me once and smiled and then she turned and blushed a little. I put down the wax can and gave her an inquirin' look. The lady takes a deep breath and comes up with, "Do you live in Harlem, Mildred?" [. . .] she backed away and retired to the living room and I could hear her and the husband just a-buzzin'. A little later on I was in the kitchen washin' glasses. I looks up and there she was in the doorway, lookin' kind of strained around the gills. First she stuttered and then she stammered and after beatin' all around the bush she comes out with, "Do you have a health card, Mildred?"

That let the cat out of the bag. I thought real fast. Honey, my brain was run-nin' on wheels. "Yes, Mrs. Jones," I says, "I have a health card." Now Marge, this is a lie. I do not have a health card. "I'll bring it tomorrow," I add real sweet-like. [. . .] "Mildred," she said, "I don't mean any offense, but one must be careful, mustn't one?"

Well, all she got from me was solid agreement. "Sure," I said, "indeed one must, and I am glad you are so understandin' 'cause I was just worrying and studyin' on how I was goin' to ask you for yours, and of course you'll let me see one from your husband and one for each of the three children." [. . .] "Mil-dred, you don't have to bring a health card. I am sure it will be all right."

I looked up real casual kind-of and said, "On second thought, you folks look real clean, too, so . . ." And then she smiled and I smiled and then she smiled again . . . Oh, stop laughin' so loud, Marge, everybody on this bus is starin'.
(Nischik 58-9)

This narrative reveals typical features of oral storytelling: the teller (1) introduces the story by mentioning what it is about, (2) specifies who takes part in it at which place and time, (3) talks about the de-velopment of a conflict, (4) its evaluation, (5) its resolution, and (6) finally marks that the story has come to an end and takes the lis-tener back to the here and now (Martinez/Scheffel 146). In most oral stories, the narrator's explanations and evaluations are promi-nent at the turning point between the complication and the reso-lution of the problem, but they occur throughout the story in order to repeatedly convey its significance to the listener (Martinez/Schef-fel 146). In this case, Mildred explains to her listener that her lie is the key problem before she introduces her clever resolution with implicit irony: "Well, all she got from me was solid agreement."

Her story reverses the stereotype of the inferior poor black woman on the level of the story and the discourse. She turns the tables on her employer, who displays prejudice and anxiety. Mildred presents herself as a self-reliant actor and as a clever storyteller with a voice of her own. She not only informs and entertains her friend but creates a black female bond against discrimination.

In everyday life, the actual teller of the story is identical with its first-person narrator, and the real listener with the **addressee** (*Adressat*) in the story. In Alice Childress's simulated first-person narrative, *the real author is as different from the narrator as the addressee from the real reader*. Regardless of the question whether the real reader of this story is black or white, the *story implies a reader*, who would be able to understand and appreciate that the story is critical about conflicts of class and race and gender: the employer worries about Mildred's residence in Harlem, consults her husband before she acts, uses "white" language, and is outwitted in the end. In turn, *real readers construct an image of the implied author from the whole text*, someone who would be responsible for the values and the structure of the story. Here, the implied author would question the racist and patriarchal white culture and promote a resourceful black culture and identity. Thus, a **model of narrative communication** would distinguish between the real author (Alice Childress) and her readers (you and me), the implied author and reader, the narrator and the narratee (Mildred and Marge) and the figures who talk to each other on the level of the story (Mildred and the white lady):

Fig. 3.1

Model of narrative communication (compare Jahn and Nünning 285).

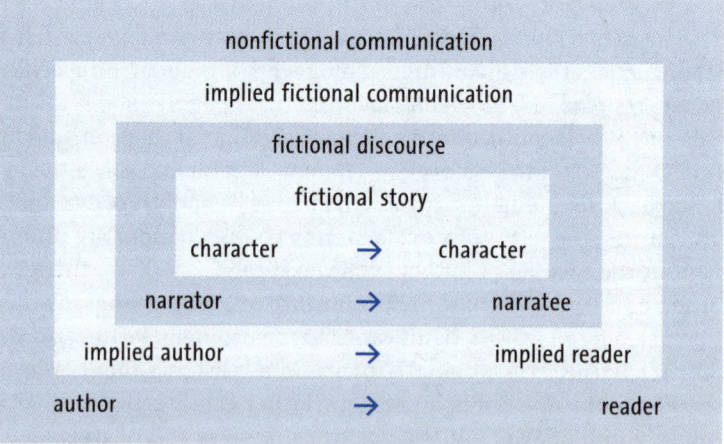

Short stories resemble oral stories in small size, flexible subject matter, style and form. They often concentrate on one character, action, place and time, and select a particular moment of crisis, reversal and insight. Short stories tend to be less explicit than oral stories and therefore demand great attention to details, images, beginnings and endings. They compensate for brevity by being ambiguous, allusive and suggestive.

Due to their sheer size, **novels** (*Romane*) have the option to present a great number of characters and strands of action (*Handlungsstränge*) as well as comprehensive descriptions of both external settings and "internal experientiality", such as scenes of consciousness (Fludernik 79-80, 158). They can probe the depth of characters, discuss a range of different perspectives and give a large panorama of society.

The basic strategies of narrative analysis are useful to explore how short stories and novels construct fictional worlds. You can analyse a narrative by beginning with the story or the discourse. We start with the discourse because it determines the quantity and quality of information about the story.

Discourse | 3.2

The communication in the text between a narrator and a narratee can be analysed according to the following questions: Who speaks to whom? Which position does the narrator have inside or outside the world of the story? In which way and in which order does the narrator speak about which characters and events? Two major approaches dominate this field, Franz K. Stanzel's concept of three narrative situations, and the structuralists' more detailed analysis of the verbal, visual and temporal organisation of narrative discourse, following Seymour Chatman and Gérard Genette among others.

Narrative situations | 3.2.1

Stanzel's **first-person narrator** (*Ich-Erzähler*) shares the characters' world. The **authorial narrator** (*auktorialer Erzähler*) is beyond the characters' world and looks at it from the outside but also has the ability to look into characters. The **figural narrative situation** (*personale Erzählsituation*) *has no visible narrator and presents events through a character's perspective.*

Who tells a story?

Fig. 3.2

An illustration of Daniel Defoe's (1660-1731) Robinson Crusoe (1719). The Englishman Defoe was an entrepreneur, secret agent, editor and writer. He published widely on education, commerce and politics before turning to novels, such as the allegorical narrative of the colonial and Puritan Robinson Crusoe or the fictional autobiography of the thief and prostitute Moll Flanders (1722). Due to the rather simple, straightforward style and the detailed descriptions of circumstances, Defoe's novels are considered an early form of realism. Separated from his family, Defoe died in hiding from his creditors.

First-person narrators   The first-person narrator is involved in the world of the story. The extent and variation of the temporal and cognitive distance between the **narrating I** (*erzählendes Ich*) and the **experiencing I** (*erlebendes Ich*) determines the quality of the narrative. For example, in the beginning of Daniel Defoe's (1660-1731) *Robinson Crusoe* (1719), the *narrator looks back with regret at the former disobedience* of his parents, who did not want him to go to sea:

> I consulted neither father or mother any more, nor so much as sent them word of it; but leaving them to hear of it as they might, without asking God's blessing, or my father's, without any consideration of circumstances or consequences, and in an ill hour, God knows, on the first of September 1651 I went on board a ship bound for London. Never any young adventurer's misfortunes, I believe, began sooner, or continued longer, than mine. (31)

The narrator also reveals his *past* perspective, for example by quoting from his *diary*, which *vividly conveys the immediate emotional impact of his recent experience on the island*:

> September 30, 1659. I, poor miserable Robinson Crusoe, being shipwreck'd, during a dreadful Storm, in the offing, came on shore on this dismal unfortunate island, which I called the Island of Despair, all the rest of the ship's company being drowned, and my self almost dead.
> All the rest of that day I spent in afflicting my self at the dismal circumstances I was brought to, viz. I had neither food, house, clothes, weapon, or place to fly to, and in despair of any relief, saw nothing but death before me [. . .]. (87)

Robinson forms the *centre of his own story* (**I-as-protagonist**), whereas the first major female English author Aphra Behn (1640-89) uses the *first person as a minor character and observer* (**I-as-witness**) in her exotic narrative *Oroonoko, or the Royal Slave* (1688). She comments on the natural limits of awareness without direct access to others' feelings and thoughts: "I was myself an eye-witness to a great part of what you will find here set down; and what I could not be witness of, I receiv'd from the mouth of the chief actor in this history, the hero himself" (NAEL 1: 2171). The narrator as witness often juxtaposes his/her own point-of-view with that of the protagonist and of society, revealing interesting contradictions and conflicts between positions.

Aphra Behn (1640-1689) was the first English-woman to make a living from writing. She was well-known for her daring lifestyle and literary output. She worked as a spy and served a term in prison for debt. Her satirical plays focus on sexual relationships and her colourful novel Oroonoko (1688) on the evil effects of slavery without, however, opting for equality among the races and social ranks.

Fig. 3.3

The rise of the first-person narrative between the sixteenth and the nineteenth century can be explained in various ways. Of course, oral stories about personal experience privilege the first person. In addition, diaries, letters, essays and autobiographies offer models of writing in the first person, which are connected to the central position of the individual since the early modern age in Western culture. For example, Puritanism demands individual inspiration and responsibility for moral acts, the soul and the personal relation to God, inspiring soul-searching diaries and spiritual autobiographies. Empiricism favours individual experience as against traditional authority. Capitalism idealises the individual *homo oeconomicus*, whose self-interest would also promote public welfare. The bourgeois society does away with the absolutist external control of its subjects and demands the citizen's internal discipline and civilised behaviour. The concepts and values of Puritanism, em-

Reasons for telling first-person narratives

pirism and capitalism pervade Benjamin Franklin's (US, 1706-1790) famous autobiography (1771-88) about his rise from rags to riches. The self-made man does not hesitate to proclaim himself a role-model and a representative of his society:

> Having emerg'd from the Poverty and Obscurity in which I was born and bred, to a State of Affluence and some Degree of Reputation in the World, and having gone so far thro' life with a considerable share of Felicity, the conducing Means I made use of, which, with the blessing of God, so well succeeded, my Posterity may like to know, as they may find some of them suitable to their own Situations, and therefore fit to be imitated. (43)

Sentiment (*Empfindung, Empfindsamkeit*) as a new eighteenth century ideal is promoted and explored in the English novelist Samuel Richardson's (1698-1761) **epistolary novel** (*Briefroman*) *Pamela, or Virtue Rewarded* (1740). Pamela's letters explore in detail her intense emotional responses to her encounters with the wealthy and unscrupulous Mr. B., who pursues her as a sexual object but is tamed by her virtue and marries her in the end. In sum, religious, philosophical, social and economic ideas stress the prominence of the individual, who finds an appropriate form of self-expression in first-person narratives.

Authorial narrators

In opposition to the subjective presentations of the world in the first person, the objective authorial narrator is detached from the characters and their concerns. The **authorial narrative** *offers a godlike panoramic view from an Olympic position outside and above the story world*. The misleading term "authorial" narrator does not mean that this narrator is identical with the real author. The fact that authorial narrators behave like the creators of their world is an artistic choice. The *authorial narrator mediates between the world of the characters and that of the reader, creating the illusion of a fictional world but also breaking it by intrusive comments and reader addresses*. The English novelist Henry Fielding (1707-54) introduced the authorial narrative in *The History of Tom Jones, a Foundling* (1740):

> Reader, I think proper, before we proceed any farther together, to acquaint thee, that I intend to digress, through this whole history, as often as I see occasion: of which I am myself a better judge than any pitiful critic whatever […] I have told my reader in the preceding chapter, that Mr. Allworthy inherited a large fortune; that he had a good heart, and no family. Hence, doubtless, it will be concluded by many, that he lived like an honest man, owed no

one a shilling, [...] And true it is, that he did many of these things; but, had he done nothing more, I should have left him to have recorded his own merit [...] Matters of a much more extraordinary kind are to be the subject of this history, or I should grossly misspend my time in writing so voluminous a work; and you, my sagacious friend, might, with equal profit and pleasure, travel through some pages [...] (Bk 1, ch. 2 and 3; 26-27)

Being **omnipresent** (*überall anwesend*) and **omniscient** (*allwissend*), the authorial narrator can see into the future, read various characters' thoughts and even their subconscious. Sharing his/her distance and supernatural insight with the reader, he/she can expose secrets that characters hide from each other or those that are hidden from themselves with the effect that the reader gains an insight into hypocrisy and blindness. *The authorial narrator's superior insight conveys the notion that the world is transparent and comprehensible.* This optimistic view, which prevailed from the middle of the eighteenth to the nineteenth century, is loosely connected to the idea that the universe is ruled by divine laws and by providence. The authorial narrative situation can be seen as an imitation of the divine perspective on the human world, which may parallel religious faith or compensate for its absence.

The omniscient narrator's insight into characters sometimes merges into the characters' view of the world, approaching figural narrative. The **neutral scenic narrative** of action and dialogues as if in drama is a borderline case between the authorial and the figural narrative situation because the perspective is external but the narrator nowhere present.

The term *personale Erzählsituation* (**figural narrative situation**) wrongly suggests that the narrator takes the shape of a fully blown person, but it actually refers to the character's perspective. Readers get the impression that they share the thoughts, feelings and perceptions of a character, who serves as a (subjective) **reflector** of the fictional world. Figural narratives *show scenes in the world* through the eyes of characters, whereas first-person and authorial narrators often foreground their discourse and *tell us about the world* with a certain distance. Reality television serves as a good example for the difference between figural narrative and first-person narrative. Reality television which reenacts crimes presents the views of characters in action and the description of their experience in voice-over at the same time. The combination of the immediate visual

Figural narrative situation

Showing versus telling

presence of the subjective perspective, simulated with a hand-held camera, and the parallel third-person description is akin to figural narrative. These scenes are often framed by retrospective first-person comments from the victims or the perpetrators of the crimes and by more or less neutral explanations from experts.

Fig. 3.4

The Irishman James Joyce (1882-1941) left Catholicism and Ireland behind in 1904, only to return to his home country time and again in his collection of short stories, Dubliners *(1914), his autobiographical* Portrait of the Artist as a Young Man *(1916), and his singular novel* Ulysses *(1922), which delineates a single day in the life of three inhabitants of Dublin, establishing a mock-heroic correspondence of their ordinary modern lives to Homer's* Odyssey. *Joyce's experiments with language and style to convey subjective experience culminated in* Finnegan's Wake *(1939).*

Figural narrative texts show third-person characters' perspectives:

through the eyes of a child

Once upon a time and a very good time it was there was a moocow coming down along the road met a nicens little boy named baby tuckoo. . . .
His father told him that story: his father looked at him through a glass: he had a hairy face. [. . .]
When you wet the bed, first it is warm and then it gets cold. His mother put on the oilsheet. That had the queer smell.
(James Joyce, GB, 1882-1941, *A Portrait of the Artist as a Young Man*, 1916, 1)

The beginning refers to a story that the father told his little son. The second sentence suggests that the little boy perceived this story. The choice of words imitates a small child's language to some extent. The father certainly looked at him through a monocle and not a simple glass. The illusion of an immediate access to a third person's mind is particularly interesting if that character could not or would not talk about him- or herself to anyone. In addition, the information is not filtered, as it would be in a first-person narrative due to the fear of exposing oneself to others. Who would volunteer information on wetting the bed? The increasing use of figural narrative towards the end of the nineteenth century relates to the decline of trust in "omnipotent" and reliable authorities (and authorial narrators), to advances in psychological research into mental processes and to the rise of impressionism in painting.

Voice and focalisation

Gérard Genette was neither happy with Stanzel's concept of the narrative situation nor with the broad use of the term **point-of-view** (*Gesichtspunkt, Standpunkt*) because both combine the way a narrator tells a story and how its world is perceived. Instead, he made a clear difference between the questions "Who speaks?" (voice) and "Who perceives?" (focalisation; Genette 64, German trans. 132). The question of the **voice** can be extended to *"Who speaks to whom from which position in relation to the story?"* **Focalisation** has "perceptual, psychological and ideological facets" (Rimmon-Kenan 82), which are *sense impressions, emotional and cognitive processes and a system of norms.*

In order to answer the question "Who speaks?", we have to find who and where the narrator is in the first place. In some cases, the invisible, **covert narrator** (*verborgener Erzähler*) is merely *a voice that reports information.* The author passes on the task of evaluating the story to the reader. In contrast, an **overt narrator** (*expliziter Erzähler*) appears as a *mediator in the discourse.* Overt narrators introduce themselves and the stories to the reader and give comments that guide the readers' understanding. There are many variations in between a mere neutral voice and a narrator who seems to be a complex character.

Who speaks …

What is the narrator's position? A **heterodiegetic narrator** (*heterodiegetischer Erzähler*) does not belong to the world of the characters. A **homodiegetic narrator** (*homodiegetischer Erzähler*) belongs to the story world and is called an **autodiegetic narrator** if he/she tells the story of his/her own life. These technical terms roughly correspond to Stanzel's third-person and first-person narrative situation.

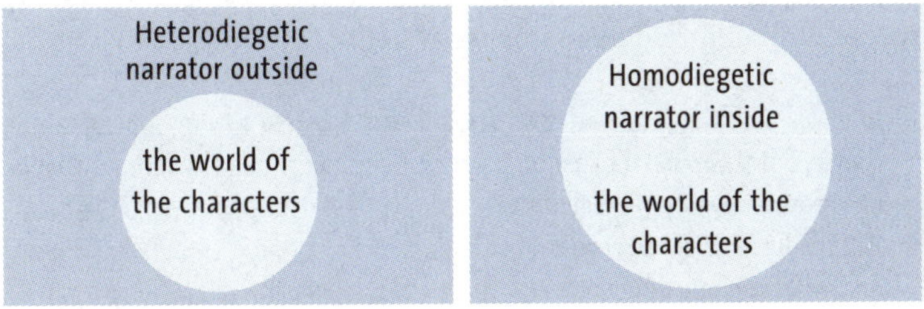

… from which position …

Heterodiegetic
narrator outside

the world of
the characters

Homodiegetic
narrator inside

the world of the
characters

Fig. 3.5

Heterodiegetic and homodiegetic narrators.

...in which part
of a narrative?

In a story-within-the-story, an **embedded narrative** (*Binnenerzählung*) within a **frame narrative** (*Rahmenerzählung*), the **intradiegetic narrator** tells his/her embedded story from within the primary or frame narrative, which is told by the **extradiegetic narrator**. What is the use of this distinction? Framing narratives directs the reader's attention to the ways and uses of storytelling itself in the specific transition zones between one story and another, and indirectly in the relationship between the embedded and the frame narrative. In *The Scarlet Letter* (1850), the American novelist Nathaniel Hawthorne (1804-64) introduces the story about a proud adulteress in Puritan Salem in the 17th century with a contemporary scene from the 19th century, "The Custom House". In this frame, the narrator, who was suffering from bureaucracy and the oppressive atmosphere, found the fascinating papers and documents of a story that he has (re)constructed. The embedded story of the Puritan past presents both the origins and a mirror image of New England culture in the nineteenth century.

Fig. 3.6

Extradiegetic and intradiegetic narrators.

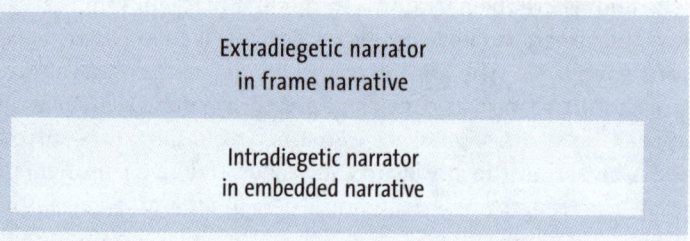

Extradiegetic narrator
in frame narrative

Intradiegetic narrator
in embedded narrative

The narrator's presentation of him/herself and the story leads us to the question whether he/she is **reliable** (*zuverlässig*) or **unreliable** (*unzuverlässig*). In general, an omniscient and detached heterodiegetic narrator inspires confidence. We have to be more careful with homodiegetic narrators because of their limited perception and insight. In Charlotte Perkins Gilman's (US, 1860-1935) story "The Yellow Wallpaper" (1892), the autodiegetic narrator confronts the reader with different assessments of her condition:

> John is a physician, and perhaps – (I would not say it to a living soul, of course, but this is dead paper and a great relief to my mind –) perhaps that is one reason I do not get well faster.
> You see he does not believe I am sick!
> And what can one do?

> If a physician of high standing, and one's own husband, assures friends and
> relatives that there is really nothing the matter with one but temporary nerv-
> ous depression – a slight hysterical tendency – what is one to do? (NAAL 2: 649)

If the female narrator maintains – in secret and against male authority – that her health is even worse than "nervous depression"
and a "hysterical tendency", how far does the reader believe her
version of the story? What, in turn, should the reader make of her
husband's downplaying her illness? This ambiguous situation
draws the reader's attention to the question of reliability, a narrator's or a character's trustworthiness, social position, (hidden) motives and strategies. We hardly trust a narrator who openly con-
fesses to uncertainty, mental problems or profoundly disagrees
with what everybody else says. However, his/her unfamiliar perspective also gives new insight into society.

The reader has basically three strategies to *test the reliability of a*   Checking
narrative, to check its (1) consistency, (2) coherence and (3) correspondence.   reliability
(1) A consistent narrative does not reveal contradictions between
the narrator's words and acts, values and judgements, self-image
and images by others, his/her version of events and those of others.
(2) A coherent narrative presents a story in which one event leads
to another without significant temporal or logical gaps. (3) There is
no direct correspondence between reality and fiction, which creates its own world, but rather one between the fictional models of
reality and the dominant view of the world at the time of writing.
The contextual frames of reference (historical background) define
implicit and explicit norms, such as the "nature", relationship and
function of men and women, black and white, rich and poor, the
individual and society, insider and outsider, home and abroad, reason and emotion, good and evil, etc. Of course, the criterion of correspondence is more helpful with realistic stories than fantastic
ones, which have more options to create alternative worlds. In
Donald Barthelme's (US, 1931-89) short story "The Baby" (Nischik
52-54), the self-righteous first-person narrator is obsessed with the
breaking and enforcement of rules in education. He punishes his
baby for tearing pages out of a book by locking her up for hours.
This treatment, the narrator continues, was "worrying my wife.
But I felt that if you made a rule you had to stick to it" (52). His
view of education verges on tyranny and contradicts both his wife's
and our contemporary notion of the psychology and upbringing of

babies. In the end, he has sentenced the baby to years of confinement and realises that he has a problem:

> I solved it by declaring that it was all right to tear pages out of books, and
> moreover, that it was all right to have torn pages out of books in the past
> [...] The baby and I sit happily on the floor, side by side, tearing pages out of
> books, and sometimes, just for fun, we go out on the street and smash a
> windshield together. (54)

Unreliability

We do not only question the narrator's judgement but also his
basic perception of reality when he tells us that "We gave the baby
some of our wine, red, white, and blue, and spoke seriously to her"
(53). The narrator gives no hint that his statement is ironic or
metaphoric. In literal terms, giving wine to a baby would be irre-
sponsible, but giving blue wine and arguing seriously with a baby
makes us ask whether the narrator is in his right mind. However,
we can read this statement as authorial irony about the United
States because the colours of the national flag are transferred to
those of an intoxicating drink. Strange characters and unreliable
narrators defamiliarise the vision of the world and challenge our
views. Thus, Barthelme's story gives rise to a discussion of the relationship between the individual and society, the questions of freedom, responsibility and justice in education and in the law.

The focus of
perception

There is no statement and no observation without an observer.
Focalisation (*Fokalisierung*) *asks who perceives what in which way.* You can
spot the focaliser by tracing the reference of the verbs of perception, feeling and thinking to the subject of the statement. **Internal
focalisation** locates the perspective within a character, limiting the
information to his/her perceptual and conceptual grasp of the
world. Internal focalisation can vary between **fixed focalisation**,
which is restricted to one and the same perspective throughout the
narrative (Joyce, *Portrait of the Artist as a Young Man*), **variable focalisation**, which presents different scenes through different perspectives
(Wilkie Collins, GB, 1824-89, *The Woman in White*, 1860), or **multiple
focalisation**, which invites comparisons between several perspectives
of the same event (Julian Barnes, GB, 1946-, *Talking It Over*, 1991). **External focalisation** presents information of characters' external behaviour, such as speech and action, excluding feelings and
thoughts. The awkward term **zero focalisation** does not mean that
no perspective is given but that the perspective cannot be attrib-

uted to someone in particular or has no restrictions and thus can vary, such as that of Stanzel's omniscient narrator. The question is whether the different points-of-view can be subsumed under **one comprehensive or monologic view** of the world or fall apart into **conflicting or dialogic perspectives**, multiplying options to make sense of the world. In detail, a narrator has different options to represent a character's mental processes and utterances, which can be ordered along a line that ranges from (diegetic) telling to (mimetic) showing:

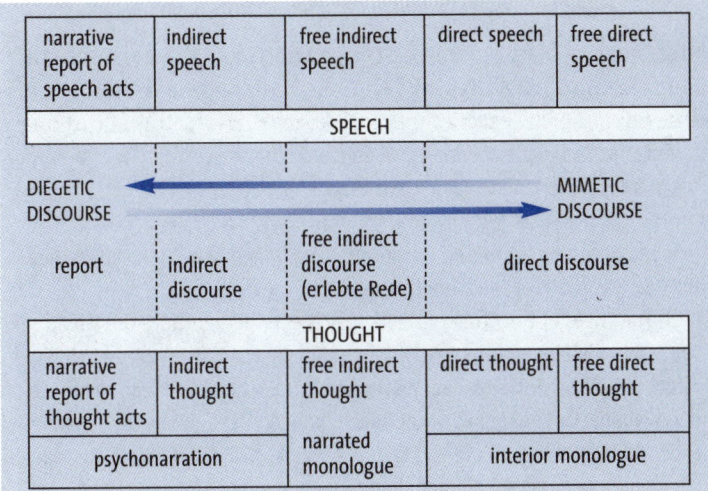

Fig. 3.7

Narrative representation of characters' words and thoughts (Jahn and Nünning 294).

The following examples clarify the narrator's choice between different forms of revealing the characters' inner lives:

Example	Type	Characteristics
Mary pondered her next move	report of thought act	narrator's summary
Mary wondered what she should do	indirect thought	narrator = main clause, character = subordinate clause
What on earth should she do now?	free indirect thought	character's language with shift in person and tense
She thought, "What on earth shall I do now?"	direct thought	character's language unshifted
What on earth shall I do now?	free direct thought	no reporting clause; no quotation marks

Fig. 3.8

Narrative presentations of consciousness (Jahn and Nünning 295).

The **narrative report** (*Erzählerbericht*) represents a character's speech or thought in the narrator's style. Often, it takes the form of a summary, as in the beginning of Chinua Achebe's (Nigeria, 1930-) story "Dead Man's Path":

> Michael Obi's hopes were fulfilled much earlier than he had expected. He was appointed headmaster of Ndume Central School in 1949 [. . .] Obi accepted this responsibility with enthusiasm. He had many wonderful ideas and this was an opportunity to put them into practice. (Nischik 67)

A later passage from the same story reveals how the narrator shifts his representation of Ms Obi's thoughts and words in indirect discourse (id; *indirekte Rede/Gedankenwiedergabe*), free indirect discourse (fid; *freie indirekte Rede, erlebte Rede*), narrative report (nr; *Erzählerbericht*), and direct discourse (dd; *direkte Rede*):

> (id) She began to see herself already as the admired wife of the young headmaster, the queen of the school.
> (fid) The wives of the other teachers would envy her position. She would set the fashion in everything . . . (id) Then, suddenly, it occurred to her that there might not be other wives. (nr) Wavering between hope and fear, she asked her husband, looking anxiously at him.
> (dd) "All our colleagues are young and unmarried," he said with enthusiasm, (nr) which for once she did not share. (Nischik 68)

In a perfect example of *zero focalisation*, the heterodiegetic narrator zooms into and out of the wife's mind and presents her husband's utterance from the outside. The narrator introduces her reflection with the tag clause "She began to see" and paraphrases the content of her thought in indirect discourse. The phrase "queen of the school" is ironic because it suggests a traditional role that contradicts the couple's idea of modernisation. The focalization foregrounds her revealing dreams of prominence in free indirect discourse, exposing their narcissistic quality. The narrator moves a step back and records the change of her thought in indirect discourse. The specific thoughts of hope and fear are not given in detail because it seems more important that her expectations will be disappointed. The narrator does not quote her question, which is implied in her thought, but her husband's answer. Her emotional response is summarized in a matter-of-fact style that prevents the

Fig. 3.9

The Nigerian Ibo Chinua Achebe (1930-), who emigrated to the US, stresses the didactic and mediating functions of journalism and literature. His novels, beginning with Things Fall Apart (1958), provide a fictional chronicle of Nigeria from precolonial to neo-colonial times. He assesses the impact of culture and society on the individual and of Europe on Africa. Achebe enriches the English language with Ibo turns and phrases (usu. in translation), creating a unique atmosphere and communicating African perspectives to readers of English.

reader's identification with her. The narrator exposes the gendered difference between Mr and Ms Obi's "wonderful ideas", stressed by the fact that she does not reveal these thoughts to her husband, who may disapprove of them. However, her secret aspiration to become "the queen of the school" also reflects back on his presumption of an absolute leading role in the village.

Free indirect discourse (*erlebte Rede*) lies on the border between telling and showing. The narrator marks mediation by transforming the first person and present/future tense to the third person and past tense/conditional: "The wives of the other teachers would envy her position" would have been "The wives of the other teachers will envy my position." Often, *free indirect discourse mixes the narrator's and the character's voices and views*. Virginia Woolf's (GB, 1882-1941) novel *To the Lighthouse* (1927) explores how a six-year-old son perceives his father:

> He hated him for coming up to them, for stopping and looking down on them; he hated him for interrupting them; he hated him for the exaltation and sublimity of his gestures; for the magnificence of his head; for his exactingness and his egotism (for there he stood, commanding them to attend to him); but most of all he hated the twang and twitter of his father's emotion which, vibrating around them, disturbed the perfect simplicity and good sense of his relations with his mother. (36-7)

Whereas the repetition of the third-person pronoun and the verb stresses the intensity of the son's hate, the father's particular characteristics are given in the narrator's elaborate words, which reveal a distance towards the boy's strong feelings (cp. James Joyce, *A Portrait of the Artist as a Young Man*, see above, 3.2.1, 68).

Fig. 3.10

The English novelist, critic and publisher Virginia Woolf (1882-1941) was a sensitive intellectual. Her experimental style, above all the use of leitmotifs and stream of consciousness in the novels To the Lighthouse *(1927) or* The Waves *(1931), represents fleeting impressions and inner experience. Woolf's witty essay* A Room of One's Own *(1929) expresses her feminist stance on the socio-cultural hindrance to the development and expression of women's creativity. She suffered from depressions and drowned herself.*

Monologue

The free direct representation of an "ordinary" stream-of-consciousness in **interior monologue** (*innerer Monolog*) faithfully *quotes* the character's thoughts. Narrative mediation gives way to the character's psychological association. Being half asleep in bed, Molly Bloom thinks about her first encounter with her husband at the very end of James Joyce's *Ulysses* (1922):

> [...] all the queer little streets and pink and blue and yellow houses and the rosegardens and the jessamine and geraniums and cactuses and Gibraltar as a girl where I was a Flower of the mountain yes then I put the rose in my hair like the Andalusian girls use or shall I wear red yes and how he kissed me under the Moorish wall and I thought well as well him as another and then I asked him with my eyes to ask again yes and then he asked me would I [...] (643-44)

The showing of free direct thought gives readers an "immediate" insight into another person's mind, which is inaccessible to them in real life.

3.2.3 | Time

A *present narrator tells a past story* at a variable point of time after its last event. Even utopian novels or science fiction, which deal with the future, usually tell stories as if they happened in the past. *The narrator has many options to shape the story by manipulating the temporal duration, order and frequency of relating story elements.* Often, the specific temporal organisation of the story is called a **plot** in contrast to Foster's definition of plot as the logical structure of a story (see above, 3.1, 60).

The **duration** of a narrative (*Erzähldauer*) results from the relationship between the **discourse time** (*Erzählzeit*, roughly: the time you need in order to tell and listen or read the story) and the **story time** (*erzählte Zeit*). We are all bored by people who tell never-ending stories because they do not select important things but dwell on every detail with minute attention. We expect narrators to omit aspects of no importance (**ellipsis**; *Auslassung*), telescope or zoom events of average or minor importance (**summary**; *Raffung*), and show events of importance in *the same time of their occurrence* (**scene**; *szenische Darstellung*) or even in slow-motion (**stretch**; *Zeitdehnung*; Chatman 67-68). A **pause** in the relation of events occurs at the description of the setting, reflections or comments. Of course, all of these techniques can be turned to particular uses: the narrator may omit an important feature for reasons of suspense, briefly mention fundamental incidents in order to focus on their effects, and expand short events for comic or symbolic purposes.

Laurence Sterne's (GB, 1713-68) novel *Tristram Shandy* (1759-67) is, among many other things, a comic novel about writing a novel and a book on time and timing. Tristram Shandy's intention is to give a complete picture of his life from its very beginning, "to go on tracing everything in it, as Horace says, *ab Ovo*" (from the very beginning, vol. I, ch. 4) rather than **in medias res** (*in voranschreitender Handlung*). In the fourth volume of the book, the autodiegetic narrator Tristram has not yet proceeded farther than the first day of his life. He is afraid that he will never be able to tell the story of his life because a day of his life contains much more than he can write of in one day, and so his writing will never catch up with the life he lives. Frequently, he interrupts the story for reflections on the process of his writing, for general considerations and reader addresses, for example:

Discourse time versus story time

> I enter upon this part of my story in the most pensive and melancholy frame of mind [...]
> – I won't go about to argue the point with you, – 'tis so, – and I am persuaded of it, madam, as much as can be, 'That both man and woman bear pain or sorrow, (and, for aught I know, pleasure too) best in a horizontal position.'
> (Vol. III, ch. 28-29)

Temporal order

In addition, Tristram struggles with the **order** of the narrative. A simple oral story begins with the beginning, arranges the events in chronological sequence and ends with the ending. Where do you begin with the story of a life? Tristram does not begin with his birth but the strange circumstances of his conception. Instead of omitting details himself, he gives readers who are not as curious about it the advice to skip parts of the text. His attempt to trace relationships between everything that is remotely connected to the story of his life leads to frequent interruptions, **associative digressions** (*Abschweifungen*), and an **anachronic** (non-chronological) combination of diverse stories about his father and his uncle rather than himself. The narrator interrupts the present chronology of the story and connects it to the future by **flashforward** (prolepsis; *Vorausdeutung*) and to the past by **flashback** (analepsis; *Rückgriff*). Besides the beginnings, endings are of prime importance for the interpretation of a story. Sterne's novel does not end with Tristram Shandy's practical achievements or conclusive opinions, but with an embedded nonsensical story, which reflects the playful book as a whole.

How many times
is something told?

A short fairy tale or a short story will usually relate every event or situation once. In a novel, the **frequency** of referring to events or situations can be handled in a more flexible manner. Tristram Shandy comes back repeatedly to his birth because being intent on telling everything, he digresses and has to return in order to relate particular circumstances. A significant variation of frequency is the repetition of the same situation by various narrators or focalisers. Julian Barnes's (GB, 1946-) novel *Talking It Over* (1991) is about an eternal triangle of two friends who fall in love with the same woman. The novel sports the motto "*He lies like an eye-witness*", which prepares the reader for the protagonists' different subjec-

Fig. 3.11

Cover of Talking It Over *(1991) by Julian Barnes (1946-). The highly sophisticated, ironic and versatile English author is fascinated with obsessive relationships, the arts, French culture and the (re)constructions of individual and collective memory. His novel* Flaubert's Parrot *(1984) delineates the futile but entertaining attempt to reconstruct literary biography. In* A History of the World in 10 1/2 Chapters *(1989), outsiders revise stories of chaos and survival from the Biblical Flood to the* Titanic. *Under the pen-name of Dan Kavanagh, he writes detective novels, such as* Putting the Boot In *(1985).*

tive versions of the same situations. The reader can reconstruct the basic external events, which, however, are of less importance than the differences between the first-person narratives. It is ironic that although the characters never seem to agree with each other at any given moment, they gradually change and take over the others' perspectives and positions in the triangle.

Story

| 3.3

There are good reasons for paying close attention to the content apart from the discourse because one can tell the "same" story in many different ways. The cognitive framework of everyday experience greatly helps us to understand realistic stories, which depict plausible characters and actions in probable circumstances. However, narrative literature often adds figural meaning to the literal one of the content.

The **setting** (*Schauplatz*) of a story is more than simply the time and place when and where the story happens. Look at a scene from the beginning of Charlotte Brontë's (GB, 1816-55) novel *Jane Eyre* (1847) and mark the symbolic meaning of the setting. The orphan Jane was excluded for alleged misbehaviour from the happy gathering of her foster-family in the living-room:

The meaning of the setting

> A small breakfast-room adjoined the drawing-room, I slipped in there. It contained a book-case; I soon possessed myself of a volume, taking care that it should be one stored with pictures. I mounted into the window-seat: gathering up my feet, I sat cross-legged, like a Turk; and, having drawn the red moreen curtain nearly close, I was shrined in double retirement.
> Folds of scarlet drapery shut in my view to the right hand; to the left were the clear panes of glass, protecting, but not separating me from the drear November day. At intervals, while turning over the leaves in my book, I studied the aspect of that winter afternoon. Afar, it offered a pale blank of mist and cloud; near, a scene of wet lawn and storm-beat shrub, with ceaseless rain sweeping away wildly before a long and lamentable blast. (39-40)

The house of Jane's foster-family does not offer her the warmth of a home. She responds to her exclusion by the double retreat into the room next door and a precious private space of her own, marked off by the permeable boundary of the curtain. The colour red returns as a symbol of her passions, which are the cause of her sepa-

Semantic space

ration from the other children and made her rebel against being abused. The curtain is not quite closed and the window offers a view, signifying that her place as an outsider is neither here nor there but in-between, subject to influences from the private and the public sphere, society and nature. The bleak and freezing afternoon, however, does not provide an escape from her situation but rather mirrors her inner desolation. So does the shrub in the storm-driven rain, which adds to the sad and melancholy effect of the setting. Throughout the novel, oppressive houses, exclusion and inclusion, retreats into private places, vistas through windows, escapes and the change of seasons form the literal and symbolic locations of Jane's internal and external development.

Functions of settings

Settings have many functions. Even detailed descriptions of places and objects never come up to the fullness of phenomena which the real world offers to perceptive observers but form verbal scaffolds that the reader imaginatively transforms into pictures. Within the fictional world, settings serve as *locations for characters in action*, and provide *a scenery and an atmosphere characters perceive and respond to* in various ways. In addition, settings acquire *aesthetic meaning* in terms of their symbolic function and in comparison to similar or opposite settings in the whole story. Finally, the setting is *related to the social, political and cultural field* in the sense of social inclusion and exclusion as well as the drawing and transgression of boundaries marked by race, class, gender, region, nation, etc.

Who's in the story?

The term "character" suggests an interesting and unusual individual in real life. The **fictional character** in a text is made of words and influenced by literary, historical and cultural concepts and conventions. In opposition to the theatre, where an actor performs

Fig. 3.12

Charlotte Brontë (1816-1855), the daughter of an Irish clergyman in England, worked as a governess and teacher. Her experience fed into her novels, such as Jane Eyre (1847) and Villette (1853), long-time favourites with female readers in particular due to the portrayals of poor but honest and self-confident young women, who fight for independence in a world dominated by men and money.

a role on the stage, the story merely presents the verbal skeleton of a figure, which the reader imaginatively fleshes out in a similar way as the sketch of the setting. However, the narrative is superior to the theatre in representing the inner lives of fictional characters (by internal focalisation). A character can be defined by:

▶ a name, which suggests an individual,
▶ a bundle of character traits (psychological disposition),
▶ the internal activities of perceptions, emotions, thought and subconscious phenomena, and
▶ the external appearance and activities of speech and action.

Characterisation is given **directly** by the self-image in comparison to images by the narrator or other characters, and **indirectly** by the quantity and quality of perceptions, emotions, thought, speech and action.

Conception of characters in narrative texts

▶ **Flat** or **round** (simple types or complex individuals)
▶ **Static** or **dynamic** (unchanging or developing)
▶ **Transparent** or **opaque** (fully explained, closed or enigmatic, open)
▶ **Psychological** or **transpsychological** (ordinarily or extraordinarily self-aware and perceptive; Pfister, *Theory* 176-83; see 4.6)

The fictional character is positioned within a **constellation of characters**, which can be analysed according to (1) the **social structure** of the fictional world (generation, gender, class, race, etc.), (2) the **structure of perspectives** (including the narrator's and the characters' concepts and values), and (3) the **aesthetic structure** of similarity and contrast, symmetry and asymmetry.

In addition, the character is related to the **structure of action** (*Handlungsstruktur*) or the plot in the sense of a logical connection between individual actions. An action is of importance if it leads to a change in the plot. A minimal **action** can be seen as *sequence of three states:* (1) *a situation that reveals the option to act,* (2) *the refusal to take action or the realisation of a possible action, and* (3) *the failure or success of the action* (Ludwig 133). Besides actions, an analysis of the plot also includes **incidents** (*Ereignisse*) if they change the circumstances and thus lead to a new situation. In the text as a whole, the

The structure of action

beginning, the turning points and the ending are of crucial importance (see above, 3.2.3, 76-79). If characters achieve their goals, resolve conflicts or die, if the good are rewarded and the bad are punished (**poetic justice**), we talk about the **closure** of a narrative (*geschlossenes Ende*) rather than an **open ending**. The particular significance of beginnings and endings becomes especially apparent if you rewrite them. In Charlotte Brontë's novel *Jane Eyre*, the heroine falls in love with Mr Rochester, who keeps his wife, a madwoman, locked up in the attic. The white Caribbean Jean Rhys (1894-1979) presents Mrs Rochester's early life in *Wide Sargasso Sea* (1966), explaining how the sensitive, beautiful Caribbean heiress went mad, living with the man who married her for financial reasons but did not love her. – Charles Dickens (GB, 1812-70) altered the ending of his novel *Great Expectations* (1860-61) in order to meet readers' demands for a happy ending. The first version ended on a sober note: after many years spent abroad, the disillusioned hero meets again the woman he loved in vain, but now he keeps his distance towards her, who haughtily rejected him before. The second version leaves them walking hand in hand in the mellow light of the evening. – Some women authors rewrite fairy tales, transforming gender roles, focalisation and especially the endings. Thus, Angela Carter's (GB, 1940-92) Little Red Riding Hood sleeps with the wolf in the end, and Sara Maitland's (GB, 1950-) wicked stepmother tells Cinderella to work rather than daydream of Prince Charming ("The Company of Wolves", 1979, "The Wicked Stepmother's Tale", 1987, in Puschmann-Nalenz 35-56, 81-92).

Rewriting stories

Fig. 3.13

Charles Dickens (1812-1870), who suffered from his father's bankruptcy as a child, succeeded in making a comfortable living from writing. His novels, first published in serial form in periodicals, still fascinate readers across the world due to their great sense of humour, concise character sketches, sentimental melodrama and social criticism. The Pickwick Papers (1836-37) represent his early, light-hearted comic mode, the autobiographical David Copperfield (1849-50) his ironic but reconciliatory vision, and Great Expectations (1860-61) a more sarcastic and pessimist mood.

Comprehensive structures of action often follow conventional patterns, such as the courtship or **marriage plot**, a love story with its "appropriate" ending, or an **initiation plot**, a story of growing up and achieving maturity. In cases of **multiple strands of action** (*mehrsträngige Handlungsführung*), an analysis of the relationships between plots should complement that of particular plots.

Characters can be analysed according to their mere function within the action or as individual agents. The functional view of a character is not interested in its psychological dimension but rather in its position as the subject or object of the action, the sender or receiver, helper or opponent. In this view, characters can assume various functions at the same time or in succession. This form of analysis is more adequate for texts that use stereotypical characters and emphasise action, such as fairy tales, soap-operas and adventure novels. For example, James Bond is sent on a mission by the secret service, fights the opponent, meets a beautiful woman, who is an object in the game or turns from an opponent to a helper; Bond defeats his opponent and retrieves a material good or creates a general good by saving the world (receiver) from evil.

In opposition to novels of action, novels of character demand a more detailed analysis of the interrelationship between character and action. In order to become an *agent* in the first place, a character needs to have the *ability, motivation and intention to act, and has to be in the position to act* (Ludwig 148).

The relationship between characters, actions and circumstances (setting in the sense of situation and incidents) helps to explain the dynamics of a story:

Functions of characters

The dynamics of a story

Characters

↗ ↘

Circumstances ⟷ **Actions**

A fictional character's psychological disposition or potential is realised in internal and external actions (or inaction due to fear, weakness, laziness). Either way, action or inaction indirectly characterise the figure. The particular circumstances that characters live in have a certain influence on their material and psychological existence. In reverse, characters perceive, react to and change circumstances, which may offer or restrict options to act.

3.4 | Fiction and metafiction

In a historical perspective, the options of how to tell stories have expanded. **Non-realistic** narratives (myths, parables, tales, etc.) have existed since time immemorial. The term **romance** has been applied to medieval stories of heroic knights and to *non-realist narratives about extraordinary lives, incidents and settings, including supernatural intervention.* Since the eighteenth century, **realistic** *narratives have created the* **illusion** *of a probable world by imitating external reality.* The representation of external reality has shifted to that of internal reality or the consciousness of reality in modernist narratives since the late nineteenth century. After the second world war, **anti-illusionist postmodernist fiction**, *which takes up the subjective, ambiguous and fragmentary style of modernist texts, refuses to tell realistic stories any longer and rather talks about fiction itself.* John Barth's (US, 1930-) ironic "Life-Story" (1968) is a case in point because it does not tell the story of someone's life but rather discusses how to tell it:

> Without discarding what he'd already written he began his story afresh in a somewhat different manner. Whereas his earlier version had opened in a straightforward documentary fashion and then degenerated or at least modulated intentionally into irrealism and dissonance he decided this time to tell his tale from the start to finish in a conservative, "realistic," unself-conscious way. He being by vocation an author of novels and stories it was perhaps inevitable that one afternoon the possibility would occur to the writer of these lines that his own life might be a fiction, in which he was the leading or an accessory character. He happened at the time* to be in his study [...]
> *9:00 A.M., Monday, June 20, 1966 (NAAL 2: 2144)

The writer is no longer an author in the traditional sense of a god-like creator because he seems to lack control over his story. The statement that the writer aspires to a "realistic" version is qualified by the inverted commas, which make the reader wonder what "realistic" means. The story will neither be realistic nor come into being in the first place. The following sentences and the footnote suspend the clear separation between the author, the third-person narrator and the writer in the story. The writer in the story has the same profession as the author. The beginning of the sentence, "He being by vocation an author", refers to the writer in the story, who needs not to be "the writer of these lines", who could be the author or the third-person narrator. The fact that the writer within the fictional story gets the idea that "his own life might be a fiction" is as paradoxical as the expression "perhaps inevitable". The footnote, a feature of documentary texts, points to an identity between the author and the writer by referring to a plausible time and date of writing. If the writer's own life was a fiction, a fictional story would be the most "realistic" form to represent it. Barth teases the reader, who expects to find "life" in this story, by telling that the narrator himself prefers traditional romances, tales of adventure and realistic narratives to experimental literature (NAAL 2: 2145). The ambiguous, confusing discourse criss-crosses the boundaries between fiction and fact, challenging the reader's predilections and assumptions about the representation of reality.

In a way, postmodernist (meta)fiction continues the tradition of Sterne's *Tristram Shandy*, which plays with the conventions of literature and highlights discourse rather than story. The heyday of postmodernism in the 1960s and 70s was informed by the post-war questioning of authorities, conventions and progress. Instead, subjective perspectives, relative values and shifting identities became prominent, which were linked to uncertainty, alienation and chaos, but also promised liberating alternatives to outdated and restrictive traditions. Although the days of radical postmodernism are past, its legacy is still visible in the mingling of the serious and the comic mode, high and low art, literature and theory, life and art, and in the foregrounding of the processes of writing and reading rather than the story.

Guiding questions and exercises   3.5

The following set of questions serves as a rough guideline to interpretations. Ideally, a thorough analysis would deal with both story and discourse in any order. A research paper could deliver a comprehensive analysis of a short story but not of a novel due to its sheer amount of information. The intrinsic analysis of a novel can (1) combine discourse and story with regard to a few selected scenes, (2) examine one level in detail and sketch the other, (3) concentrate on either the story or the discourse, or (4) focus on one question or topic only (time, settings, characters, etc.). Some questions overlap: for example, an analysis of characters includes characterisation by internal and external action, and in turn, action needs characters as agents or functions in opposition to happenings without human intervention. An enquiry into intertextual relationships of novels needs to restrict the number of general features and of details under discussion even more. An extrinsic approach to a short story or a novel often begins with an analysis of the context, continues with that of the text, explains the relationship between them, or relates features of context and text in a parallel succession of comparisons. An up-to-date interpretation would combine an appropriate contemporary approach to literature (see ch. 5) with questions on analysing narrative.

Guiding questions for analysing narrative

A) Discourse

1 How is the story related? Why did the author choose this particular form of narrative communication? Decide whether to use Stanzel's or Genette's model:

▶ Which narrative situation prevails? (Stanzel)
- ▹ Authorial (third-person narrator outside of the story world, omniscient, intrusive),
- ▹ first-person (narrating I vs. experiencing I; protagonist vs. witness),
- ▹ figural (third-person narrator outside story world, figure as reflector),
- ▹ neutral scenic (external perspective on dialogue and action).

▶ Who speaks to whom from which position and in which way? (Genette)
- ▹ Covert or overt narrators and narratees,
- ▹ heterodiegetic (third-person) or homodiegetic/autodiegetic (first-person) narrators,
- ▹ extradiegetic (frame) narrators or intradiegetic (embedded) narrators.

▶ Where and to which extent does the narrator show the story, tell the story, or reflect about the story or storytelling itself?

▶ How reliable or unreliable is the narrator?

2 Who perceives what in which way? (Focalisation)
- ▶ External, internal or zero focalisation,
- ▶ fixed, variable or multiple focalisation,
- ▶ monologic or dialogic structure of perspectives.
- ▶ How are the characters' thoughts, feelings and words mediated?
  - ▶ Narrative report, indirect discourse, free indirect discourse, direct discourse, interior monologue.

3 What is the duration, order and frequency of mediation? (Time)
- ▶ How does the discourse time relate to the story time?
  - ▶ Ellipsis, summary, scene, stretch, pause.
- ▶ Where does the narrative begin?
  - ▶ *Ab ovo* or *in medias res.*
- ▶ Does the narrative follow the chronological order of events or rearrange it?
- ▶ Does the narrator anticipate the future or look back into the past?
  - ▶ Flashforward/prolepsis or flashback/analepsis.
- ▶ Does the narrator relate an event, which regularly happens, once only or a single event several times in various versions?
- ▶ How does the objective, chronological time relate to the subjective, psychological time?

B) Story

1 When and where does the story take place? What is the function of the setting and the circumstances?
- ▶ Single setting or multiple settings/circumstances,
- ▶ objective location and perceived atmosphere,
- ▶ relationship between internal space and external space (subjective mind, private home vs. world outside),
- ▶ social, political, cultural spaces and boundaries (inclusion, exclusion, transgression),
- ▶ symbolic function (semantic space, externalised mirror-image of character),
- ▶ selection of contemporary or historical setting (relationship to cultural context).

2 Who takes part? What is the significance of the fictional characters?
- ▶ (Telling) name,

▶ psychological disposition,

▶ internal activities (perceptions, emotions, thought and sub-conscious phenomena),

▶ external appearance and activities (speech, action),

▶ non-psychological construction without inner depth, psychological one with plausible behaviour, trans-psychological one with superior insight,

▶ position within the social structure (generation, gender, class, race, etc.),

▶ direct or indirect characterisation by self and others (overlaps with focalisation),

▶ position within the structure of perspectives (overlaps with focalisation),

▶ position within aesthetic structure: major or minor character, similar/opposed to others, flat type or round character, well-defined (closed) or fuzzy and obscure (open) figure.

3 What is the structure and function of the action?

▶ Chronological order and logical order?

▶ Are the beginning, middle and ending clearly marked?

▶ Is the action linear, circular or fragmentary?

▶ Does chance or action propel the plot?

▶ How do the internal action and the external action relate to each other? (Parallel or different conflicts within and between characters?)

▶ How does the action relate figures and circumstances?

▶ How do multiple strands of action correspond to each other?

C) **Why does the narrative combine this particular discourse with this story?**

Test: What would happen if someone else told or perceived the story, if the beginning or the ending were changed, if another character was foregrounded or placed in another setting or society, if different actions were highlighted, condensed or omitted?

Does the narrative use a particular image, idea or phrase as a recurrent leitmotif?

What does the narrative do to the reader?

▶ Suspense,

▶ manipulation of empathy or ironic distance,

▶ motivation of political/cultural/aesthetic reflection and awareness or escapist fantasy, etc.

D) Extrinsic approach

▶ In which way does the text interact with other texts/media? Are newspapers, pictures, music, film or theatre singular events in the story or of structural value for the narrative?

  ▷ E.g. inclusion of factual information, news clippings and/ or novel as "faction", a blending of fact and fiction,

  ▷ description of pictures and/or graphic depiction of still lives and landscapes,

  ▷ music as topic and/or musical rhythm of structures,

  ▷ theatrical performance of characters in the novel, theatrical technique of representing dialogues, or presentation of the novel as a puppet show manipulated by the narrator,

  ▷ talking about film or using cinematic techniques, such as short scenes and quick transitions.

▶ How does the text relate to cultural contexts?

  ▷ Social, political and economic ideas and situations,

  ▷ positions in philosophy, art and science.

Exercise 1

Analyse the voice, focalisation and the setting of Ernest Hemingway's (US, 1898-1961) "Banal Story", taking into account its title (Nischik 41-45).

So he ate an orange, slowly spitting out the seeds. Outside, the snow was turning to rain. Inside, the electric stove seemed to give no heat and rising from his writing-table, he sat down upon the stove. How good it felt! Here, at last, was life.

He reached for another orange. Far away in Paris, Mascart had knocked Danny Frush cuckoo in the second round. Far off in Mesopotamia, twenty-one feet of snow had fallen. Across the world in distant Australia, the English cricketers were sharpening up their wickets. There was Romance.

Patrons of the arts and letters have discovered The Forum, he read [...]

(Nischik 41)

Fig. 3.14

The American war correspondent, novelist and short story writer Ernest Hemingway (1899-1961) was as famous for his adventurous life-style as his themes of sports, war, danger, death and for his "masculine", simple, spare and detached style. His characters display heroic ambition, experience loss and stoically bear disillusionment in his short story collections Men Without Women *(1927) and* Winner Take Nothing *(1933), in his war novels* A Farewell to Arms *(1929) and* For Whom the Bell Tolls *(1940). The man, who turned into a myth during his life-time, suffered from depression and shot himself.*

Exercise 2

Analyse the beginning of Rose Tremain's (GB, 1943-) story "My Wife is a White Russian" (Bradbury 382-388).

> I'm a financier. I have financial assets, world-wide. I'm in nickel and pig-iron and gold and diamonds. I like the sound of all these words. They have an edge, I think. The glitter of saying them sometimes gives me an erection. I'm saying them now in this French restaurant, where the table-cloths and the table-napkins are blue linen, where they serve sea-food on platters of sea-weed and crushed ice. [. . .] Opposite me, the two young Australians blink as they wait (so damned courteous, and she has freckles like a child) for me to stutter out my hard-word list, to manipulate tongue and memory so that the sound inside me forms just behind my lips and explodes with extraordinary force above my oysters: 'Diamonds!'
> But then, I feel a soft, perfumed dabbing at my face. I turn away from the Australians and there she is. My wife. She is smiling as she wipes me. Her gold bracelets rattle. She is smiling at me.
> (Bradbury 382)

Analyses: see below, 228-229.

Bibliography | 3.6

PRIMARY SOURCES

Abrams, M. H., et al., eds. *The Norton Anthology of English Literature*. 7th ed. 2 vols. New York and London: Norton, 2000. (=NAEL 1 and 2)

Barnes, Julian. *Talking It Over*. London: Cape, 1991.

Baym, Nina, et al., eds. *The Norton Anthology of American Literature*. 3rd ed. 2 vols. New York and London: Norton, 1989. (=NAAL 1 and 2)

*Bradbury, Malcolm, ed. *The Penguin Book of Modern British Short Stories*. London: Penguin, 1988.

Brontë, Charlotte. *Jane Eyre*. Ed. Q. D. Leavis. London: Penguin, 1986.

Defoe, Daniel. *Robinson Crusoe*. Ed. Angus Rose. London: Penguin, 1985.

Dickens, Charles. *Great Expectations*. Complete, authoritative text with biographical and historical contexts, critical history, and essays from five contemporary critical perspectives. Ed. Janice Carlisle. Boston: Bedford Books of St. Martin's Press, 1996.

Fielding, Henry. *The History of Tom Jones*. Ed. R. P. C. Mutter. Rpt. London: Penguin, 1985.

*Ford, Richard, ed. *The Granta Book of the American Short Story*. London: Granta, 1993.

Franklin, Benjamin. *Autobiography*. Eds. Leonard W. Labaree, Ralph L. Ketcham, Helen C. Boatfield and Helene H. Fineman. New Haven and London: Yale University, 1964.

Hawthorne, Nathaniel. *The Scarlet Letter and Selected Tales*. Ed. Thomas E. Connolly. Harmondsworth: Penguin, 1970.

Hill, Susan, ed. *The Penguin Book of Contemporary Women's Short Stories*. Harmondsworth: Penguin, 1995.

Joyce, James. *A Portrait of the Artist as a Young Man*. Ed. Seamus Deane. Harmondsworth: Penguin, 2000.
—. *Ulysses*. Student's Edition. Eds. Hans Walter Gabler, Wolfhard Steppe, and Claus Melchior. Harmondsworth: Penguin, 1986.

*Nischik, Reingard M., ed. *Short Short Stories Universal*. Stuttgart: Reclam, 1993.

Puschmann-Nalenz, Barbara, ed. *Ten British Women Writers. Contemporary Short Stories*. Stuttgart: Reclam, 2000.

Richardson, Samuel. *Pamela, or Virtue Rewarded*. Eds. Thomas Keymer and Alice Wakely. Oxford and New York: Oxford University Press, 2001.

Sterne, Laurence. *The Life and Opinions of Tristram Shandy, Gentleman*. Ed. Graham Petrie. Harmondsworth: Penguin, 1967.

Woolf, Virginia. *To the Lighthouse*. Orlando: Harcourt Brace Jovanovich, 1989.

SECONDARY SOURCES

*Abbot, H. Porter. *The Cambridge Introduction to Narrative*. 2nd ed. Cambridge: Cambridge University Press, 2002. (Very accessible textbook for students and teachers; relates the analysis of narrative in literature, film, drama and comics to the universal and everyday ordering of events in time; recommends primary and secondary literature in each chapter).

*Ahrens, Günter. *Die amerikanische Kurzgeschichte. Theorie und Entwicklung*. Stuttgart et al.: Kohlhammer, 1980. (Very readable systematic and historical introduction).

Bal, Mieke. *Narratology. Introduction to the Theory of Narrative.* 2nd, rev. ed. Toronto: University of Toronto Press, 1998. (Very clear and helpful).

Bauer, Matthias. *Romantheorie.* 2nd, rev. ed. Stuttgart and Weimar: Metzler, 2005. (Very clear overview of historical theories about the novel from antiquity until today, foregrounding different contemporary approaches).

*Bode, Christoph. *Der Roman. Eine Einführung.* Tübingen and Basel: Francke, 2005. (Excellent, vivid, sophisticated and comprehensive introduction to analysing novels, using many German, English and American examples).

Borgmeier, Raimund, ed. *Englische Short Stories von Thomas Hardy bis Graham Swift.* Stuttgart: Reclam, 1999. (Short interpretations).

Chatman, Seymour. *Story and Discourse: Narrative Structure in Fiction and Film.* 2nd ed. Ithaca: Cornell University Press, 1980. (Readable basic study).

Emory, Elliott, ed. *The Columbia History of the American Novel.* New York: Columbia University Press, 1991. (Comprehensive overview of novel writing from the United States, Canada, the Caribbean and Latin America).

Fludernik, Monika. *Towards a 'Natural' Narratology.* Repr. London and New York: Routledge, 2002. (Comprehensive study of narrative forms from the Middle Ages until today).

Genette, Gérard. *Narrative Discourse Revisited.* Reprint. Trans. Jane E. Lewin. Ithaca: Cornell University Press, 1990. (Selection of essays on key categories of narrative analysis).

—. *Die Erzählung.* Trans. Andreas Knop, ed. Jürgen Vogt. Munich: Fink, 1994. (Original theory; at times difficult, in-depth study of Proust).

Hanke, Michael, ed. *Amerikanische Short Stories des 20. Jahrhunderts.* Stuttgart: Reclam, 1998. (Brief and helpful interpretations).

Hanson, Clare. *Short Stories and Short Fictions, 1880-1980.* London: Macmillan, 1985.

Herman, David, ed. *Narratologies: New Perspectives on Narrative Analysis.* Columbus: Ohio State University Press, 1999.

Jahn, Manfred. *Narratology: A Guide to the Theory of Narrative. Part III of Poems, Plays, and Prose: A Guide to the Theory of Literary Genres.* English Department, University of Cologne. Version: 1.7. 2003. <http://www.uni-koeln.de/~ame02/pppn.htm>. Date of access: 29 August 2007. (Short and accessible overview).

Jahn, Manfred, and Ansgar Nünning. "A Survey of Narratological Models." *Literatur in Wissenschaft und Unterricht* 27 (1994): 283-303. (Very useful and simple explanation of key concepts).

*Korte, Barbara. *The Short Story in Britain. A Historical Sketch and Anthology.* Tübingen and Basel: Francke, 2003. (Very good and readable, systematic definition of genre, historical overview and texts).

*Ludwig, Hans-Werner. *Arbeitsbuch Romananalyse.* 6th ed. Tübingen: Narr, 1998. (Excellent introduction: very readable and critical presentation of systematic approaches with many diagrams and quotes from theoretical sources and illustrations from primary texts).

Lubbers, Klaus. *Typologie der Short Story.* 2nd ed. Darmstadt: WBG, 1989. (Systematic depiction of types, subject matter and techniques of short stories).

Lubbers, Klaus. *Die englische und amerikanische Kurzgeschichte.* 2nd ed. Darmstadt: WBG, 2001. (Short interpretations of American and some British short stories).

*Martinez, Matias, and Michael Scheffel. *Einführung in die Erzähltheorie.* 7th ed. Munich: Beck, 2007. (Very helpful introduction to structuralist analysis of narrative, incl. chapter on narrative in disciplines beyond fiction).

May, Charles E. ed. *The New Short Story Theories*. Athens: Ohio University Press, 1994. (Presents essays on key elements of short fiction, on various subgenres, such as the tale, the fable or the novella, and the historical and international development of the genre).

Nünning, Ansgar, ed. *Unreliable Narration. Studien zur Theorie und Praxis unglaubwürdigen Erzählens in der englischsprachigen Erzählliteratur*. Trier: WVT, 1998. (Major collection about un/reliability in narrative texts).

Nünning, Ansgar, and Vera Nünning, eds. *Multiperspektivisches Erzählen. Zur Theorie und Geschichte der Perspektivenstruktur im englischen Roman des 18. bis 20. Jahrhunderts*. Trier: WVT, 2000. (Useful studies on a large variety of multiple narrative perspectives).

Nünning, Ansgar/Vera Nünning, eds. *Erzähltheorie transgenerisch, intermedial, interdisziplinär*. Trier: WVT, 2002. (Covers narrative structures in the arts, music, comics, movies, hyperfiction and historiography).

Nünning, Vera, and Ansgar Nünning, eds. *Erzähltextanalyse und Gender Studies*. Stuttgart and Weimar: Metzler, 2004. (Explains how gender influences all aspects of writing and reading fiction, such as the construction of and response to narrative discourse, characters and plots).

*Prince, Gerald. *A Dictionary of Narratology*. Rev. ed. Lincoln and London: University of Nebraska Press, 2003. (Very useful, short and clear definitions of key terms for narrative analysis).

Richetti, John J., John Bender, Deirdre David and Michael Seidel, eds. *The Columbia History of the British Novel*. New York: Columbia University Press, 1994. (Comprehensive and accessible coverage of major genres, authors and works from Defoe in the 18th century to women's novels of the 1980s and early 1990s).

*Rimmon-Kenan, Shlomith. *Narrative Fiction. Contemporary Poetics*. 2nd ed. London: Routledge, 2002. (Excellent presentation of structuralist approach to narrative).

Schlager, Neil, and Josh Lauer, eds. *Contemporary Novelists*. 7th ed. Contemporary Writers Series. Detroit: St. James-Gale Group, 2000. (Brief biographical and bibliographical information on primary texts and selected secondary material, often with a short critical essay).

Shaw, Valerie. *The Short Story. A Critical Introduction*. 7th impr. London et al.: Longman, 1995. (Systematic analysis of key problems).

Stanzel, Franz. *Theorie des Erzählens*. 7th ed. Göttingen: Vandenhoeck und Ruprecht, 2001. (Very readable original study of narrative situations).

Steinecke, Hartmut, and Fritz Wahrenburg, eds. *Romantheorie: Texte vom Barock bis zur Gegenwart*. Stuttgart: Reclam, 1999. (Comprehensive, annotated and illuminating selection).

Wenzel, Peter, ed. *Einführung in die Erzähltextanalyse: Kategorien, Modelle, Probleme*. Trier: WVT, 2004. (Concise and critical discussion of the key areas of narrative analysis).

* Strongly recommended.

Drama $|4$

Contents

4.1	Dramatic text and theatrical performance	96
4.2	Verbal communication	99
4.3	Character and action	105
4.4	Place and time	115
4.5	Guiding questions and exercises	120
4.6	Bibliography	126

Abstract

This chapter will point out the differences between reading drama as a literary text and as a script for a theatrical performance. It is of great interest to explore the relationships between the verbal communication in the text and the audiovisual communication in the theatre, between character and actor, action in drama and stage performance, fictional location and stage-design, fictional time and performance time.

4.1 | Dramatic text and theatrical performance

All the world's a stage,
And all the men and women merely players.
They have their exits and their entrances,
And one man in his time plays many parts.

Shakespeare, *As You Like It*, 2.7, 1598-1600.

[W]hile he certainly felt rather often
that he was merely acting his own role or roles
he had no idea who the actor was.

John Barth, "Life-Story", 1966.

Performing roles is of crucial importance on the stage of our social lives. You will find directors, actors and spectators among children playing mother and child, in families organising dinners or weddings and in companies designing corporate identities or sales strategies. Apart from deliberate acting in games, social rituals and deceptions, our everyday behaviour often erases the difference between "being oneself" and performing a role. Race, class, gender, generation and situation provide numerous role patterns, which we become aware of if someone violates norms and patterns. Take for instance a white "boy" acting like a black rapper (Eminem), a man dressing like a woman (*Tootsie*) or a child behaving like an adult while explaining software to a teacher in the classroom.

The negotiation of social norms and roles in interactions are of particular interest in dramatic dialogues. Dramatic texts may give stage directions in the **secondary text** (*Nebentext*) but mainly present the direct communication among characters in dialogues in the **primary text** (*Haupttext*). Drama shows characters interacting here and now and is therefore more immediate than narrative texts, in which a narrator tells a story from the past.

Fig. 4.1 |

Dramatic communication.

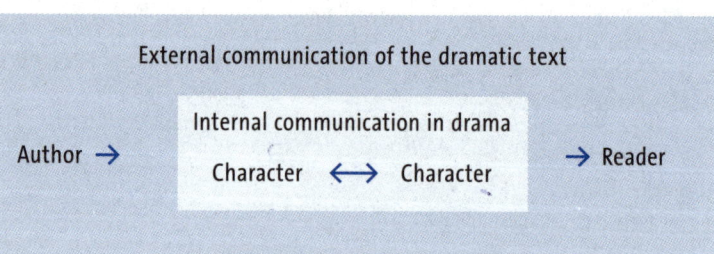

External communication of the dramatic text

Internal communication in drama

Author → Character ⟷ Character → Reader

A theatrical performance on stage replaces the individual reader's imagination as a site of realising the fictional dramatic world. The theatre company, including the producer, director, designers, technicians and actors, transforms the dramatic text into a multi-media performance. *Each performance is an unrepeatable, simultaneous and collective production and reception, in which actors play characters in fictional settings for spectators* (Fischer-Lichte, *Semiotics* 15-17). The spectators' response to the players forms an essential part of the dynamics of a performance as a unique event:

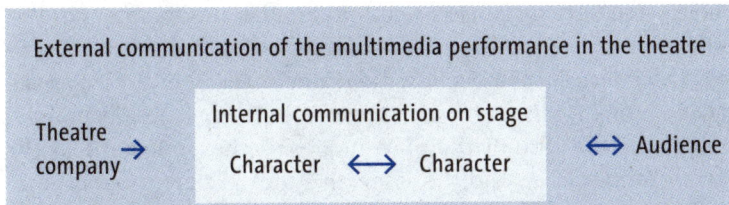

| **Fig. 4.2**

Theatrical communication.

Performances always exceed the text, no matter whether it gives no, few or many stage directions. Stage directions about the choice of actors, their appearance and performance, the stage design, lighting and music suggest one way of staging a play but hardly exhaust the possibilities of a performance. The following table shows thirteen sign-systems of the theatre according to Tadeusz Kowzan:

Auditive signs (actor)	Visual signs (actor)		Visual signs (outside the actor)	Auditive signs (outside the actor)
Time	Space and time	Space	Space and time	Time
Auditive signs	Visual signs			Auditive signs
Actor			Outside the Actor	
Spoken text	Expression of the body	Actor's external appearance	Appearance of the stage	Inarticulate sounds
1 Word 2 Tone	3 Mime 4 Gesture 5 Movement	6 Make-up 7 Hair-style 8 Costume	9 Properties 10 Settings 11 Lighting	12 Music 13 Sound effects

Fig. 4.3

Kowzan's classification of theatrical sign-systems (in Aston and Savona 105).

A traditional analysis of the dramatic text would be restricted to the verbal sign-system only. We will deal with the use of verbal communication, characters, action, space and time both in the dramatic text and in the theatrical performance.

In general, the spectator, who is aware of the fact that everything on the stage serves as a sign, will have an advantage over characters on stage, to whom their gestures, external appearance, objects and circumstances are often familiar and therefore of less informational value. The **external communication** *of the whole performance to the audience provides more information than the* **internal communication** *between characters on stage.* Often, reviews, rumours, brochures, the title of the play, its genre, the prologue and the form of the theatre and the stage give the spectators advance information. For example, the characters usually do not know whether they live in the world of comedy or tragedy, which provides patterns for their actions. William Shakespeare's promising title *As You Like It* (1600) suggests that the good characters, who are driven into exile, will not come to serious harm, whereas Romeo's and Juliet's plan to outwit their parents will fail because their tragic fate is announced in the prologue. **Dramatic irony** *exploits the difference between external and internal communication because it means that a character, as opposed to the spectators, is not aware of the implications and consequences of what he/she says or does.* Thus, Romeo, who thinks that Juliet is dead, is amazed at Juliet's lifelike beauty and kills himself in grief (5.3.90-121) shortly before she wakes up.

Fig. 4.4

James Northcote, Romeo and Juliet *5.3, 1792.*

Verbal communication

Dramatic language is based on, but differs from, ordinary language due to dramatic conventions and theatrical requirements. Dramatic speech addresses both the characters on stage and the spectators in the theatre. The lack of a narrator in most forms of drama demands that characters foreshadow events, present retrospectives, comment upon events or summarize actions. Characters do not always speak "ordinary" prose. For example, Shakespeare has his aristocrats talk in blank verse (iambic pentameter). We accept monologues as perfectly normal on stage but consider them to be rather odd in real life. When we overhear a conversation in a noisy pub, we do not understand everything because we do not hear some of the phrases or miss the reference and the context. In the theatre, a whisper, which means to exclude all but one or a few listeners on stage, is usually loud enough to be heard by everyone in the audience. Speech on stage must be comprehensible (unless intentionally obscured) because the spectator can hardly ask a character to repeat or explain what he/she said.

Dialogue or polylogue, talking in turns by two or more speakers, is the hallmark of drama. In dialogues, fictional characters or figures
- present themselves directly to others,
- characterise other figures,
- characterise themselves indirectly through the content, style and manner of their replies,
- exchange information,
- negotiate meanings and relationships in discussions or quarrels,
- plan and perform actions,
- create a particular mood and atmosphere.

We can analyse the content (what), manner (how) and function (why) of an individual speech by itself and in relationship to the preceding and following speeches by the same character and others. For example, the simple remark "I am cold" expresses that the speaker is feeling chilled, but may also reveal that the he/she is ill, lonely, feels alienated from his/her partner, implies that the speaker wants the addressee to shut the window in that room or to pay more attention. The *norms for co-operative communication* help to understand dramatic speech: speakers should respect each other and tell the truth, give the adequate amount of information and say in a comprehensible

Dramatic language

Analysing dramatic language

way what is relevant to the matter at hand. The intentional or un-intentional violation of these rules in a dialogue reveals incompetence, alienation, domination or deception. In addition, it matters how often and how long someone speaks, who interrupts whom and how often. Dominant characters are usually given more and longer speeches in order to reveal their individual complexity, their prominence as agents or their social power.

Particular forms of
dialogues

A particular dramatic form of dialogue is the **line-by-line exchange** *(Stichomythie)*, which may convey passion or wit but also reticence and alienation. In the English playwright George Etherege's (ca 1634-91) comedy of manners *The Man of Mode* (1676; see p. 109) the aggressive Dorimant tries to seduce Bellinda and gradually talks her into coming to his apartment on the following morning:

BELLINDA   I tremble when you name it.
DORIMANT Be sure you come.
BELLINDA   I sha' not.
DORIMANT Swear you will.
BELLINDA   I dare not.
DORIMANT Swear, I say!
BELLINDA   By my life, by all the happiness I hope for –
DORIMANT You will.
BELLINDA   I will.
(3.2)

Her resistance crumbles as his entreaties become more urgent. He appeals to her in more and more dominant imperatives, whereas her resistance seems half-hearted from the start. Her trembling could be an expression of rage in response to his impertinent demand, of fear or of excitement. Her subsequent replies point to the latter emotion. She may have wanted to say that her life and happiness depended upon staying safely at home but he cuts her short and leads her into temptation.

In *The School for Scandal* (1777), a play in the tradition of the comedy of manners by the Anglo-Irish playwright Richard Brinsley Sheridan (1751-1816), Lady Teazle displays her sarcasm in **repartees** (witty replies):

MRS. CANDOUR   They'll not allow our friend Miss Vermilion to be handsome.
LADY SNEERWELL Oh, surely she's a pretty woman.

CRABTREE	I am very glad you think so, ma'am.
MRS. CANDOUR	She has a charming fresh color.
LADY TEAZLE	Yes, when it is fresh put on.
MRS. CANDOUR	Oh, fie! I'll swear her color is natural – I have seen it come and go.
LADY TEAZLE	I dare swear you have, ma'am – it goes of a night, and comes again in the morning. (2.2)

We find many line-by-line exchanges in the **absurd drama** of the 20th century, albeit with a very different function because here, *long pauses, short utterances* and *replies signify skepticism in language* as a means of communication. In an absurd world that does not make sense, characters without a definite identity, a coherent past or a promising future spend or rather waste time together but remain lonely. In *Endgame* (1958) by the Irish writer Samuel Beckett (1906-89), Clov and Hamm are dependent upon, but dislike, each other:

CLOV	Why do you keep me?
HAMM	There's no one else.
CLOV	There's nowhere else. [Pause.]
HAMM	You're leaving me all the same.
CLOV	I'm trying.
HAMM	You don't love me.
CLOV	No.
HAMM	You loved me once.
CLOV	Once!

(NAEL 2: 2474)

The curt remarks lead to nowhere. The characters would part from each other but Hamm has no other person to take care of him and Clov has no other place to go to. In spite of their alienation, they maintain (but do not develop) their relationship by talking to each other, which sounds more like a repeated performance than an intimate conversation.

Fig. 4.5

*The Anglo-Irish novelist and dramatist Samuel Beckett (1906-1989) developed a unique style and vision of the **absurd**. He depicted both the comic aspects and the despair of grotesque characters, who are reduced to existential needs, caught in repetitive communication, cyclical actions and barren, adverse circumstances. Living mainly in France, Beckett often wrote in French and translated his texts into English, such as the play* En attendant Godot/Waiting for Godot *(1952/55) and the novel* Malone meurt/Malone dies *(1951/58).*

Function of monologues

If the dialogue is completely dominated by one character or if two or more characters share one and the same opinion, dialogues tend to become monologic. In turn, a monologue tends towards a dialogue if a character addresses him/herself, being torn between two positions, or if he/she speaks to a potential but absent addressee. A **monologue** is a speech that is addressed to nobody on stage but expresses a character's inner life to the audience. The monologue is called **soliloquy** if the speaking character is alone (Latin *solus*) on stage. *In addition to expressing emotions and judgements about the self and others, monologues reveal information about off-stage characters and incidents, point to past or future events and expose intentions, consequently creating suspense, sympathy or antipathy.* In William Shakespeare's (1564-1616) *King Lear* (1605/06), for example, the "bastard" Edmund ironically justifies his evil action by the mean and contemptible character that "unnatural" society attributes to him. The poetic alliteration between "brand", "base" and "bastardy" stresses how the mere term "bastard" stamps a bad image on someone. Edmund questions the function of the word "legitimate" in a metalingual reflection. He rebels against the cultural norm that disapproves of illegitimate children and foreshadows his plot to displace his legitimate brother by writing a slanderous letter:

> Thou, Nature, art my goddess, to thy law
> My services are bound. Wherefore should I
> Stand in the plague of custom, and permit
> The curiosity of nations to deprive me,
> For that I am some twelve of fourteen moonshines
> Lag of a brother? Why bastard? Wherefore base?

[...] Why brand they us
With base? With baseness, bastardy? Base, base?
[...] Well then,
Legitimate Edgar, I must have your land.
Our father's love is to the bastard Edmund
As to th' legitimate. Fine word, "legitimate"!
Well, my legitimate, if this letter speed
And my invention thrive, Edmund the base
Shall [top] th' legitimate. I grow, I prosper:
Now, gods, stand up for bastards!
(1.2.1-22)

William Shakespeare (1564-1616) wrote intricate sonnets and narrative verse before turning into an actor and playwright, who owned shares in a professional theatre that enjoyed great popularity due to its bad reputation of good entertainment (and moral corruption). Borrowing heavily from European history, legend and literature, he considerably enriched the English stage and language.

Fig. 4.6

Both dialogues and monologues serve particular **theatrical functions**. Initial speeches are often intended for the audience rather than for the characters because they introduce both the present world on stage and its off-stage extension, and initiate or foreshadow actions. Speech triggers off action, such as the "bastard" Edmund's accusation of his father as a traitor, who is thereupon blinded by his enemies (*King Lear* 3.7). Speech itself can be action: take for instance a performative promise, curse or banishment. Often, conflicts are enacted in verbal struggles, which range from a harmless battle of wits to a painful quarrel between serious antagonists. Towards the ending of plays, speeches terminate the action, form judgements and draw conclusions.

In opposition to **Aristotelian drama**, which is defined by the immediate presentation of characters in speeches and a coherent sequence of actions, **epic drama** uses narrative techniques, such as a

Aristotelian versus epic drama

figure who introduces characters and conveys the (episodic or open-ended) action of the play to the spectators. The American playwright Thornton Wilder (1897-1975) created an **epic narrator** in *Our Town* (1938), the "Stage Manager". He addresses the audience and describes the world of a prototypical small town, which the spectator's imagination has to flesh out since the neutral stage is almost empty. He introduces the characters and the action, sometimes even takes over minor parts, interrupts the play, presents retrospectives and foreshadowings:

> Here's the Town Hall and Post Office combined; jail's in the basement. [...]
> First automobile's going to come along in about five years – belonged to Banker Cartwright, our richest citizen ... lives in the big white house up on the hill. [...] (Two arched trellises, covered with vines and flowers, are pushed out, one by each proscenium pillar.) There's some scenery for those who think they have to have scenery. This is Mrs. Gibb's garden. Corn ... peas ... [...]
> Nice Town, y'know what I mean? Nobody very remarkable ever come out of it, s'far as we know. (7-8)

The narrator in epic drama

Manfred Pfister remarks about the Stage Manager: "Transcending the merely explanatory and reflective function of the chorus, he appears as the fictional and authorial subject presenting the internal dramatic system" (*Theory* 75-76). The effect is ambiguous: history is presented here and now in order "to bring the events home more emphatically" (Pfister, *Theory* 76). This narrator, who is ironic at times, creates a distance between the audience and the dramatic world and its characters, whose ordinary lives serve as a parable of our own, in order to promote reflection rather than identification. The Stage Manager, who is responsible for the stage-design, belittles those who prefer realistic illusion by his condescending statement about those spectators who expect scenery. The praise of the "Nice Town" is ironically counteracted by the question and the implication that its culture apparently does not foster remarkable talent but only mediocrity.

Other forms of epic communication, which also occur in Aristotelian drama, include the title of the play, the stage directions, the **prologue**, **epilogue**, **report** (*Bericht*) and the **aside** (*Beiseite-Sprechen*; Pfister, *Drama* 123). A chorus or an actor *ex parte* (not acting his/her part) speaks the prologue and the epilogue, which frame the dramatic world, leading the spectators into, and out of, the dramatic illusion by advance information or retrospective judgement, by an appeal to the spectators' imagination and goodwill. The prologue frequently supports the exposition and goes hand in hand with reports about events before or beyond the present situation. The **aside** excludes other characters present on stage. The aside can simply be "overheard" by the spectators, a fact that maintains the immediate presence of the dramatic world on stage, or can directly address the audience (*ad spectatores*) and mediate between the world on stage and that of the audience in the theatre.

Usually, neither the epic narrator's perspective nor that of a single character can be identified with the author's opinion. Rather, *the interplay and development of perspectives in relationship to the stage directions or the performance have to be taken into account in order to understand the meaning of the play as a whole.* However, you can hardly analyse every single speech and all of its relationships with others, but you have to isolate major characters' important conflicts and stages of development and select the appropriate scenes for close readings. The various perspectives in a play can share or move towards similar basic assumptions and value judgements in a monologic way or contradict each other without any possibility of a compromise or an alternative in a dialogic way.

Network of perspectives

Character and action | 4.3

In everyday life, our image of people depends upon many sources and kinds of information, such as who gives us which sort of information about them before we meet them, how our experience of individuals relates to the images others have of them and the images they have of themselves, whether they confirm or disappoint our preconceptions, where we meet them and how they behave towards us and others. When we meet someone for the first time, we often form an image of him or her within seconds without being fully aware of it. The first direct impression is often based on the person's age, gender, colour of skin and hair, size, posture, clothes, movements, charisma, facial expression, gestures and voice in addition to what he/she says and does. Drama imitates many of these sources and kinds of information in order to construct fictional characters or figures to be performed by actors. Our image of a human being may be based on little or wrong information in a chance situation and is therefore subject to future changes. The image of a dramatic figure is defined by all the information given within the limits of the play on the basis of dramatic conventions. *Drama constructs a* **fictional character** *as a complex sign defined by psychological disposition, external appearance, speech, action, relationships to other characters and to circumstances.*

Dramatic conventions influence both the **conception of characters or figures** and the **styles of acting**.

Conception of characters in dramatic texts

- ▶ **Flat** or **round** (simple types or complex individuals)
- ▶ **Static** or **dynamic** (unchanging or developing)
- ▶ **Transparent** or **opaque** (fully explained, closed or enigmatic, open)
- ▶ **Psychological** or **transpsychological** (ordinarily or extraordinarily self-aware and perceptive; Pfister, *Theory* 176-83)

Acting

The actor impersonates a character, identifying with the role, or shows the character, maintaining a distance towards the role. The styles of acting are related to differences in the design and function of the character, genre and theatre.

Forms and functions of theatre

In general, tragic characters tend to be round and tragic action linear, comic characters to be flat and comic action complicated. Both genres reveal characters' blindness and mistakes, surprising discoveries and reversals of situations, but the kinds and consequences of weaknesses and changes are different. In ordinary life, many people call any unexpected death a tragedy, whether caused by slipping on the peel of a banana or into the crevice of a glacier. According to Aristotle, **tragedy** *requires a serious and coherent action and an intermediate or mixed but consistent and noble character, whose fortune turns from good to bad because of an error. The tragic action incites terror because something like it may happen to us and invites pity because we empathise with the suffering hero/ine* (Aristotle 100). If the protagonist is of a high social status, the reversal or fall appears to be more tragic because of the greater loss *(Fallhöhe)*. The protagonist's suffering due to his/her **recognition** *(anagnorisis)* of his mistake or guilt compounds the effect of his loss

Tragedy

This world is a comedy to those that think, a tragedy to those that feel.
Horace Walpole, Letter to Anne, Countess of Upper Ossory, 16 August 1776

(Aristotle 99). Our identification with the tragic hero/ine and our experience of **pity and fear** *(Mitleid und Furcht)* takes the effect of a **catharsis** *(Reinigung, Klärung;* Aristotle 95), presumably some form of detachment from these emotions.

Shakespeare's powerful King Lear wants to pass on the responsibility for his country by dividing it up among his daughters according to the level of their love for him. Being blinded by the flatteries of his two older daughters and offended by his youngest daughter's sober response, the enraged king gives all his land to his deceitful daughters and banishes the latter.

Fig. 4.7

Johann Heinrich Füssli, King Lear 1.1, 1792. The furious King Lear dismisses his youngest daughter from his court because he considers her to be disloyal. His loss of emotional control foreshadows that of his country to his older daughters, who watch the spectacle with cool detachment.

However, her sisters drive their father from court and into despair, which he suffers from immensely (with a limited degree of insight).

William Shakespeare, King Lear *(Klaus Michael Grüber, director, Berlin 1985). Having lost his kingdom, Lear is reduced to a mad, homeless beggar in need of help. In this performance, the choice of a child as Lear's guide highlights the king's deviation from his socio-political function as the wise father and leader of his country.*

Fig. 4.8

Aristotle's model of tragedy was based on specific examples of ancient tragedy. The conception of the characters and the action vary to some extent. The reversal of fortune may be initiated by fate (the gods) or the force of circumstances (e.g. poverty and tuberculosis), a flaw in character (e.g. rage, credulity), an error of judgement (e.g. misplaced trust or a misinterpreted situation) or subconscious forces (e.g. the death-drive). The **domestic tragedy** *(bürgerliches Trauerspiel)* replaces noblemen and public life by middle-class characters and private life because these would bring pity and fear as well as a moral message closer to the middle-class audience of the 18th century. In the 20th century, the American Eugene O'Neill (1888-1953) succeeds in depicting modern secular life with tragic grandeur, drawing on psychoanalysis and ancient tragedy. He combines external social and economic conflicts *and* devastating internal conflicts of outsiders and lost souls in a mix of realist and symbolic elements in style, as in his masterly trilogy *Mourning Becomes Electra* (1931) about a family in the context of Puritanism and the American Civil War (see also exercise 2, p. 124-125).

Comedy *often stages ordinary people of the middle or lower classes as flat types with stereotyped forms of behavior that may hold the mirror up to society for its pleasure or education.* Spectators may identify with the superior **wit** *(geistreicher Witzbold)* and laugh at the inferior **dupe** *(Tölpel).* Comic characters reveal shortcomings *(Schwächen)*, make mistakes, violate rules and are frustrated by failure, but their weaknesses, transgressions and defeats as well as the consequences are not as serious as in tragedy. The action is usually marked by stock elements, such as cross-dressing, deception, mistaken identities, surprising turns and revelations, all of which may transgress the laws of probability. In general, quarrels are settled without any serious harm to either party, such as the battle of wits and/or the sexes, and poetic justice prevails in the end.

Romantic comedies differ to some extent from satiric comedies in tone, the selection of characters, the pattern of the plot and the response invited from the spectators. The *light-hearted* **romantic comedy** *conceives romantic lovers, who are able to remove impediments to happiness, often with supernatural help, and a happy ending that integrates almost everyone.* The happy ending represents the ideal commonwealth of good life and harmony. *The romantic comedy favors tolerant humor and entertainment.* Shakespeare's romantic comedy *As You Like It* (1600) displays its cultural function as wish-fulfillment in

Comedy

the title. Political rivalry for power, which drove the legitimate ruler and the potential lovers Orlando and Rosalind into exile, is overcome by the wonderful change of the usurper in pursuit of his enemies in exile. Here, all forms of love-relationships are budding. Rosalind, cross-dressed as Ganymede, educates her ignorant lover. In the end, the political enemies are reconciled, the right couples married and almost everyone returns with the legitimate ruler to the court. This romantic comedy suggests that private experience (e. g. love) in a sphere that is segregated from the ordinary world (as the space of the theatre is from that of the real world) provides alternative solutions to public problems (power).

Satiric comedies *subject individual flaws and social vices to ridicule for the sake of the spectators' laughter, recognition and motivation to amend the problems.* The sharp focus on blatant transgressions and their bad social consequences, which can hardly be tolerated, stresses the relevance of values and rules. Instead of reconciliation, **poetic justice** is called for in order to drive the moral message home that virtue is rewarded and vice is punished. The English playwright Ben Jonson's (1572-1637) **comedy of humours** attacked the negative ruling passions of characters, such as greed, arrogance and stupidity in *Volpone, or the Fox* (1606). The comedy of humours is based on a psychology that defined types of human beings according to their disposition, related to bodily fluids: the sanguine, phlegmatic, choleric and melancholic. Jonson's satire hit hard because the worst offenders are members of the social establishment, a nobleman, an old gentleman, a merchant and a lawyer, who should embody rather than mock traditional values, but who meet their deserved end (see also p. 114). The **comedy of manners** *(Sittenkomödie)*, which thrived in the second half of the 17th century, was less strict in moralising than its predecessor, the comedy of humours. The comedy of manners celebrated sophisticated taste and manners, delighted in battles of wit and the sexes and in worldly pleasures as opposed to naivety, sobriety and hypocrisy. The objects of laughter were those who failed to meet these elevated standards because they were morally and intellectually innocent or exaggerated fashionable style or behaviour. In *The Man of Mode* by George Etherege (see also p. 100), the rake or womaniser Dorimant is able to manipulate women until he finds his equal in the witty Harriet, as opposed to Sir Fopling Flutter, whose extraordinary efforts to dress fashionably and converse politely fail miserably to achieve the intended effect. Oscar Wilde's *Importance of Being Earnest* (see pp. 112-113) builds on the tradition of the comedy of manners in his delineation of fashionable society and witty conversations, which do not always go together.

Beside the dramatic genre, the theatrical form privileges certain kinds of characters and acting. In **non-illusionist theatre**, roles are more often displayed than embodied. In medieval Christian plays on simple open-air stages, it would have been presumptuous for a craftsman to identify with, rather than to show, Christ or the devil. Medieval **morality plays** displayed Everyman's moral struggles on the way to salvation and personified abstract concepts, such as Folly or Temptation, which were didactically exposed to the audience. In satires or soap operas actors tend to exaggerate roles, which are often reduced to static stereotypes or stock characters, such as the cunning old man, the rich bitch and the innocent beauty. **Illusionist theatre** privileges rounded, complex individuals, which call for impersonation. The realist theatre of the 19th century presented transpsychological protagonists, whereas the naturalist theatre in the late 19th century stressed that the characters' ordinary psychological insight falls short of understanding their own existence. In the 20th century, **anti-illusionist, radical and experimental theatre** deconstructs the notion of consistent and independent individuals and tends to stress the theatrical quality of the performance (Aston/Savona 91-95; Pfister, *Theory* 177-83).

Dramatic figures characterise themselves and others directly in dialogues and monologues, indirectly in the way they talk and how they interact with others (verbal style and attitude). In addition to the verbal characterisation by the figures themselves, the stage directions and the performance provide authorial non-verbal information about characters and their positions in relationship to others.

The actor's **performance** is marked by

Actor

▶ the manner and timing of entrances and exits,

▶ the external appearance: stature (*Statur*), physiognomy (*Physiognomie*), costume (*Kostüm*), mask (or make-up: *Maske*) and hairstyle (*Frisur*),

▶ body language: facial expression (*Mimik*), gesture (*Gestik*), choreographic grouping (*Gruppierung*) and movement (*Bewegung*),

▶ the characteristic vocal quality (or timbre: *Stimmqualität*), pitch (*Stimmlage*), volume (*Lautstärke*), stylistic features (*Figurenstil*) and the delivery of speeches, varying according to pace (*Sprechge-*

schwindigkeit), rhythm (*Rhythmus*), intonation (*Melodie*), emphasis (*Betonung*) and emotional tone (*Tonlage*).

The individual character is also defined by his/her position within the **constellation of characters** (*Struktur des Personals*). Dramatic texts usually present a list of roles (*dramatis personae*), which ranks characters according to social position, generation and gender. The performance unfolds a character's relationship to others in a sequence of scenes with specific **configurations of characters** (*Konfiguration*). The number of *dramatis personae* is usually limited for pragmatic reasons, i.e. the number of actors in a company and the amount of characters and relationships an audience can reasonably absorb during the two or three hours of the performance. Often, characters appear in pairs, which call for comparisons of similarities and differences between them: ruler and counsellor, master and servant, husband and wife, parent and child, brother and sister, lover and beloved. A character can serve as a mirror of or a **foil** for another one inverting the other's features, setting off their particular strengths and weaknesses. In *Romeo and Juliet*, the old Montague and the old Capulet harbour the same old hate for each other, as opposed to their children's love for each other. The romantic Juliet, in turn, is juxtaposed to her pragmatic nurse as the sentimental Romeo is to his light-hearted friend Mercutio, who is murdered by the passionate Tybalt. Romeo's rival for Juliet is the noble Paris, whose conventional considerations of marriage are opposed to the lover's passion. A partner, such as Friar Laurence, can serve as a **confidant/e** (*Vertraute/r*), whose interaction with a major character allows the audience insight into the protagonist's private feelings and thoughts. It is useful to capture the characters' basic positions, roles and relationships towards each other in a diagram:

Characters in pairs

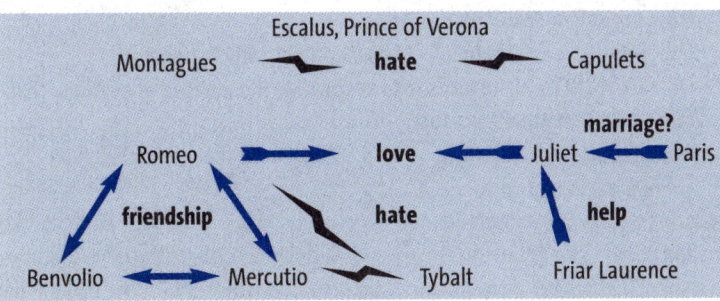

Fig. 4.9

Diagram of relationships between characters in Romeo and Juliet.

The relationships between characters reveal shared concerns but also **conflicts, motivated by an imbalance of power,** by differences in passions, opinions and interests. The central conflict is enacted in the struggle between the **protagonist** (*Hauptfigur*) and the **antagonist** (*Widersacher*) or adverse circumstances. In opposition to an event that may be caused by nature or chance, external action traditionally requires a character's motivation, intention and ability to change a situation, which can be impeded by powerful forces or circumstances. Of course, a character can also act from impulse or habit, leading to consequences beyond his/her intention and control.

As in ordinary life, it is worthwhile to observe how the various signs that define a character agree or disagree with each other. For example, the question is how a character's status, position and appearance compare to what he/she says in which manner and in which type of language (restricted or elaborated code, standard, dialect, sociolect, individual style/ideolect). In *The Importance of Being Earnest* (1899), for example, the Anglo-Irish author Oscar Wilde (1856-1900) presents the elegant and arrogant Lady Bracknell, who is unaware of the fact that she undermines her pretension to superiority when she tests her daughter's suitor. Her questions and ridiculous replies to Jack Worthing's embarrassed answers contradict any serious values:

> LADY BRACKNELL   Do you smoke?
> JACK   Well, yes, I must admit I smoke.
> LADY BRACKNELL   I am glad to hear it. A man should always have an occupation of some kind. There are far too many idle men in London as it is. How old are you?
> JACK   Twenty-nine.
> LADY BRACKNELL   A very good age to be married at. I have always been of the opinion that a man who desires to get married should know either everything or nothing. Which do you know?
> JACK [After some hesitation.]   I know nothing, Lady Bracknell.
> LADY BRACKNELL   I am pleased to hear it. I do not approve of anything that tampers with natural ignorance.
> (NAEL 2: 1771)

Words and acts

It is also of interest to see whether *words agree with acts, support acts or differ from acts* (Pfister, *Theory* 44), whether a humiliated character (1) says "I tremble with rage" and does so, (2) says "I tremble with

Fig. 4.10

The Anglo-Irish author Oscar Wilde (1854-1900) was as least as famous for his scandalous lifestyle as for his provocative epigrams, his fairy-tales, his aestheticist novel The Picture of Dorian Gray *(1890) and his witty comedies, such as* Lady Windermere's Fan *(1892) and* The Importance of Being Earnest *(1895). Having been imprisoned for homosexual activities for two years, he was divorced and spent the last years of his life in exile in France.*

rage" with rolling eyes and raising a fist in complement or (3) utters that sentence in a calm and firm voice, conveying irony by the discrepancy between content and form. Samuel Beckett presents a case of extreme discrepancy between verbal and bodily performance at the very end of the first and second acts in *Waiting for Godot* (1952):

ESTRAGON   Well, shall we go?
VLADIMIR   Yes, let's go.
(They do not move.)

Here, the difference between their words and acts expresses a lack of motivation, intention or ability in a situation with little meaning and less change, which are typical features of the **absurd drama.**

Events and actions follow the chronological arrangement of the **story** (*Geschichte*), "whereas the plot already contains important structural elements, such as causal and other kinds of meaningful relationships, segmentation in phases, temporal and spatial regroupings, etc." (Pfister, *Theory* 197). The Aristotelian or **closed form** (*geschlossene Form*) of drama conceives characters as agents in a coherent story with a well-defined beginning, a logical development in the middle and a solution to the conflict at the end. Often, the five acts of the closed form present a plot in the shape of a pyramid:

Story and plot

(3) climax
(*Höhepunkt*)

(2) complication
(*Steigerung*)

(4) reversal
(*Fall, Umkehr*)

(1) exposition
(*Einleitung*)

(5) catastrophe/dénouement
(*Katastrophe/Lösung*)

Fig. 4.11

Closed form of plot in five acts.

For example, Ben Jonson's satiric comedy *Volpone* (1607) (1) introduces the avaricious protagonist Volpone (the fox) and his clever sidekick Mosca (the fly), who put up hilarious performances to pretend that Volpone is fatally ill and talk greedy acquaintances into doing favours for Volpone in order to inherit his fortune upon his death within a short time. (2) Volpone and Mosca succeed in deceiving several fools but (3) are unmasked and (4) dragged into court, where they manage to turn the tables on those who discovered their fraud. (5) Finally, the protagonists are caught because they continue to play their game to excess and turn against each other.

Fig. 4.12

The poet, critic and dramatist Ben Jonson (1572-1637), who used to be a bricklayer and a soldier, became one of Shakespeare's great if less versatile rivals. In contrast to Shakespeare, he maintained the three unities of place, time and action in drama. He excelled in the genre of the satiric comedy, ridiculing immoral passions that motivate human actions. His masterly play Volpone *(1605/06) castigates false pretence and greed.*

The **open form of drama** (*offene Form*) violates the (neoclassical) demand for the unities of time, space and action, which were thought to promote a convincing illusion of reality on stage. In the open form of drama, characters tend to be determined by circumstances rather than mastering them by goal-directed action. The scenes are often fragmentary, loosely connected to each other and may not end with a definite solution to problems. In Shakespeare's *Midsummer Night's Dream* (1594-98), young lovers flee from the court of Athens to a forest, where craftsmen rehearse a play, and where the natural and the supernatural worlds overlap. Instead of one coherent action, the **sub-plot** (*Nebenhandlung*) and the play-within-the-play add to the **main plot** (*Haupthandlung*). Love in the world of the fairies, of human beings, in fiction and on stage is fraught with difficulties because of adverse circumstances and changing passions. The lovers' passions and the craftsmen's performance are clearly beyond their control: as the lovers' affections take sudden turns, the artisans' clumsy performance turns their fictional lovers' tragedy into a farce full of exaggerated, foolish behaviour. The ruler of Athens, Theseus, and his fiancée Hippolyta seem to form the exception to the rule, but the jealous quarrel between the king of the fairies, Oberon, and his wife Titania about a boy fore-shadows problems between the future husband and wife when they will have a baby. The play is symbolic rather than realistic, and the three strands of action offer various skeptical perspectives on passionate love.

Place and time | 4.4

The **three unities** of one coherent **action**, one **place** and a performance time that comes close to the fictional **time** limit the scope of plays. In the extreme, this demand for mimesis would require the action to take place in one room in one evening, as does the English play-wright Peter Shaffer's (1926-) *Black Comedy* (1965). However, its **farcical action** of improbable surprises, ironic accidents and downright chaos at a party in an apartment that is dark because of a blown fuse de-stroys any notion of **verisimilitude** (*Wahrscheinlichkeit*).

Unity of place, time and action

In the dramatic text, stage directions and characters locate the action by descriptions of the fictional **locale** (*Ort, Schauplatz*), which is transformed on the stage by the

▶ stage design (related to the size, form and equipment of the stage), such as the setting (*Bühnenbild*) and the properties (or props: *Requisiten*),
▶ lighting (*Beleuchtung*),
▶ sound effects (*Geräusche*) and music,
▶ special effects (fog, projections, etc.).

The British playwright Peter Shaffer (1926-) acquired international fame with his fiction-al case study of a psychic and violent young boy in Equus (1973), who gouges horses' eyes, and of Mozart's jealous arch-rival An-tonio Salieri, who might have murdered Mozart, in the play Amadeus (1974), which was turned into a successful film.

| Fig. 4.13

The stage

Of course, the construction of locales is limited by the form and the technical equipment of the stage, which reflects back on the dramatic texts. **Open-air theatres** in the Middle Ages and the Renaissance did not have the intention and the technical means to create a realistic locale and did not clearly separate the stage from the audience. Medieval theatres performed in public places, on platforms and pageants (*Bühnenwagen*), carts with a symbolic stage-setting. In Shakespeare's time, big public theatres sported a large **apron stage**, which was surrounded on three sides by up to 3000 spectators. The poverty of the stage design and props was made up for by **word scenery**, characters' descriptions of locales, which allowed fast changes of place.

Fig. 4.14

Reconstruction of the Swan theatre, built in 1592 for about 3000 spectators.

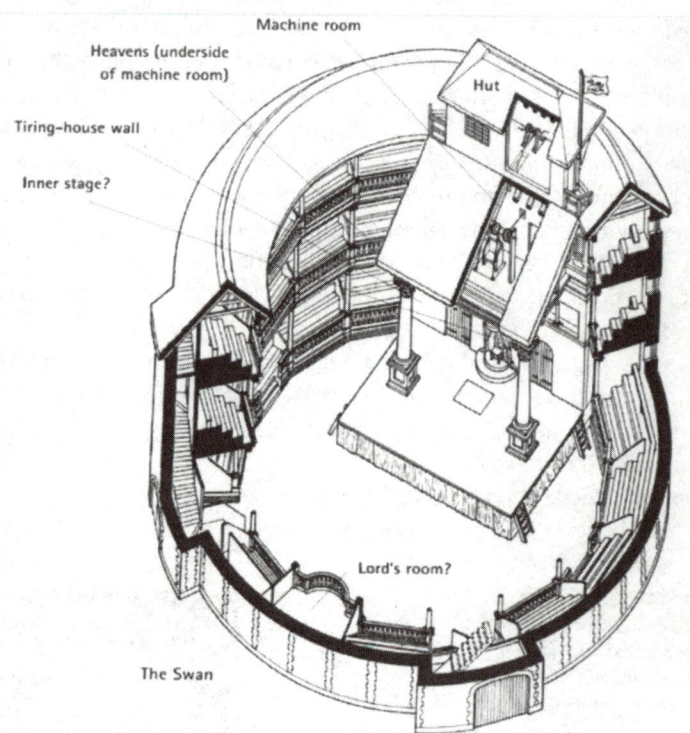

Machine room

Heavens (underside of machine room)

Hut

Tiring-house wall

Inner stage?

Lord's room?

The Swan

From the 17th century onwards, **indoor theatres** gradually separated the stage from the audience. At first, private theatres had actors perform on the proscenium stage (*Vorderbühne*) in front of a more or less elaborate setting on the scenic stage behind them.

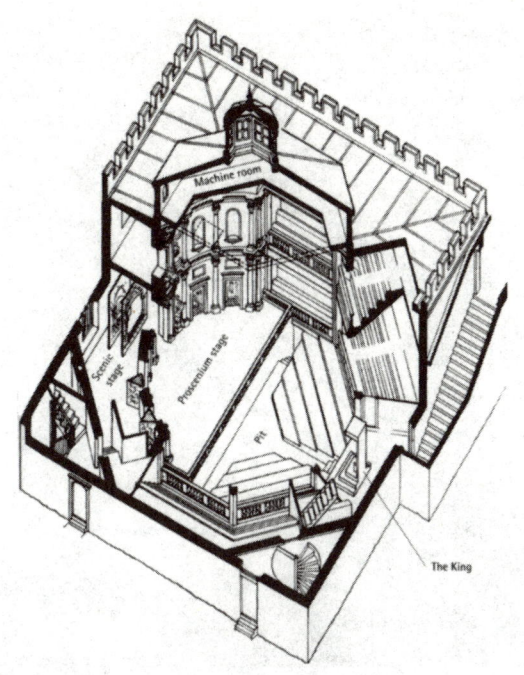

Fig. 4.15

Reconstruction of the Cockpit in Court, built in 1629-30. The King, whose position is elevated and juxtaposed to the stage, is just as important a spectacle as the action on stage.

Later, the **picture frame stage** (*Guckkastenbühne*) presented realistic settings with the help of elaborate technical equipment and gave the spectators the illusion of watching the world on stage through a "transparent" **fourth wall**. The "invisible" fourth wall separates the stage from the audience: the actors behave as if there were no spectators, who are invisible observers in the darkness of the theatre.

Whereas stage directions tend to indicate the *objective appearance* of the stage design, characters tend to express their *subjective perception* of locales in the primary text. In addition, characters mark the locale by their positions and movements, which in turn build the rhythm of the performance. The manner and meaning of entries and exits divide and connect the onstage and offstage areas, specifying whether a locale represents a place of action or rest, danger or refuge. Characters can assume the prominent central position on stage for reasons of being important or exposed to others. They can be relegated off-centre because they want to observe others or because they are excluded from others. The dynamics of spatial relationships symbolise social relationships.

Fig. 4.16

The Empire Music Hall, Newcastle, built in 1891. The advanced machinery of the picture frame stage, detailed paintings and the separation of actors and spectators help to create the illusion of observing real life in the theatre.

Task

Note the multiple significations of place and time in Beckett's *Endgame* (1958), and draw sketches of the stage design and the movements in order to visualise the stage directions and to support your interpretation:

> Bare interior.
> Grey light.
> Left and right back, high up, two small windows, curtains drawn.
> Front right, a door. Hanging near door, its face to wall, a picture.
> Front left, touching each other, covered with an old sheet, two ashbins.
> Centre, in an armchair on castors, covered with an old sheet, HAMM.
> Motionless by the door, his eyes fixed on HAMM, CLOV. Very red face.
> Brief tableau.
> [CLOV goes and stands under window left. Stiff, staggering walk.
> He looks up at window left. He turns and looks at window right.

He goes and stands under window right. He looks up at window
right. He turns and looks at window left. He goes out, comes back
immediately with a small step-ladder, carries it over and sets it down
under window left, gets up on it, draws back curtain. He gets down,
takes six steps (for example) towards window right, goes back for
 ladder, carries it over [. . .]
CLOV: [Fixed gaze, tonelessly.] Finished, its finished, nearly finished,
it must be nearly finished. [. . .] I can't be punished any more. [Pause.]
I'll go to my kitchen, ten feet by ten feet by ten feet, and wait for
him to whistle me. (Pause.) Nice dimensions, nice proportions. I'll lean
on the table, and look on the wall, and wait [. . .] (NAEL 2: 2472-73)

The naked, grey interior with small windows recalls a cold prison
cell. The bareness and Clov's isolation are enhanced by the fact that
everything is veiled: the windows, the picture (in a metaphorical
way), the ashbins and the figure in the middle of the room. Clov's
clumsy, mechanical and repetitive movements suggest that he has
been confined to this room for a long time and passes his time like
an imprisoned animal, pacing up and down but lacking its energy.
His initial words, spoken to the auditorium, are ambivalent because they promise an end to this situation and possibly a dramatic change but also suggest the end of the performance at the beginning of the play: either way, these words convey urgency and pressure. Clov's reference to punishment supports the impression that
the room is like a prison cell. The relationship between the onstage
and the offstage locales is as important as the change of locales on
stage. The kitchen seems to be *his* room as opposed to the staged
room. The exact size of the kitchen can be taken literally or read
symbolically as another prison cell, an interpretation confirmed by
Clov's ironic comment and his waiting for the whistle. The two windows connect the room with the world outside, which seems to be
just as bleak as the room inside from which the characters do not
escape.

   The relatively short **duration of a performance**, between two   Time in drama
and four hours, forces the playwright to carefully select, concen-
trate and telescope the **fictional time of a drama**, which lasts a
few hours only or many years. The dramatic action shown on stage
can be performed from the very beginning of the whole story *(ab
ovo*, early point-of-attack), start at some point during a story *(in me-*

dias res, late point-of-attack) or at the ending of a story (*in ultimas res*). If the action begins *in medias res*, **retrospectives** may provide information that explains the previous development, saving time in order to concentrate on decisive moments of the story. A play that begins at the ending of a story focuses on how it came about rather than what happened. **Foreshadowings** and time limits (a threat, deadline or case of emergency) create **suspense**. Usually, a loose succession of disconnected scenes requires a greater effort from the spectator to find meaningful links than a coherent temporal sequence of actions. *Time can be measured objectively in minutes, hours and days, perceived subjectively as boredom, pressure, etc., or interpreted symbolically.* For example, Eugene O'Neill's (US, 1888-1953) coherent play *Long Day's Journey into Night* (1940) takes place from morning to midnight, slowly unveiling repressed and painful conflicts. The course of the day symbolises the movement of life towards death both for the old parents and their sons Jamie, who has grown old before his time due to a reckless life, and Edmund, who suffers from consumption. In contrast, Wendy Wasserstein's (US, 1950-) *Heidi Chronicles* (1988) present eleven scenes in achronic order about women's lives before, during and after women's liberation between 1965 and 1989. The achronic order, which places scenes from different years next to each other, helps to underline similarities in women's positions in spite of the general trend towards women's emancipation, a fact that is supported by references to women's portraits over the centuries.

4.5 | Guiding questions and exercises

A detailed analysis of a complete drama or a performance would require a booklength study. Therefore, it is advisable to focus on one of the following tasks:
- ► to explore a topic (such as "The American Dream in Arthur Miller's *Death of a Salesman*"),
- ► to concentrate on one level (epic communication, dialogues, monologues, characters, action, place or time), or
- ► to select scenes for a comprehensive analysis of multiple aspects.

In addition, you have to decide whether to analyse the dramatic text as a literary artefact, as a script for a potential performance or the performance (or its recording) in itself. The analysis of the enactment of a text can first consider the text, then the performance, and conclude with a comparison, or compare text and performance according to selected aspects in a parallel proceeding.

Alternatively, check which current approach to literature would promise interesting results if applied to the play under discussion, and combine this approach with questions on particular features of the genre, such as the negotiation of gender constructions in the characterisation and the plot of an individual comedy.

Guiding questions for analysing drama and theatre

A) Verbal communication

1. Which forms of epic communication fulfil which functions?
   - ▶ Significance of title,
   - ▶ comments in stage directions,
   - ▶ epic narrator (outside the play or part of play; introduces and mediates play),
   - ▶ prologue and epilogue (frame, foreshadowing, retrospective, address audience),
   - ▶ report (link to the offstage world before or beyond the present scene),
   - ▶ aside (overheard or *ad spectatores*).
2. Who says what to whom in which way and for which reasons? (Dialogues and monologues).
   How do figures characterise themselves and others?
   - ▶ Direct versus indirect characterisation through content, manner and style of replies.

   What do utterances aim at?
   - ▶ Exchange of current information, retrospectives and foreshadowings, negotiation of meanings and relationships, planning and performing of actions.
3. How do the perspectives relate to each other? Why does the play select and combine these points-of-view?
   - ▶ Relationships between utterances of one character and others (quantity and quality),
   - ▶ development in sequence vs. (monologic or dialogic) structure of all perspectives.

B) Character and action

1. Which basic conceptions underlie the construction of characters in the play? What is the effect?
   ▶ Flat or round (simple types or complex individuals),
   ▶ static or dynamic (unchanging or developing),
   ▶ transparent or opaque (fully explained, closed or enigmatic, open),
   ▶ psychological or transpsychological (ordinarily or extraordinarily self-aware and perceptive).

2. How are characters designed and enacted? What do they signify?

   Which particular psychological dispositions are attributed to individual characters?

   How do stage directions define and actors perform characters?
   ▶ Impersonation or role distance,
   ▶ manner and timing of entrances and exits,
   ▶ external appearance: stature, physiognomy, costume, mask and hair-style,
   ▶ body language: facial expression, gesture, choreographic grouping and movement,
   ▶ characteristic vocal quality, pitch, volume, stylistic features,
   ▶ delivery of speeches, varying according to pace, rhythm, intonation, emphasis and emotional tone.

   Do words agree with acts, support acts or differ from acts? (Overlaps with action).

   Which particular places do characters belong to? (Overlaps with place).

   What are the characters' positions and relationships towards others?
   ▶ General constellation of characters vs. changing configurations in scenes,
   ▶ groups (families, gangs) vs. individuals (isolated individuals, outsiders),
   ▶ pairs: social (couples, master-servant, etc.) vs. dramatic (protagonist and antagonist, overlaps with action).

3. What is the structure and the function of the action?

   How is the chronological order of events and actions (story) related to the logical order and temporal presentation (plot)?
   ▶ Closed form vs. open form (coherent, linear order vs. episodic, fragmentary order).

How does the action relate to characters and circumstances?
- ► Are actions or circumstances dominant?

How is the main plot connected with the sub-plot?
- ► Links or overlaps in terms of characters, motifs, actions: similarities, differences, function as mirror or foil.

What is the function of the play-within-the-play?
- ► Limited significance as entertainment on the level of the story, more general function as mirror of play, reflection of dramatic conventions.

C) Place and time

1. Where does the story take place? Why?
   - ► Single setting or multiple settings/circumstances,
   - ► objective location and perceived atmosphere,
   - ► relationship between internal space and external space (individual consciousness, home interior vs. world outside),
   - ► social, political, cultural spaces and boundaries (inclusion, exclusion, transgression),
   - ► symbolic function (semantic space, externalised mirror-image of character).

2. When does the play take place and how is time conceived? How do you account for these choices?
   - ► Selection of contemporary or historical setting (relationship to cultural context),
   - ► objective measure of time vs. subjective perception of time (pressure, suspense),
   - ► linear, cyclical, inverted or achronic sequence of time (overlaps with plot).

3. How are the fictional locale and time presented on stage? Why?
   - ► Fictional time and location of text faithfully realised or changed by performance,
   - ► neutral, realistic or symbolic stage design, setting and properties,
   - ► lighting,
   - ► sound effects and music,
   - ► special effects (fog, projections, etc.),
   - ► relationship between fictional time and performance time,
   - ► sense of rhythm and space by change of scenes, actors' movements and actions.

D) General considerations

- ▶ How does the composition of the drama/performance relate to its topics? What is the meaning of this particular combination of form and content?
- ▶ Why does the drama relate to its cultural context in its particular ways?
- ▶ How do/did spectators respond to performances? Why?

Exercise 1

How do Arthur Miller's (US, 1915-2005) stage directions in *Death of a Salesman* (1949) characterise the protagonist (verbal and non-verbal information, setting)?

> A melody is heard, played upon a flute. It is small and fine, telling of grass and trees and the horizon. The curtain rises.
> Before us is the Salesman's house. We are aware of the towering, angular shapes behind it, surrounding it on all sides. [...] we see a solid vault of apartment houses around the small, fragile-seeming home. [...] From the right, WILLY LOMAN, the Salesman, enters, carrying two large sample cases. The flute plays on. He hears but is not aware of it. He is past sixty years of age, dressed quietly. Even as he crosses the stage to the doorway of the house, his exhaustion is apparent. He unlocks the door, comes into the kitchen, and thankfully lets his burden down, feeling the soreness of his palms. A word-sigh escapes his lips – it might be "Oh, boy, oh, boy." [...]
> LINDA, his wife, has stirred in her bed. She gets out and puts on a robe, listening. Most often jovial, she has developed an iron repression of her exceptions to WILLY's behavior – she more than loves him, she admires him, as though his mercurial nature, his temper, his massive dreams and little cruelties, served her only as sharp reminders of the turbulent longings within him [...]
> (NAAL 2: 1996-97)

Exercise 2

Analyse the relationship between the external situation, the action and the dialogue of Tyrone, an old but vital actor, and his son Edmund, both of whom are drunk. They meet in the barely lit living-room around midnight in a summer house surrounded by a wall of fog, which is pierced by sounds of a foghorn in the fourth act of Eugene O'Neill's autobiographical *Long Day's Journey into*

Night (1941; first prod. 1956):

EDMUND   She's [the mother] coming downstairs.

TYRONE   We'll play our game. Pretend not to notice and she'll soon go up again.

EDMUND   [Staring through the front parlour – with relief.] I don't see her. She must have started down and then turned back.

TYRONE   Thank God.

EDMUND   Yes. It's pretty horrible to see her the way she must be now. With bitter misery. The hardest thing to take is the blank wall she builds around her. Or it's more like a bank of fog in which she hides and loses herself. Deliberately, that's the hell of it! You know something in her does it deliberately – to get beyond our reach, to be rid of us, to forget we're alive! It's as if, in spite of loving, she hated us!

TYRONE [remonstrates gently]   Now, now, lad. It's not her. It's the damned poison.

EDMUND [bitterly]   She takes it to get that effect. At least, I know she did this time! [abruptly] My play, isn't it? Here. [He plays a card.]

TYRONE [plays mechanically – gently reproachful]   She's been terribly frightened about your illness, for all her pretending. Don't be too hard on her, lad. Remember she's not responsible. Once that cursed poison gets a hold on anyone –

EDMUND [His face grows hard and he stares at his father with bitter accusation.]   It never should have gotten a hold on her! I know damned well she's not to blame! And I know who is! You are! Your damned stinginess! If you'd spent money for a decent doctor when she was so sick after I was born, she'd never have known morphine existed! [...]

TYRONE [goaded into vindictiveness]   Or for that matter, if you insist on judging things by what she says when she's not in her right mind, if you hadn't been born she'd never – (NAAL 2: 1358-59)

Analyses: see appendix, 229-230.

The American Eugene O'Neill (1888-1953) used elements of ancient Greek tragedy in staging modern American life. He transforms the concept of fate as an external force of divine intervention into the internal force of inescapable psychic conflicts. The pessimistic assessment of human suffering from neurosis and complexes flies in the face of the American optimistic trust in self-reliance. The tragic trilogy Mourning Becomes Electra *(1931) confronts the passions of desire and revenge in the American Civil War.*

| Fig. 4.17

4.6 | Bibliography

PRIMARY SOURCES

Aristotle. Poetics. *The Norton Anthology of Theory and Criticism*. Eds. Vincent B. Leitch et al. New York and London: Norton, 2001, 90-117.

Beckett, Samuel. *Waiting for Godot. A Tragicomedy in Two Acts*. Ed. Manfred Pfister. Stuttgart: Reclam, 1987.

—. *Endgame. The Norton Anthology of English Literature*. Eds. M.H. Abrams, et al. 7th ed. Vol. 2. New York and London: Norton, 2000. 2472-99. (NAEL 2)

Etherege, George. *The Man of Mode. Restoration and Eighteenth-Century Comedy*. Ed. Scott McMillin. New York: Norton, 1973. 79-152.

Gilbert, Helen, ed. *Postcolonial plays: an Anthology*. London and New York: Routledge, 2001.

Jonson, Ben. *Volpone. Three Comedies*. Ed. Michael Jamieson. London: Penguin, 1972. 49-174.

Miller, Arthur. *Death of a Salesman. The Norton Anthology of American Literature*. Eds. Nina Baym, et al. 3rd ed. Vol. 2. New York and London: Norton, 1989. 1996-2056. (NAAL 2)

O'Neill, Eugene. *Long Day's Journey into Night. The Norton Anthology of American Literature*. Eds. Nina Baym, et al. 3rd ed. Vol. 2. New York and London: Norton, 1989. 1302-75. (NAAL 2)

Shakespeare, William. *The Riverside Shakespeare*. Ed. G. Blakemore Evans. 2nd ed. Boston: Houghton Mifflin Company, 1997.

Sheridan, Richard Brinsley. *The School for Scandal. Restoration and Eighteenth-Century Comedy*. Ed. Scott McMillin. New York: Norton, 1973. 277-340.

Wasserstein, Wendy. *The Heidi Chronicles and Other Plays*. New York: Vintage, 1991.

Wilde, Oscar. *The Importance of Being Earnest. A Trivial Comedy for Serious People*. Ed. Manfred Pfister. Stuttgart: Reclam, 1990.

Wilder, Thornton. *Our Town. A Play in Three Acts*. Ed. Eva-Maria König. Stuttgart: Reclam, 1984.

GUIDES TO THEORY AND INTERPRETATION

Asmuth, Bernhard. *Einführung in die Dramenanalyse*. Stuttgart: Metzler, 2004.

*Aston, Elaine, and George Savona. *Theatre as Sign System. A Semiotics of Text and Performance*. London: Routledge, 1991. (Very readable and systematic).

*Fielitz, Sonja. *Drama. Text & Theater*. Berlin: Cornelsen, 1999. (Very readable and useful overview, includes historical survey and reference to film analysis).

Fischer-Lichte, Erika. *Semiotik des Theaters. Eine Einführung*. 3 vols. 4th ed. Tübingen: Narr, 1994. *The Semiotics of Theatre*. Transl. Jeremy Gaines, and Doris L. Jones. Bloomington/Indianapolis: Indiana University Press, 1992. (Major study; shortened translation preferable for beginners).

Klotz, Volker. *Geschlossene und offene Form im Drama*. 14th ed. München: Hanser, 1999.

Müller, Klaus. *Das amerikanische Drama. Eine Einführung*. Berlin: ESV, 2006. (A good combination of historical overviews and discussions of individual authors and plays, mostly 20th century; white male canonical authors, but also ethnic and female playwrights).

*Pfister, Manfred. *Das Drama: Theorie und Analyse* 11th, revised ed. München: Fink, 2001. The Theory and Analysis of Drama. Trans. John Halliday. Cambridge: Cambridge University Press, 1988. (Excellent standard work, well structured and readable, very useful technical terms).

Platz-Waury, Elke. *Drama und Theater. Eine Einführung.* 5th ed. Tübingen: Narr, 1999. (Readable, systematic and historical introduction).

Szondi, Peter. *Theorie des modernen Dramas.* 25th ed. Frankfurt/Main: Suhrkamp, 1999.

Wallis, Mick, and Simon Shepherd. *Studying Plays.* 2nd ed. London: Arnold, 2002. (Very helpful guide to understanding plays).

GENERAL SOURCES

Artslynx International Arts Resources. Ed. Richard Finkelstein. updated regularly. Date of access: 1 December 2007. <http://www.artslynx.org>. (International arts resource registers directors, actors, diverse forms of theatre, magazines, organizations; sections on the visual arts, film, etc.).

*Banham, Martin, ed. *The Cambridge Guide to Theatre.* Cambridge: Cambridge University Press, 2000. (Concise information about playwrights, directors, actors, theatres and movements around the world, including overviews of national traditions).

—. *The Cambridge Guide to African and Caribbean Theatre.* Cambridge: Cambridge University Press, 2000. (Entries about national traditions, theatre companies, individual playwrights, list of primary works and highly selective lists of secondary works).

Benson, Eugene, and L. W. Conolly, eds. *The Oxford Companion to Canadian Theatre.* Toronto: Oxford University Press, 1989. (Covers individual playwrights, plays, genres, forms, theatres and companies; gives further reading).

Berney, K.A., and N.G. Templeton, eds. *Contemporary American Dramatists.* London: St James Press, 1994. (Biographical and bibliographical information mostly on American, Australian, British and Canadian playwrights; lists of primary works and sometimes of critical studies).

Bigsby, Christopher. *Contemporary American Playwrights.* 2nd ed. Cambridge: Cambridge University Press, 2000. (Brief biographical and bibliographical information).

*---. *Modern American Drama, 1945-2000.* 2nd ed. Cambridge: Cambridge University Press, 2001. (Good overview of postwar American drama and theatre).

Bigsby, Christopher, and Don Wilmeth, eds. *The Cambridge History of American Theatre.* 3 vols. Cambridge: Cambridge University Press, 1998-2000. (Comprehensive overview).

Bordman, Gerald. *The Oxford Companion to American Theatre.* 3rd ed. New York: Oxford University Press, 2004. (Focuses on Broadway theatres, summarises plays and comments on performances).

Brown, John Russell, ed. *The Oxford Illustrated History of Theatre.* Reprint. Oxford: Oxford University Press, 2001. (Collection of articles that focus on central European traditions).

Die Deutsche Shakespeare-Gesellschaft e.V. Updated regularly. Date of access: 1 December 2007. <http://www.shakespeare-gesellschaft.de/>. (Numerous links to online and offline material on Shakespeare, incl.performances, pictures, courses, etc.).

The German Society for Contemporary Theater and Drama in English (CDE). Date of access: 1 December 2007 . <http://www.contemporary-drama.de>. (Bibliographies on all aspects of drama and theatre in English; many links to journals, theatres, performances, etc.).

Goetsch, Paul. *Bauformen des modernen englischen und amerikanischen Theaters.* 2nd ed. Darmstadt: WBG, 1992. (Explains differences between realist, expressionist, epic and absurd theatre).

Grabes, Herbert. *Das amerikanische Drama des 20. Jahrhunderts.* Stuttgart: Klett, 1998. (Brief overview).

Hartnoll, Phyllis, ed. *The Oxford Companion to the Theatre.* 4th ed. Oxford: Oxford University Press, 1983. (Phyllis Hartnoll and Peter Found edited a shorter and updated paperback: *The Concise Oxford Companion to the Theatre.* 2nd ed. Oxford: Oxford University Press, 1996. This companion covers the international theatre of all ages, the technical conditions and styles of theatres, major dramatists, performers, directors and festivals).

*Innes, Christopher. *Modern British Drama: The Twentieth Century.* Rev. and updated ed. Cambridge: Cambridge University Press, 2002. (Very valuable standard book; covers major playwrights, plays and forms in five sections: context, modernism, social and realist theatre, comic and poetic theatre).

The Internet Shakespeare Editions. 1996-2003. 1 December 2007. <http://web.uvic.ca/shakespeare>. (Editions of Shakespeare's plays and those of his contemporaries; selected secondary material about Shakespeare and the Renaissance; links to online journals).

*Kennedy, Dennis, ed. *The Oxford Encyclopedia of Theatre and Performance.* 2 vols. Oxford: Oxford University Press, 2003. (Covers a huge range of international theatrical traditions and performances of all kinds, and provides explanations of key concepts and approaches to drama and theatre).

Krieger, Gottfried. *Das englische Drama des 20. Jahrhunderts.* Stuttgart: Klett, 1998. (Brief and selective overview).

Mengel, Ewald. *Das Englische Drama des 20. Jahrhunderts. Eine Einführung in seine Klassiker.* Tübingen: Stauffenburg, 2004.

Mr. William Shakespeare and the Internet. Version 4.0. Ed. Terry A. Gray. 1995-2003. 1 December 2007. <http://shakespeare/ palomar.edu/>. (Large amount of useful material about Shakespeare for students).

Müller, Klaus Peter, ed. *Englisches Theater der Gegenwart. Geschichte(n) und Strukturen.* Tübingen: Narr, 1993. (Good essays on theatres, genres and movements, women in theatre, new media, political and historical theatre).

Riggs, Thomas, ed. *Contemporary Dramatists.* 6th ed. Contemporary Writers Series. London: St. James, 1998. (Biographical and bibliographical information on contemporary playwrights, including selective lists of critical writings).

Rusinko, Susan. *British Drama 1950 to the Present. A Critical History.* Boston: Twayne, 1989. (Essays about authors, focus on Beckett, Osborne, Pinter and Stoppard).

*Schabert, Ina, ed. *Shakespeare-Handbuch.* 4th ed. Stuttgart: Kröner, 2000. (Comprehensive standard reference work about Shakespeare's time, life, work and reception).

*Schnierer, Peter Paul. *Modernes englisches Drama und Theater seit 1945. Eine Einführung.* 2nd ed. Tübingen: Narr, 2001. (Very readable overview of major developments in postwar drama, including sample passages from plays).

*Trussler, Simon. *The Cambridge Illustrated History of British Theatre.* Cambridge: Cambridge University Press, 2000. (Excellent and comprehensive study of British drama, theatre, actors, all forms of staged entertainment and the audience in cultural context).

UK Theatre Web. 2003. Updated daily. Oxon. 1 December 2007. <http://www.uktw.co.uk/>. (Listings of contemporary performances of all kinds).

*Wells, Stanley, and Margreta de Grazia, eds. *The Cambridge Companion to Shakespeare.* Cambridge University Press, 2001. (Comprehensive standard reference work in English on Shakespeare's time, life, work and reception).

Wilmeth, Don B., and Tice L. Miller, eds. *The Cambridge Guide to American Theatre.* Updated ed. Cambridge: Cambridge University Press, 1996. (Brief articles on individuals, plays, performances of all kinds and theatres).

The WWW Virtual Library: Theatre and Drama. Ed. Barry Russel. Date of access: 1 December 2007. <http://vl-theatre.com/>. (International and multilingual virtual library of plays and theatres; provides texts and pictures of performances; links to conferences and online journals).

*Strongly recommended.

Literary Theory

Contents

5.1	Author	135
5.1.1	Psychoanalysis	137
5.2	Text and code	143
5.2.1	New Criticism	143
5.2.2	Formalism, structuralism and semiotics	145
5.2.3	Deconstructivism, post-structuralism and postmodernism	150
5.3	Context	155
5.3.1	Marxism and cultural materialism	155
5.3.2	New Historicism	161
5.3.3	Feminism and gender studies	164
5.3.4	Postcolonialism and multiculturalism	169
5.4	Reader	175
5.5	Bibliography	180

Abstract

Literary theories provide stepping stones for informed readings of literature. They offer reasons, perspectives and concepts for particular approaches to the text, its aesthetic codes, its production, reception and representation.

A professor must have a theory
as a dog must have fleas.
H. L. Mencken.

If you know what they mean,
things make sense.
Bob Perelman, "4. Clippings," 1988.

This chapter continues the sketch of literary theories given in the introduction (review chapter 1.1) and complements the sections on poetry, narrative and drama. In many cases, particular questions concerning poetry, narrative or drama are based on specific literary theories (the rhetoric of poetry, structure of narrative, semiotics of the theatre). The British Terry Eagleton, professor of literary and cultural theory, has an appropriate answer to those who think that theory spoils the fun of reading literature: "without some kind of theory, however unreflective and implicit, we would not know what a 'literary work' was in the first place, or how we were to read it. Hostility to theory usually means an opposition to other people's theories and an oblivion of one's own" (viii). It is important to acquire not only one but various theories since not every approach generates interesting results with any kind of text. An approach adopts a certain perspective and highlights some aspects of a text while disregarding others. The reader has to ensure that the information ignored is not important to the issue in question. Otherwise, the validity of the interpretation, which depends upon adequate answers to the questions raised, is compromised.

Many theories of literature are challenging. Literary theory has taken up ideas from philosophy, psychology, sociology, linguistics and cultural theory. Students are often confused at first since many contemporary theories undermine "self-evident" ideas about who we are, how language and representation work and what an appropriate reading of literature is. However, rather than rejecting theory, it is relevant to become aware of one's own basic concepts of literature and other ideas of literature that can help us to develop new insights.

The changes in literary theories can be related to the history of the so-called Copernican revolutions, which triggered fundamental alterations in understanding God, human beings and the world. A brief survey introduces major shifts. Copernicus's (1473-1543) scientific explanation that the world moves around the sun shocked the Catholic belief in the motionless centre of the universe and in the eternal truth of the Bible, which placed human

Copernicus

beings in the centre of the cosmos under divine rule. Immanuel
Kant (1724-1804) challenged two fundamental beliefs in things
that are beyond experience: metaphysical concepts, such as God
or immortality, which could not be proven, and the idea of the
objective knowledge of the world as it is because the world we
know is always formed by the structure of human perception.
Charles Darwin's (1809-82) theory of evolution reduced human
beings from divine creatures and potential angels to descendants
from apes. His contemporaries were not only disturbed by the
questioning of Christian dogma but also by the idea that evolution and progress can be reversed by regression and decadence.
Karl Marx's (1818-83) theory of the determination of existence by
economic conditions and material forces undermined the notion
of individual human beings as the shaping forces of history.
Sigmund Freud (1856-1939) saw psychoanalysis as an insult of the
self-love of human beings because he questioned the dominant
function of consciousness in human beings, whose drives (*Triebe*)
and unconscious or subconscious were beyond its control. Ferdinand de Saussure (1857-1913) initiated the **linguistic turn** in literary
studies because he claimed that *language is a system that creates
meaning by itself instead of expressing individual intentions or mirroring
the world*. The **cultural turn** was initiated by theories which claim
that *identity, truth and meaning are not simply given but cultural constructions and subject to change*. Psychoanalysis, structural linguistics and cultural theories dismantle concepts of the stable, coherent identity of a unique, autonomous and rational individual, of
language as a neutral medium of intentional communication and
of universal truths and values. These attacks on liberal humanist
ideals do not merely destroy traditional notions but open up new
perspectives to see ourselves, literature and the world in new
ways (Tyson 2-3).

Kant

Darwin

Marx

Freud

de Saussure

Three tendencies characterise many approaches to literature
since the 1960s:

► Meaning is less based on factual reality or the individual mind
but rather on texts, linguistic and cultural conventions.

► Reading is no longer understood like cracking nuts, revealing
the meaning concealed beneath the surface in the "depth" of
the text but rather like taking strands from texts and weaving
patterns of meaning.

► Instead of adding up towards a definite or unifying result (A and

B = C), readings tend to arrive at contradictory or indeterminate meanings (A versus B = X).

The following presentation of theories parallels the model of literary communication introduced in the beginning of this book. The theories are grouped around the elements and relationships of literary communication that they primarily explore, the author's production of the text, the text itself, the linguistic and aesthetic codes, the historical and cultural context and the reader's reception of literature. Some theories deal with various dimensions of literary communication, and some approaches take up ideas from several theories and put them to new uses. For example, feminism and postcolonialism could be located in all extrinsic fields of the diagram. Psychoanalysis, structuralism and post-structuralism have influenced feminism and postcolonialism, which are concerned with social and historical contexts but also the production, codes and reception of literature.

Fig. 5.1

Fields of literay theories, some of which cover more areas than the ones marked here.

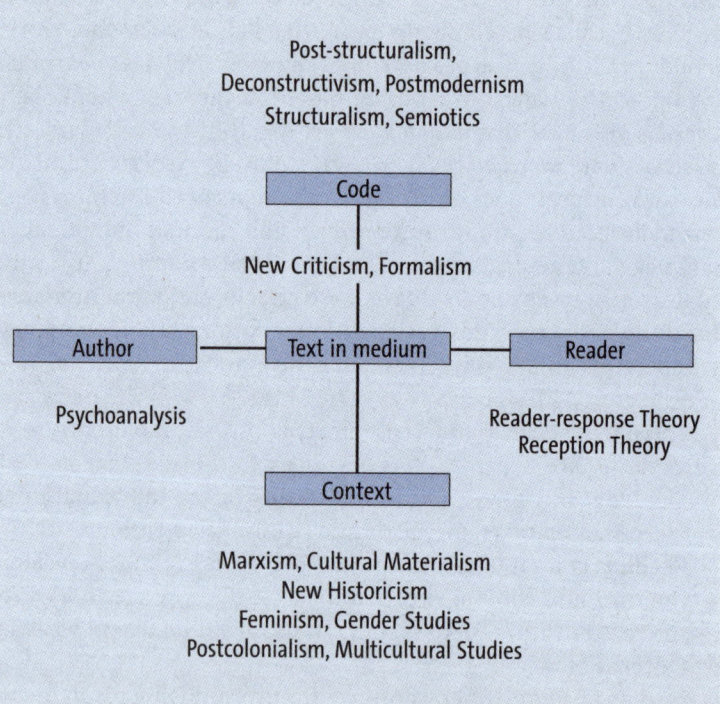

Post-structuralism,
Deconstructivism, Postmodernism
Structuralism, Semiotics

Code

New Criticism, Formalism

Author — Text in medium — Reader

Psychoanalysis

Reader-response Theory
Reception Theory

Context

Marxism, Cultural Materialism
New Historicism
Feminism, Gender Studies
Postcolonialism, Multicultural Studies

I will briefly present the central assumptions, aims and concepts of each theory in response to others. The major insight of each approach will be juxtaposed to its blind spot. A selection of key questions serves as a guideline for putting the approach into use. An example and a brief exercise – where particularly needed or possible within the allotted space – conclude the presentation. For the sake of brevity and accessibility, the presentation of current approaches and scholars is highly selective and most quotes will be taken from major anthologies rather than individual works of theory.

Author | 5.1

The idea that individual authors and their creation of the work are of prime importance for its understanding is essentially Romantic but persistent, as the constant flow of biographies reveals. Author-centered approaches considered three aspects to be important: historical evidence, the conscious intention and the unconscious or subconscious.

The **positivist biographical approach**, which originated in the 19th century, records "positive" (certain, objective) facts about an author's life and times, which are considered to be the cause of his/her literary output. The approach seems to be attractive because it "grounds" the ambiguous literary text in palpable facts. However, the approach requires interesting biographical facts in the first place, which are often hard to come by, especially if personal documents and other sources are scarce or if the personal data hardly bear any relationship to the literary work. In addition, if the biographical approach is used in a stereotypical way, it reduces literature to an effect of reality and underestimates that the author's intention and aesthetic aims may carry him/her far away from factual experience. Parallels between an author's life and work suggest cause and effect, but differences are more difficult to understand. Thus, rather than asking how the text mirrors life, it is more interesting to ask how life is transformed in the literary text, and how to account for its reasons.

Biographical questions

> ▶ Which aspects of the author's life and times are relevant to the text?
> ▶ What are the functions of autobiographical elements and their transformation? Do aesthetic invention or psychological motivation account for the changes?

Example

Wordsworth's "Daffodils"

Wordsworth's poem "I wandered lonely as a cloud" (see 2.3) is based on a walk with his beloved sister Dorothy, who wrote about it in her diary (NAEL 2: 391). Although he probably used her diary to compose his poem because there are verbal echoes, he did not mention her. It would not amount to a satisfactory interpretation to say that he lied since we know that literature does not have to be literally true. But why did he exclude her from his text? In terms of the artistic intention, Wordsworth wrote a poetological poem, which explains the creation of a poem in the unique and solitary poet's mind. An inspiring subjective encounter of nature served as a counterpart to society, which he considered to be alienating. This intense sense experience at times "flash[es] upon that inward eye" (NAEL 2: 285), and the resulting happiness is expressed in this text. The poem illustrates his idea of poetry as an expression of "emotion recollected in tranquillity" (NAEL 2: 250; feminists have more to say about this intertextual relationship as an exploitation of female creativity.)

Hermeneutics, the theory of interpretation, also places authors in their historical context but rejects the scientific explanation of cause and effect in favor of the humanist understanding of individual motivation and intention. The process of understanding, as we have seen in the first chapter of this book, is based on the reader's presupposition. Thus, it is a difficult if not impossible leap from our understanding of a text to finding the answer to the teacher's question everyone knows: "What was the author's intention?" The American scholar E. D. Hirsch, Jr. (1928-), who advocates an extreme position within hermeneutics, claimed that the author's intention determines the meaning of a text. He concedes that the fixed **mean-**

ing of a text (*Sinn*) hardly ever corresponds to its **significance** (*Bedeutung*) for readers, which can change over time. Nevertheless, he proclaims that readers should aim at an *objective interpretation* of the author's meaning in the text as opposed to the *more or less subjective criticism* of its significance for us (Hirsch in Leitch 1686).

New Critics, who focus on the text itself, regard the search for authorial intention as invalid and an answer to this question as **intentional fallacy** (*intentionaler Trugschluss*) because here, readers mistake their own understanding for the author's meaning. Structuralists and post-structuralists go further and deny the importance of the author, maintaining that meaning is based on processes in language itself and defined by the reader (see 5.2.2 and 5.2.3). However, psychoanalysis also undermines intention as the central source of meaning without neglecting the author.

Psychoanalysis 5.1.1

Our understanding of literary characters is usually based on popular psychology, such as understanding aggression as a response to frustration. Psychoanalysis would not necessarily disregard these views but seriously question that we are aware and in control of what we are doing by rational and conscious decisions. Apart from dreams, the slip of the tongue (*Freudscher Versprecher*) probably is the most familiar evidence of the unconscious or subconscious in everyday life (it also occurs in writing: in spite of being consciously open to semiotic theory, I wrote "sigh" instead of "sign"). The Romantics discovered the relevance of the unconscious but Sigmund Freud elevates it to the central problem of the human psyche, *decentering the conscious self*, which had formed the core of identity: "I think, therefore I am" (Descartes). Freud's model of the human psyche consists of three areas, the **super-ego** (*Über-Ich*), which contains the social and cultural norms, the **id** (*Es*), which harbours the drives (*Triebe*) and the rational **ego** (*Ich*), which tries to mediate between social norms and individual drives. These three parts roughly correspond to the conscience, the unconscious and the consciousness. In spite of decentering the individual, Freud aimed at an integrated self with some insight into the subconscious and the rational management of life, mediating between individual needs and social norms.

Freud's model of the human psyche

Fig. 5.2

The Austrian Sigmund Freud (1856-1939) developed the theory of psychoanalysis as a model of the human psyche related to social and cultural pressures. His focus on the dominant forces of sexuality, repression and the unconscious has been as disturbing as influential. Among his major works are Die Traumdeutung *(1899;* The Interpretation of Dreams), *which understands dreams as a working through of desires, fears and problems of everyday experience, and* Drei Abhandlungen zur Sexualtheorie *(1905;* Three Essays on the Theory of Sexuality).*

Freud identifies childhood as the formative period of identity and (sexual) desire (*libido, Eros*) as the predominant motivation (besides the destructive death drive: *Thanatos*). Infant libidinal energy moves from oral and anal to phallic pleasure, which goes along with the discovery of the sexual difference between the penis and the vagina. Freud attributes penis envy to girls and the anxiety of castration to boys (in a patriarchal model of gender). In the beginning, the infant directs all its libidinal energy upon itself in a **narcissistic** way, but later projects his/her desire upon objects (Freud in Kimmich 163). Problems arise if the self is caught up in one of his/her stages of infant development and in narcissistic self-love, being unable to form mutually satisfying relationships with others.

Psychological conflicts

The family becomes the first site of psychological conflicts between individual desire and social rules. According to Freud's interpretation of the **Oedipus complex**, the son first imitates the father as a model (identification) and later rivals his father for the love of the wife and mother (object-choice). The boy's "identification with his father then takes on a hostile coloring and becomes identical with the wish to replace his father in regard to his mother as well" (Freud, qtd. in Rivkin and Ryan, henceforth RR, 438). In a parallel and equally ambivalent way, a little girl identifies with her mother and desires to replace her mother as the lover of her father. Since these children's desires for their parents are illegitimate, as expressed in the **incest taboo**, they may be accompanied by guilt.

Social norms make individuals repress their desires, which live a life of their own in the subconscious but resurface in what is called the **return of the repressed** (*Rückkehr des Verdrängten*). Often, the return of the repressed reveals the **uncanny** (*das Unheimliche*), something that is *heimlich* in the sense of familiar and secret and at the same time *unheimlich*: "this uncanny is in reality nothing new or foreign, but something familiar and old – established in the mind that has been estranged only by the process of repression [. . .] something which ought to have been kept concealed but which has nevertheless come to light" (Freud, qtd. in RR 429). Freud relates the uncanny to "the idea of a 'double' in every shape and degree, with persons [. . .] doubling, dividing, interchanging the self" (qtd. in RR 425).

While Freud does not ignore the conscious creation of art, he is more interested in the expression of the unconscious as a revelation of the author's core psychological conflicts. He considers *literature to work like dreams* because the overt or **manifest** meaning on the surface of the text conceals the **latent** or covert meanings in the hidden depth of the text. *Criticism resembles therapy*: the reader reveals what has been concealed and subjects the unconscious to rational interpretation. Two patterns of dreams and texts have to be deciphered: **condensation** (*Verdichtung*), which combines and concentrates multiple experiences in complex images, and **displacement** (*Verschiebung*), which substitutes one thing for another closely related to it. The death of a relative may trigger the dream of a bird that is flying away, expressing a feeling of loss, the soul leaving the dead body, etc., or the dream of a strange character, dressed in black, haunting the dreamer.

On the part of the author, writing can reveal the return of the repressed, a dreamlike wish-fulfilment or serve as a therapy parallel to the talking cure the client is subjected to in psychoanalysis. The psychoanalytic approach, while concentrating on the origin of conflicts, can be applied to the production of literature, to the work itself and to its reception.

Art and dreams

Freudian psychoanalytic questions

▶ What do images and what do conflicts between and within characters reveal or conceal? How do characters' words, acts, emotions and subconscious states relate to each other? Do forms of repression, repetition, doubling and the uncanny mark conflicts of social conventions and individual desire?

▶ In which way do the manifest and the latent elements of the text reveal the author's conscious craft or subconscious conflicts?

▶ What is the function of writing for the author? (Wish-fulfillment, escapism, therapy, etc.).

▶ What is the effect of the text on the reader? Does my response reveal subconscious motives? Does a text allow us to imaginatively reenact subconscious conflicts?

Examples

Freud's interpretation of Hamlet's hesitation to kill the murderer of his father, which has fascinated and puzzled generations of spectators and critics, is a famous example of psychoanalytic criticism. Freud sees the Oedipus complex at work in Shakespeare's *Hamlet*. Hamlet's uncle Claudius killed Hamlet's father and married his mother, fulfilling Hamlet's secret Oedipal desire. Thus, the uncle serves not only as Hamlet's opponent but also as his *alter ego*. The great success of the play with spectators is explained in a similar way since the play shows the fulfillment (Hamlet's uncle), the repression (Hamlet) and the punishment of the forbidden Oedipal desire (the deaths of Claudius and Hamlet).

Robert Louis Stevenson's (GB, 1850-94) *Dr. Jekyll and Mr. Hyde* (1886) is one of the most famous literary expressions of the uncanny and doubling. The educated gentleman Dr. Jekyll lives up to Victorian ideals and his alter ego Mr. Hyde embodies antisocial drives. Jekyll's repetition-compulsion (*Wiederholungszwang*) motivates him time and again to transgress social norms in the body of the uncanny Mr. Hyde. Jekyll's rational ego (the "I") is no longer master in his own house and of his own self: "Think of it – I did not even exist" (Stevenson 90). When Jekyll realises that he has lost control over his passions and can no longer change from Hyde into the respectable citizen, he commits suicide.

Exercise

Interpret the limerick "Three blind mice" (read the text in 2.1; the appendix gives an interpretation).

The French psychoanalyst and critic Jacques Lacan reverses Freud's insight that literature works like dreams, taking into account the linguistic turn: the individual subject (Latin *subjectum: unterworfen*) comes into being in language, and *the unconscious is structured like a language* (Barry 111). According to Lacan, the subconscious process- es of condensation and displacement follow the patterns of metaphor and metonymy. If you are secretly afraid of the fact that you will not meet the deadline of your paper, you may dream of missing a train (metaphor) or of no longer knowing how to write any more or of writing words that disappear (metonymy).

Lacan

Due to his understanding of the psyche as a linguistic process, Lacan has been associated with post-structuralism. Like Freud, Lacan regarded the child's early development as crucial for human identity and its problems. Whereas the baby has no conception of an identity apart from its mother (narcissism, symbiotic unity where it is the center of desire), the discovery of its **mirror image** ini- tiates the imaginary sense of the self as an individual. If a baby re- alises for the first time that the movements in the mirror are an image of its own behavior, it develops a visual sense of itself as a person apart from others, especially its mother. Instead of recog- nizing the identity of the self and its mirror image, Lacan stresses the separation of the observer from his/her image, the other. The identification with the specular image, Lacan maintains, forms a matrix (pattern) of identity formation that precedes "the dialectic of identification with the other" (qtd. in RR 442) and its conception as a subject in language.

Mirror stage

Learning language provides the infant with a **symbolic order** (here, symbolic does not refer to the rhetorical figure but to words used as signs). In opposition to the baby's symbiotic unity with the mother, the infant is now subject to the symbolic order, which Lacan associates with the father, because language embodies patri- archal rules, knowledge and power. The acquisition of the "father's language" goes along with the birth of the unconscious because the desire for the lost unity with the mother or the mother as ob- ject has to be repressed. According to Lacan, the **split** between the self and the mirror image, the "I" and the "me", the signifier and the signified, the self and the m/other, the consciousness and the subconscious, generates the desire for unity, which is unattainable, so that lack and **absence** become central features of the subject's identity in language.

- ▶ Does the text reveal conflicts of the mirror stage or the entry into the symbolic order?
- ▶ In which way is the speaking subject different from or undermined by what he/she says about him/herself?
- ▶ How is the conscious search for meaning, order, unity or an object/other frustrated by subconscious elements?

Example

Barthelme's "The Baby"

Donald Barthelme's short story "The Baby" (see 3.2.2; Nischik 52-54) can be read in Freudian and Lacanian terms. Freudian psychoanalysis would stress that the father has a strong super-ego, projects his own drive of destruction onto his baby and punishes it for what he would like to do. The ending, which appears to be completely arbitrary, acquires a psycho-logic in Freudian terms as the return of the repressed in the father's indulgence in destructive behaviour. In a Lacanian perspective, the story reveals the baby's subconscious resistance against being separated from its mother and subjected to the law of the father. The baby continues to tear pages out of books that the father offers to it in spite of – or rather because of – knowing what will happen. These books represent the father's symbolic order, which is enforced by the baby's separation from the mother, which may have been the (jealous) father's subconscious motive all along, treating the baby as if it already knew language and could be held responsible for transgressions against his order. However, the regressive return of the father to tearing pages out of books with the baby in the end reveals that he subconsciously suffers from the split self due to his own entry into the symbolic order, which separated him from his own mother.

The psychoanalytic approach has met with criticism that considers it arbitrary because it privileges subconscious revelation to conscious communication. What is more, if psychoanalytic critics and their readings are in turn subjected to psychoanalytic interpretation, their special interest in the sexual motives and subconscious repression of authors appear to be an outcome of their own problems or projections. While the psychoanalytic interpretation of fictional characters and relationships can be fruitful, we must not forget that they are, after all, aesthetic creations and not real people. Both Freud and Lacan have been criticized by feminists for their "phallocentric" construction of human identity and gender, which privileges male over female identity. Nevertheless, the unconscious is one of the central concepts of contemporary thinking and figures in various forms in recent political, cultural and feminist theory.

Text and code | 5.2

All of the subsequent approaches in this section are sometimes labeled text-centered because they neglect the dimensions of expression, mimesis and reception or conceive writing and reading as (inter)textual processes rather than intentional acts.

New Criticism | 5.2.1

The Anglo-American New Critics (1920s-60s) reject the extrinsic readings of literature in favour of an **intrinsic approach** (*werkimmanenter Ansatz*). They denigrate an interpretation that refers to the author's expression as intentional fallacy. They also oppose an impressionist reading as an affective fallacy because it allows the critic's emotions to attribute significance to the text. Literature is regarded as an *autonomous aesthetic object independent of authorial intention, historical circumstances and its emotional effect upon the reader*. In this respect, they follow Matthew Arnold's interest in an "objective" theory of art and criticism (see 1.1), and T.S. Eliot's ideal of the poet's impersonality.

The tag "objective approach" for New Criticism is misleading. While ignoring a subjective response to the text, the interpretation of the text as an object and its reading are not free from any consideration of values. The mere recognition and understanding of a text as a work of art implies intersubjective values, which the reader of a certain sensibility can find materialised in the literary text (see Wellek and Warren 156, 250). Important literature, the New Critics maintain, has an intrinsic value of its own, revealing universal meaning.

Since "a literary work of art is not a simple object but rather a highly complex organisation of a stratified character with multiple meanings and relationships" (Wellek and Warren 27), it requires **close reading** (*detaillierte textimmanente Lektüre*). Close readings aim at the exact description and sound interpretation of form and content, including metre, rhythm, rhyme, imagery, grammar and verbal meaning. In contrast to expository prose, literature is considered to be especially sensitive to and rich in connotative meanings. The **denotation** (*Grundbedeutung*), which refers to the primary meaning or the referent of words, is not more relevant in literature than the **connotation** (*Mitbedeutung*), the secondary meaning, such as the association of fox and cleverness or steel and coolness. Connotations follow conventions of style, register, region or history.

Task

Look up the different connotations of African-American, Black, Afro, negro, nigger and coon.

The method of New Critics corresponds to their ideal of art, using rhetoric and poetics to scrutinize a text for *the aesthetic organisation of its elements into an organic whole*. They appreciate complex texts that are rich in imagery, ambiguity, irony and paradox, for example poetry or Shakespeare's plays.

New Critical questions

▶ Do denotative and connotative meanings, literal and metaphorical meanings generate a complex unity of the text?
▶ Does the composition integrate content and form? Does the work of art create a whole or fail to do so?
▶ Do the particular positions of the text allow for generalization or even universal truth?

The conservative New Critical conception of universal values in life and in (high-brow) literature was attacked by virtually all extrinsic positions as being unhistorical and far too general. Close readings were held to be inappropriate because they avoided addressing the importance of readers, history and culture to literature. Deconstructive critics would scorn the New Critical attempt to subsume ambiguous and paradoxical meanings under an idealising concept of unity rather than acknowledging irreconcilable contradictions.

Formalism, structuralism and semiotics | 5.2.2

Like the New Critics, Russian Formalists (1910s-30s) largely ignore authorial intention, historical circumstances and the effect upon the reader. However, they are more interested in the general (linguistic) features of literature than the unique individual work of art that the New Critics privilege. The *author is no longer considered an original genius but a craftsman or writer, who works with artistic devices*. In a simplified way, *formalism is concerned with the deviation of literature from ordinary language, structuralism with the system of literature itself* (as *langue*), *which enables the generation of actual texts* (as *parole*). Sometimes, semiotics or semiology is used in a similar way as structuralism, at other times, a difference is made between the structuralist focus on the abstract system of signs and the semiotic interest in the communicative process of encoding and decoding signs by users.

These approaches refuse the idea of literature as authorial expression and concentrate on textual structures or on readers, who use their literary competence in order to structure texts. In general, semiotics and structuralism are either used in an intrinsic way, practicing close textual analysis, or in an extrinsic way, reading cultural systems of fashion, food, film, sports, etc., as if they were texts.

Saussure's linguistics has profoundly influenced the following approaches. According to Saussure, language cannot be defined as the expression of intentions or the mirror of reality but as *a system of dynamic relationships between signs*, which generates meaning in itself. The virtual system of the rules and signs of language (*langue*) **is realised** in individual performances (*parole*) **with a difference,** which can change the meanings of signs and rules in the long run. Saussure's definitions of the sign and its meaning were groundbreaking. A sign does not connect a name and a real thing but rather a **sound image** or **graphic image** (**signifier**, *Signifikant*) and a **mental concept** (**signified**, *Signifikat*) in an **arbitrary** (*arbiträr, willkürlich*) relationship. René Magritte's painting illustrates this insight:

The meanings of signs are defined by the relationships between **paradigms** (*Paradigma*, *Beispiel*), that is by differences from other signs within the same category. The subject in the sentence "The cat is on the sofa" is meaningful since the subject is not the dog or the elephant. It may be difficult to understand Saussure's statement that language creates meaning based on the difference between signs rather than the content of individual signs. If "black" means the opposite of "white" and we only know what "black" means if it is related to "white", it is hard to see how one can choose between paradigms of colors if none of them means anything as such. However, Saussure's insight that **binary oppositions** form the basic semantic units of a language, such as man/woman, earth/sky, human/animal, etc., is generally accepted. Sentences mean something by the **selection of paradigms** and their **syntagmatic combination**: "The cat/dog is/sleeps under/behind the armchair/sofa." Saussure's concepts have influenced the definition of literature as a system, writing and interpretation as competence (*langue*) put into performance (*parole*), and meaning as a relationship between signs.

Shklovsky's theory of deviation

The Russian writer Viktor Shklovsky defines literature by its **deviation** (*Abweichung*) *from the conventional rules of language*. Literature does not differ in content from ordinary language because it deals with topics from everyday life, for example education, love, morals, money and death. Literature foregrounds *how* it expresses content.

Literature can be defined as *the sum or the system of stylistic devices*, which raises our awareness of language and **defamiliarises** (*verfremden*) our perception of the ordinary world that is so familiar to us that we no longer notice it: "'If the whole complex lives of many people go on unconsciously, then such lives are as if they had never been.' And art exists that one may recover the sensation of life; it exists to make one feel things, to make the stone *stony*" (Shklovsky 9 qtd. in RR 16). Art raises our awareness for language and life, Shklovsky maintains, by describing things as if they were unknown, compelling readers to slow down and concentrate on their new perception.

The formalists find many of these deviant stylistic devices in poetry, which uses metre, rhythm, rhyme and imagery, and sometimes violates semantic, grammatical and syntactical rules. In narrative, formalists comment on the functional use of the perspective and the plot, which draw the reader's attention to *how* something is seen and to connections between the events of a story (see 3.3). Formalists are also interested in metafictional, self-referential narrative texts, which foreground their literary devices, such as Sterne's *Tristram Shandy* (see 3.2.3).

However, literary language is not *per se* different from ordinary language and sometimes uses and endorses its readers' stereotypes. Ordinary language itself, especially oral discourse, is full of imagery, grammatical and syntactical deviations from elaborated language. Language is not a univocal system but reveals many differences according to region, class, gender, generation, styles, registers and individuals. Novels, drama and also modern poetry often explore the various uses of ordinary language, defamiliarising literary conventions (see RR 19).

The Russian linguist and literary critic Roman Jakobson moved from formalism to structuralism and semiotics. Jakobson developed an influential model of communication, which served to define the aesthetic function of literature in a slightly different way than Shklovsky. According to Jakobson, language has six functions: the emotive, referential, conative, phatic, poetic and metalingual function. The **emotive or expressive** function externalises a speaker's emotions and thoughts, and the **referential** serves to convey information. The **conative or imperative** function aims at convincing the addressee, and the **phatic** serves to maintain the contact with the addressee (e.g. the particle "well..." or the tag "...isn't it"). The **poetic or aesthetic** function reflects on the structure of the utterance itself, for

Functions of language

example its diction, whereas the **metalingual** refers to the codes used in this process of communication (e.g. questions about the use or meaning of a specific phrase). Jakobson stressed that *literature foregrounds the poetic or aesthetic function*, which points to its use of language at the expense of the referential function.

His definition of poetry in particular has acquired fame because it explains its characteristic repetition of diction, metre and rhyme: "The poetic function projects the principle of equivalence from the axis of selection into the axis of combination" (qtd. in Ludwig 18). This means that a poem asks us not only to see similarities and differences between the choice of "house", "hut" or "hovel" in the paradigms for "building", but also between these words and those connected to them through syntactic or poetic means: for example, "the metrical parallelism of lines or the phonic equivalence of rhyming words prompts the question of semantic similarity and contrast" (Jakobson qtd. in RR 79).

The limerick "Three blind mice" combines words not only according to the rules of semantics and syntax but also according to poetic similarities, for example, rhyme ("Three"/"See"), assonance ("blind mice") and alliteration ("cut"/"carving", see 2.1, 23). *Form follows function* according to structuralists. The *basic binary opposition* in the poem is rendered equivalent by rhyme: "blind"/"sight", paralleled by the assonance "mice"/"wife". The opposition of blindness and insight is equivalent to that of animal and human being. However, the poem implicitly establishes an equivalent opposition in life/poem, stressing its own function as art to make us see something that we have ignored in life. Structuralism would be interested in *how the poem generates meaning, not what it means*. The interpretation of its content would be of interest to the psychoanalytic critic (see 7.1).

Structuralism is very useful for the analysis ·of poetry, but it achieved greater prominence in the theory of narrative, establishing a detailed system of narrative voice and focalisation, time and the function of characters and plots (see 3.2.2-3.3).

Structuralist Questions (compare the guiding questions in 2.5, 3.5, 4.5)

▶ What are the central elements, their relationships and their functions within a genre?
▶ What are the fundamental semantic, syntactic, rhetorical and

poetic binary oppositions and equivalences in the text under analysis? How are they interrelated and what is their function in comparison to the conventions of the genre?

▶ How does the fictional model of reality relate to other cultural models of reality, such as designed by the systems of kinship, psychology or the law?

Determine the fundamental binary oppositions and equivalences in Phillis Wheatley's poem "On being brought from Africa to America" (see 2.3) on the level of semantics, sound and metre. Find out how these oppositions relate to each other and how their combination changes in the poem. Compare the realignment of oppositions to those of Christian culture and North American slavery and explain its function (see Zapf, *Literaturgeschichte* 1-34, 402-406; for an answer, see 7.1).

It has been debated to which extent the insight resulting from the structuralist approach reveals patterns implied in the object or imposed by the critics (cp. Eagleton 116, 122). The Marxist scholar Terry Eagleton conceded that the basic insight of structuralism into the construction of meaning by "shared systems of signification" (107) forms a decisive advantage over the liberal humanist conception of meaning as originating in a unique individual or in universal ideas. However, he criticises that structuralism goes too far in eliminating the human subject and in isolating literature from the material conditions of social practices and historical changes (Eagleton 109-114). Structuralism in the narrow sense of establishing rather static systems seems to be outdated. Semiotics in the general sense of understanding various fields of culture as system *and* communication is still flourishing. For example, Erika Fischer-Lichte developed a semiotic understanding of the complex theatrical system of audiovisual signs *and its communication in performances*, which helps enormously to analyse plays (see 4.1, 4.3). Roland Barthes's concise analyses of the different structures of advertising detergents and soap-powders, like Persil and Omo, or of an exhibition of photographs, *The Great Family of Man*, which presents the myth of a unity in diversity of humanity, stressing a common nature instead of cultural and historical inequality, are still relevant and entertaining (qtd. in RR 81-89).

5.2.3 | Deconstructivism, post-structuralism and postmodernism

In spite of numerous differences between them, deconstructivism, post-structuralism and postmodernism (1960s-) share a few tenets, such as dismantling the fictions of essence and truth in metaphysical philosophy, objective knowledge in rational science and universal values in liberal humanism.

The French deconstructivist philosopher Jacques Derrida questions traditional concepts of truth, based on the given identity, essence and presence of things and people in the world. According to common sense, a text *re-presents* something that is absent, as a letter conveys our thoughts to someone else in our absence. The ordinary reader of the letter would suppose that the meaning and the truth of the letter ultimately rely on the facts of our identity, our presence and our past experience in the substantial world we share. However, Derrida would stress that the letter's origin and its reference (the writer and his/her experience) are not only absent, deferred in time and space. In a more radical sense, every thing, concept or identity can only mean something in the first place due to their difference from other things, concepts or identities. Therefore, *everything is textual because it only makes sense to us due to differences from something else, as a sign in the text means something due to its differences from other signs.*

Whereas Saussure takes the relationship between signifier and signified as the two different but inseparable pages of a sheet of paper, Derrida stresses the separation between them, which renders the relationship unstable, slippery and indeterminate. He coins the artificial term differance (French **différance**), which includes the notions of "to differ" and "to defer". Differance encompasses "the sense of not being identical, of being other" (Derrida qtd. in RR 283) and of the temporal and spatial gap between signs that is necessary in order to generate meaning. This process cannot be explained by equivalent binary opposition, which defines black as not white and white as not black. Derrida *decentres the system of binary oppositions*, which organises the meaning of texts according to structuralists. Instead of forming a simple opposition of equivalent terms, binary oppositions convey a hierarchy, in which the "minor" term disturbs the stable balance. The oppositions man/woman, culture/nature, heaven/earth privilege the first term, which, however, is always "contaminated" by the **trace** of its "lesser" counterpart. If the term "civilised" needs the term "barbarian" to define it, it is difficult to use the one without a trace of the other.

> Differance is what makes the movement of signification possible only if each element that is said to be "present", [...] is related to something other than itself but retains the mark of a past element and already lets itself be hollowed out by the mark of its relation to a future element. This trace [...] constitutes what is called the present by this very relation to what it is not, to what it absolutely is not [...] (Derrida qtd. in RR 287)

If you want to know the exact meaning of a word, you look it up in a dictionary, where the word/signifier is explained by other words/signifieds, which are signifiers in themselves and in turn are explained by other words in an **endless chain of signification**. You can read the whole dictionary without getting closer to the exact meaning of the word but will rather end up with more and more words. The meaning of the word that you want to find is related to the definitions you have looked up, those you will have to look up and those you might look up. There is no logical point where to stop but a practical one. Ultimately, the complete meaning of a sign would be constituted by its differance to all other signs. In other words, the meaning of signs remains incomplete, but we accept provisional meanings for pragmatic purposes.

In sum, language consists of an *interminable play of signifiers, which disseminates or disperses rather than fixes meanings.* A deconstructive analysis proceeds in two steps. It figures out the principles that serve as the bedrock of the text, and then unearths the quicksand beneath it. Consequently, deconstructive analysis reveals *where the text says something that it does not mean*, that is multiple and contradictory meanings in addition to "obvious" ones. Something a text presents as natural, normal or self-evident would appear to be based on what is considered to be cultural, arbitrary and strange. The Eurocentric "universal" definition of humanity as mankind or "man" turns out to be an artificial patriarchal construction that serves as the norm for men and women of any culture around the world, containing (including and repressing) multiple gendered and ethnic differences, which, if addressed, question the universal assumption.

Deconstructive questions

▶ How are privileged terms of binary oppositions undermined by their negative other?

▶ Which passages present arguments or images of profound ambiguity or contradiction?

▶ What is considered to be self-evident or natural but appears to be arbitrary?

▶ Where do shifts in perspective and judgment occur and disrupt the coherence of the central argument of a text?

▶ Do blind spots or omissions hide potentially subversive information?

▶ Where do self-referential statements and intertextual links undermine basic assumptions of the text?

Examples

Macbeth

After violent struggles over life and death for honor and power, Shakespeare's Macbeth arrives at an insight which questions all of his goals and values:

> Life is but a walking shadow, a poor player,
> That struts and frets his hour upon the stage,
> And then is heard no more; it is a tale
> Told by an idiot, full of sound and fury,
> Signifying nothing. (5.5.24-28)

Hubert Zapf comments that here, life is marked by absence rather than presence, the shadow rather than the real thing; life is but a text, and what is more, one that is beyond the control of its speaker and does not make any sense; it is a sign without a referent, a signifier without a signified, or in short: nothing (201-202). However, this statement hardly represents the play as a whole because it is voiced by the hero after his recognition of the futile and amoral strife for the crown (Zapf 202), and because law and order are restored in the end.

Phillis Wheatley

In Phillis Wheatley's poem, the phrase "Christians, Negroes, black as Cain" disrupts the binary hierarchy between the heathen

Africans and the "chosen people", white American Christians. The analogy of Christians and Negroes renders white and black equivalent: evil Christians are black as Cain, Africans can be "white" as Christians. The hierarchy is even inverted: since the soul counts more than the body, the moral corruption of Christians is worse than the dark skin of the "Negroes". The intertextual reference to the Bible reveals more ambiguity and contradiction. The "black" Cain is the bad brother and negative other of the "white" Abel. The black br/other is relevant to the construction of the "pure" white individual but also (literally and metaphorically) undermines white identity as a separate racial identity: Cain *murdered* Abel and was *marked* by God in order *to protect him* from the revenge of people. Cain was white before he turned black. The black color of *Cain* is not a diabolic sign, as racists say, but rather a sign of God's mercy. If that was true, there would have been no Christian basis for the essentialist racial and religious discrimination against Africans. If the color black signifies both God's mercy and God's opponent, the devil, and if God's favorite, Abel, is killed and his killer is saved, Christian ethics and God as the transcendental principle of Christian faith (and the poem) seem to be rather arbitrary.

Roland Barthes, who developed famous structuralist/semiotic readings of cultural signifying systems, such as fashion, sports and advertisement (see above), has promoted post-structuralist positions under the influence of Derrida. In his later writings, Barthes claims that texts can hardly be reduced to binary oppositions but reveal multiple and indeterminate meanings. He argued that the *death of the author gives birth to the reader* (Barry 66): the author's "life is no longer the origin of his fictions but a fiction contributing to his work" (qtd. in RR 1474). *The reader employs codes to unfold the meanings of a text, which are potentially endless because each text (and each reading) is* **intertextual** *in a wide sense,* that is, connected not only to the texts it explicitly refers to, as Wheatley's text is based on the Bible and the genre of poetry, but to the universe of other texts:

> The intertextual in which every text is held, it itself being the text-between of another text, is not to be confused with some origin of the text: to try to find the 'sources', the 'influences' of a work, is to fall in with the myth of filiation; the citations which go to make up a text are anonymous, untraceable, and yet already read: they are quotations without inverted commas. (Barthes qtd. in RR 1473)

Writers and readers are no longer considered individuals in a psychological sense but sites of intertextual intersections, which form the basis to construct meanings. Readers do not find meaning within or outside the text but rather weave words and strands from other texts into and around the given text. Barthes distinguishes between **readerly texts,** realistic texts that are easy to decode, and **writerly texts**, experimental texts that challenge the reader to co-write the text, establishing a network of signs within this text and between this and other texts.

According to the French philosopher Jean-François Lyotard, **metanarratives**, *which combine a vision of history as progress and the justification of institutions, have lost credit in our postmodern age.* He couches his disbelief in the Enlightenment narrative in ironic terms: it is a story "in which the hero of knowledge works toward a good ethico-political end – universal peace. [. . .] The narrative is losing its functors, the great hero, its great dangers, its great voyages, its great goal" (qtd. in RR 356). Instead of enlightenment and liberation, Lyotard maintains that the dominant groups in a state "allocate our lives for the growth of power" and legitimize their wielding of power over the people by "optimizing the system's performance – efficiency" (qtd. in RR 356), His insight (from 1979) that "the growth of power, and its self-legitimation, are now taking the route of data storage and accessibility, and the operativity of information" (qtd. in RR 356) seems prophetic. In opposition to questionable grand narratives and dominant groups, *numerous small narratives give voice to multiple points of view that resist integration in a master narrative*. These counter-narratives might be texts by feminists, lesbians, American Indians, Mexican Americans, Black British, etc.

Deconstructivists, post-structuralists and postmodernists like to work with texts that discuss writing, representation or reading in a self-referential way, such as Romantic or postmodern texts (see John Ashberry, 2.5, and John Barth, 3.4). These approaches reverse the aesthetic (and moral) norms of New Critics. Instead of looking for harmony, unity, order and universal ideas, they reveal discord, contradiction, incoherence and indeterminate, relative concepts. What appears to be self-evident is revealed as arbitrary. Their sceptical relativism favours the pluralism of competing opinions and interpretations. Deconstructive readings have been attacked as "the French plague" or "Derridadaism" because being aware of indeterminacy and contradictions in every text they do not aim at coherent and conclusive interpretations but playful and associative readings/re-writings, which can be challenging and obscure. They have been accused of being destructive, dependent on the concepts they undermine and arbitrary: "anything goes." However, their insight into the contradictory and indeterminate structure of texts has sharpened readers' awareness of arbitrary claims to authority, power, truth and universal values, liberating readers from the compulsion to ignore those textual problems that cannot be integrated in a coherent interpretation.

Deconstructivism, post-structuralism and postmodernism have had an enormous impact on approaches that deal with the social and historical context, turning attention away from the mimesis of real conditions of existence to the arbitrary social construction of reality (see also Michel Foucault's post-structuralist discourse analysis in 5.3.2 New Historicism).

Context | 5.3

Many approaches reflect on the relationship between text and con-   Marx: base and
text, which is defined as social, political and economic reality or as   superstructure
a system of signifying cultural practices. Marxism, cultural materialism, New Historicism, feminism and postcolonialism primarily
deal with the holy trinity of contemporary literary and cultural theory: class, race and gender.

Marxism and cultural materialism | 5.3.1

According to Karl Marx and Friedrich Engels, the material reality of economic circumstances forms the base (*Basis, Unterbau*) that conditions the social, political and cultural life of the superstructure (*Überbau*). Marx reverses the idealist notion that consciousness determines our existence into the slogan that being determines consciousness ("*Das gesellschaftliche Sein bestimmt das Bewusstsein*"). Marxists differ in the assessment of the relationship between base and superstructure. The founders of the theory specify that it is a dialectical relationship of mutual influence but some followers hold that the base determines or conditions the superstructure. **Ideology** is usually defined as a falsifying *collectively held system of ideas and beliefs that interpret the world*. Deceptive ideology expresses the interests of those who are in power, covers up contradictions and conflicts in society and legitimises the status quo.

Fig. 5.4

The German political thinker Karl Marx (1818-83) wrote his monumental treatise Das Kapital *(1867-95) with the support of Friedrich Engels in exile in England. Marx relates the historical development of society to that of economics and politics, aiming to overcome alienating working conditions, exploitation and the class system under capitalism by proletarian revolution.*

Trying to explain how ideology works and why it has such a powerful hold on our minds, the French philosopher Louis Althusser analyses how *ideology is implemented in and by the individual*. He considers *ideology as practice, which is enacted by individual subjects in specific performances according to their conscious beliefs*, "ideology existing in a material ideological apparatus, prescribing material practices governed by a material ritual" (qtd. in RR 701). For example, we subject ourselves to the **ideological apparatuses** – systems of institutions, ideas, values, practices – of religion, education or politics when we willingly participate in church services, university courses or elections. Ideologies interpellate (address) individuals as subjects in the double sense of "(1) a free subjectivity [. . . and] (2) a subjected being who submits to a higher authority, and is therefore stripped of all freedom except that of freely accepting his submission" (qtd. in RR 701). Ideology would certainly deny that it is ideology and endorse a certain "existing state of affairs (*das Bestehende*), that 'it really is true that it is so and not otherwise'" (qtd. in RR 701). The fact that we share the attitudes and practices of these ideologies reproduces the imaginary relationships to reality that obscure relations of production and exploitation.

Literature can be identified as a mere vehicle of ideology or as a reflection on ideology if it is granted a certain degree of autonomy. In the first case, literature serves as an expression of a particular ideology of the dominant class, in the second, as a potential criticism of ideology. Both perspectives presuppose insight into the material conditions of existence and the ideology of a certain period, and appreciate the ideological function of literature rather than its aesthetic quality.

The Russian literary theorist Michail Bakhtin shared the social and political approach to literature and combined it with a closer look at the aesthetic structure of literature, especially **discourse** (*Rede*) in the novel. His basic insight is that the words (and ideas) we use have been someone else's and will be taken up by someone else, never being completely our own. According to Bakhtin, ideology is the other's discourse that tries to determine our "interrelations with the world, the very basis of our behaviour" (qtd. in RR 682). However, he introduced a difference between ideologies that gives rise to more optimism than Althusser's concept of ideology. Ideology can take the form of **authoritative discourse**, like normative ethics or the words of a conservative father, which we have to abide by, or **internally persuasive discourse**, which we adopt willingly (in RR 682-83). Authoritative discourse can be paralysing both in individuals and novels because it is essentially a monologue that stifles freedom and creativity. Bakhtin considers **monological novels** with an unqualified moral or political message an aesthetic failure. He is more interested in **dialogical novels** that question monologues and those that reveal the struggle of persuasive discourses both between and within individuals, drawing an analogy to identity-formation: "Our ideological development is just such an intense struggle within us for hegemony among various available verbal and ideological points of view, approaches, directions and values" (qtd. in RR 685). The competition of ideologies finds its equivalent in **heteroglot language**, which "represents the coexistence of socio-ideological contradictions between the past and the present, between differing epochs of the past, between different socio-ideological groups in the present, between tendencies, schools, circles and so forth" (qtd. in RR 676). For example, these differences are manifest in the different languages of generations, varying and intersecting with those of class, gender and professional background. The creative novel plays with **heteroglossia**, *the duality or multiplicity of voices between and within utterances.* Bakhtin celebrates the subversive potential of

contradictory voices in dialogical novels, which cannot be subsumed under a single overarching system or ideology. **Double-voiced
discourse** would reveal another style within an utterance, a fact that
could be exploited for ironic effects.

In his novel *The Scarlet Letter* (1850) about the failure of Puritan culture in New England, the American Nathaniel Hawthorne (1804-64)
juxtaposes the authoritarian discourse of dogmatic Puritanism,
which dominates society and politics, and the persuasive discourse
of humanist ethics, which guides the outcast Hester Prynne. The
public perception of Hester Prynne, who was condemned to wear
the scarlet letter "A" because she had committed adultery, is slowly
changing due to her charitable behavior. However, the narrator remarks with irony that the male elite of the Puritan community is
less forgiving than the people:

> The rulers, and the wise and learned men of the community, were longer in
> acknowledging the influence of Hester's good qualities than the people. The
> prejudices which they shared in common with the latter were fortified in
> themselves by an iron framework of reasoning, that made it a far tougher
> labor to expel them. (181)

The narrator undermines the legitimacy of the leading Puritan
men, who were expected to be models of virtue and wisdom but
whose narrow-minded reasoning ironically confirms rather than
questions stereotypes. The "reformed sinner" becomes the model
of true virtue without any pretension to social power as opposed to
the despotic Puritan regime.

The dialogic principle is also of relevance for drama. In Ben Jonson's play *Volpone*, the protagonist's opening speech reveals the
conflict between the discourses of economics, religion and society:

> Good morning to the day; and next, my gold:
> Open the shrine, that I may see my saint.
> Hail the world's soul, and mine.
> [...] let me kiss,
> With adoration, thee, and every relic
> Of sacred treasure in this blessed room. [...]

Thou being the best of things: and far transcending
All style of joy, in children, parents, friends,
Or any other waking dream on earth.
      […] Thou art virtue, fame,
      Honour, and all things else! (1.1.1-26)

Volpone's monologue, which takes the form of a prayer, elevates gold to the status of a sacred relic, personifies it as a saint and worships it as a divine principle ("the world's soul"). His materialism does not simply ignore and replace religion and society but couches his material values in religious and social terms. His speech is double-voiced in the sense that the style of a prayer is used to elevate a materialist doctrine that is fundamentally opposed to religious dogma. That is why Volpone's revaluation of traditional values would appear to be ironic or provocative to early 17th century spectators, who experienced the rivalry for hegemony between the capitalist discourse of competition and monetary value and the idealist discourse of cooperation and shared spiritual and moral values.

The British writer and political activist Raymond Williams is a representative of the development from Marxist literary criticism to cultural materialism, which locates a text in its material context but greatly enhances the relevance of language, communication and culture. Cultural forces coexist in complex and conflicting relationships. Dominant cultural forces have to cope with residual and emergent ones, defenders of an old order and critics who clamor for reform. In *The Country and the City* (1973), Williams delineates economic, social and political developments in connection with multiple literary responses from the Renaissance to the 20th century, e.g. the social, scientific and literary reflections of and on the changes from feudalism to capitalism in the long 18th century (in RR 508-32).

Cultural materialism

Marxist and cultural materialist questions

▶ What are the key features of the base and superstructure of the period in question?
▶ How does the text represent social and economic conflicts? Are the characters determined by circumstances or in control of them?
▶ How does the text represent ideologies? Are the narrator and

the characters aware of economic, social and ideological conflicts? Does the text explore the rivalry of ideologies for hegemony between and within characters in dialogic and double-voiced discourse?

▶ What are the political and cultural positions of the text on the material conditions, the ideological and cultural context?

A traditional Marxist would criticise Phillis Wheatley's poem for its neglect of North American slavery and capitalism. Wheatley's adherence to religion takes the effect of opium, which helps her to ignore her own economic and social situation and those of other slaves. She hopes for a solution to repression and exploitation in life after death instead of aiming at a social, economic and political change. She falls prey to the appeal of Christian faith, which lulls her into accepting the status quo.

A cultural materialist would be more careful to specify Wheatley's position in historical circumstances and in the tensions between and within cultural forces. As a slave who had the rare opportunity to learn how to read and to write, Wheatley was in a privileged position but still dependent upon the goodwill of her owner. Thus, she could only criticise slavery in an indirect way if she wanted to have any chance of publishing her poems. Her poems were first published in 1773 in London, catering to abolitionist circles. Beginning in the 1770s mainly within Great Britain, a minority among middle-class Christians opposed slavery for humanitarian reasons. Wheatley's poems dovetailed with abolitionist views of Africans, who can be converted to Christianity and raised from ignorance, endorsing the abolitionist missionary zeal. Wheatley's discussion of faith is ambivalent. It takes sides within the conflict between pro-slavery Christians, who formed the dominant cultural force in the 1770s, and the emergent faction of British anti-slavery Christians. While Wheatley cannot openly appeal to free herself and all the slaves, her claim to a soul, to conversion and to equality implies the hope for liberation from slavery as a Christian human being, which was the central argument of the British abolitionists. She shares their moral superiority by assuming the position of a preacher, who appeals to the conscience of those who discriminate against African-Americans. Thus, Wheatley's potential impact on the debate of emancipation depends upon her positioning in an ideological conflict within Christian culture.

Staunch adherents of the idea that the Marxist view of history is objective, that the base determines the superstructure and that capitalist ideology is determinist would have difficulties to convince us why their analysis escape or penetrate the dominant system. The primarily ideological view of literature could be considered as imbalanced, whereas political critics like Bakhtin and Williams open up to the aesthetics of literature. British cultural materialists share the left-winged politics of their predecessors and are interested in the critical and progressive function of literature. The New Historicists, their American colleagues, regard questions of power in history and politics with more detachment.

New Historicism

5.3.2

Some traditional historiographers claim to discover the (empirical) truth about the past, and some traditional literary critics understand literature as a mirror of reality or a creative response to objective historical circumstances. However, New Historicists (1980s-) maintain that literature does not simply reflect a "given" historical moment. The problem of historiography, they argue, lies in the contradiction between past events and their retrospective representation: the past was never the way we see it in retrospective. Historians cannot be objective because they are themselves subject to history. The past is not a stable, coherent entity, and therefore cannot serve as an objective background and reference point of literature, as Marxists see it (Selden 95). History exists in multiple sources and texts, which historiography often shapes into narratives that follow plots recalling literary genres (Hayden White). The post-structural New Historicists, Louis Montrose states, are concerned "with the historicity of texts and the textuality of history" (qtd. in RR 588):

History and literature

> By the textuality of history, I mean to suggest the cultural specificity, the social embedment, of all modes of writing – not only the texts that critics study but also the texts in which we study them. By the textuality of history, I

mean to suggest, firstly, that we can have no access to a full and authentic past, a lived material existence, unmediated by the surviving textual traces of the society in question [...] and secondly, that those textual traces are themselves subject to subsequent textual mediations when they are construed as the "documents" upon which historians ground their own texts, called "histories." (Montrose qtd. in RR 588)

New Historicists have profited from the research of Michel Foucault, who analysed the historical formation of thinking and knowledge in discourses and their relations to practices. *Discourses regulate the ways in which we think and speak about certain topics in particular forms of statements with specific functions.* For example, religious, medical and legal *discourses establish and legitimise different authorities, fields of knowledge, forms of arguments and claims to power* (The Order of Discourse). If a relative of yours died in the hospital and the doctor would remark: "God's will was done" instead of giving a medical explanation of the cause of death, you might become suspicious and resort to the authority of other doctors or employ legal discourse in order to find out whether the doctor violated medical standards and could be held responsible by the law. Foucault was particularly interested in

Knowledge and power the relationship between knowledge and power (*Wissen ist Macht*). According to Foucault, knowledge and power are used by the authorities to control individuals by external observation and discipline, but individuals have also internalised these techniques as they observe and form themselves according to the norms of certain discourses and practices (*Discipline and Punish*). For example, education, psychology and medicine have increasingly defined individuals according to sexual preferences or deviations from "normality", which in turn led people to define themselves as individual subjects along these lines (*The History of Sexuality I*). Any violation of the norm would be a part of the system. Thus, resistance is less an independent counterforce to the dominant power but rather its complement. Power generates resistance, which in turn motivates repression or containment and paradoxically legitimises those who wield power.

Example

Barthelme's "The Baby" Donald Barthelme's story "The Baby" exemplifies power, surveillance (*Überwachung*) and punishment at work. The father's educational maxim is to be strict in enforcing rules in order to prepare his baby daughter for life in society. He defines tearing pages out of a book as a transgression of his rule, ignoring the fact that the baby cannot understand it. His regulation creates the "crime", motivates the surveillance of his daughter, and legitimises her punishment. He continues to offer books to the baby, inviting her transgression, which in turn calls for and asserts his authority and power. His locking her away without any effect can be read as a comment on the failure of the American judicial system, which seems to aim at revenge rather than reform. The authoritarian father copes with his failure to change the baby's mind and behavior by arbitrarily reversing the rules, legitimising his new stance on normality and transgressive behavior.

Following Foucault, the New Historical *concept of power conceives resistance to power as a complement rather than a subversive opposition.* Literary texts are neither *per se* oppositional nor superior to the historical text. Both *literary and non-literary texts are embedded in a dynamic network of interdependent cultural discourses and social practices, circulating social and cultural energies.* For example, Stephen Greenblatt, who initiated New Historicism, compared Elizabeth I's display of power in theatrical performances on the public stage of political representation to the performance of power on the Elizabethan stage. Like in the theatre, the queen's and the king's power depend upon their self-fashioning, instigating and containing conflicts, and manipulating the imagination of their subjects. The theatre, which had a low reputation, had a subversive potential. If ordinary actors could impersonate a king, the real king might have been an ordinary human being or an impostor simply performing as the head of state. Renaissance drama thrives on conflicts, often putting the abuse of power and resistance to power on show, strategies that can be regarded as subversive. However, any reversal of the status quo is usually followed by the restoration of law and order. In addition, the potential subversion of the theatre was contained by censorship.

Elizabethan theatre

The New Historicists have been blamed for effacing the difference between documentary and fictional texts and for underestimating the critical potential of literature. However, they have been praised for research on the forms and uses of historical texts, in particular their rhetorical quality, and on the use of literature, negotiating social, political and cultural values.

5.3.3 | Feminism and gender studies

Feminists, gender theorists, lesbian and gay critics take issue with material forms of social, economic and political discrimination, with discursive gender constructions or the link between practices and discourses. Most of them assert that the notion of universal values and meanings of humanity is a patriarchal ideology which ignores the specific experience and needs of women, lesbian women and gay men. Most of them stress the difference between the **biological sex** and the **cultural construction of gender** (see 1.3) but disagree over the relative importance of these categories concerning experience, identity and representation.

The two "founding mothers" of 20th century feminism are Virginia Woolf and the French philosopher and writer Simone de Beauvoir. In *A Room of One's Own* (1929), Woolf complains that potential female authors have been frustrated because women's voices have been muted under patriarchal restrictions of women to domestic duties and that the relationship between women have been passed over in silence in fiction. Woolf calls for the androgynous writer, who uses both the male and the female aspects of the mind. De Beauvoir exposes the patriarchal myth of woman's body as nature and of her mysterious essence as her reduction to an object, "the absolute Other, without reciprocity, denying against all experience that she is a subject, a fellow human being" (qtd. in Leitch 1407). The cultural myth legitimises repression and exploitation, "for instance by refusing to grant to woman any right to sexual pleasure, by making her work like a beast of burden" (qtd. in Leitch 1409). The cultural construction of women, the question of women's identity and representation as well as their roles as writers and readers of literature have become dominant issues of feminist theory and fiction.

The American literary and cultural theorist Elaine Showalter proposes that feminist readings of literature should go beyond exposing masculine stereotypes of women. She demands a new form of **gynocriticism** that retrieves neglected literature by women, based on a female subculture, "including not only the ascribed status, and the internalized constructs of femininity, but also the occupations, interactions and consciousness of women" (qtd. in Mary Eagleton 256). American feminism goes beyond recording the female tradition and sometimes puts forth a *prescriptive concept of literature*, which is based upon its contribution to women's liberation: literature is valuable if it provides a forum for the authentic self-expression of women, raises consciousness about women's issues, presents positive role-models, fosters sisterhood and promotes "cultural androgyny [. . .,] humanizing and equilibrating the culture's value system, which historically served male interests" (qtd. in Mary Eagleton 236-37).

Toril Moi takes issue with a feminist position that searches for the direct expression of experience in a woman's text in a humanist way but reserves a deconstructive approach for texts written by men, a "'Hermeneutics of suspicion', which assumes that the text is not, or not only, what it pretends to be, and therefore searches for underlying contradictions and conflicts as well as absences and silences" (qtd. in Mary Eagleton 259).

Deconstructive feminism questions whether "authentic" female expression is possible within the **"phallo(logo)centric"** cultural construction of masculinity and femininity in patriarchal societies. French theorists have explored the possibility of an *écriture féminine* different from and beyond the masculine binary system of either/or, which positions woman as the negative Other of man. "The 'feminine', in this scheme, is to be located in the gaps, the absences, the unsayable or unrepresentable of discourse and representation" (Jacobus qtd. in Mary Eagleton 301).

Woman as the Other

The French psychoanalyst and critic Julia Kristeva claims that signs, meanings and the subject are unstable. Her concept of the **subject in process** takes into account both the patriarchal curtailing of female liberty and its subversive expression. The "subject in process" recalls "the sense of a legal proceeding where the subject is committed to trial, because our identities in life are constantly called into question, brought to trial, over-ruled." (qtd. in Mary Eagleton 351). Following Lacan, Kristeva holds that the (illusory) sense of a stable identity, initially formed by the identification with one's mirror image, exists side by side with the prelinguistic and fluid bodily experience (in Mary Eagleton 352-53). She stresses that the feminine expression of the bodily drives, which she calls "semiotic", disrupts the linear, logical and symbolic structure of "masculine" language. Whereas ordinary communication represses these forms of instability, creative writing explores it. These semiotic ruptures are primarily visible in non-linear imagery and the (bodily) sound and rhythms of poetic language and modernist novels.

For the French writer and theorist Hélène Cixous, *écriture feminine* is not self-indulgence but **politics**: "writing is precisely *the very possibility of change*, the space that can serve as a springboard for subversive thought, the precursory movement of a transformation of social and cultural structures" (qtd. in Leitch 2043). Cixous exhorts women to liberate their desire and their desire to write as women, not as neutral or masculine voices: "When someone says 'I'm not political' we all know what that means! It's just another way of saying: 'My politics are someone else's!' (qtd. in Mary Eagleton 323). Literature becomes women's politics if it "goes beyond the bounds of censorship, reading, the gaze, the masculine command, in that cheeky risk taking women can get into when they set out into the unknown to look for themselves" (qtd. in Mary Eagleton 324). Opposite to the masculine segregation of body and mind, the *female body is intricately related to writing*: "writing her self, woman will return to the body which has been more than confiscated from her, which has been turned into the uncanny stranger on display" (qtd. in Leitch 2043). Cixous stresses that it is necessary to "'de-phallocentralize' the body" (qtd. in Mary Eagleton 322) in order to liberate bodily pleasure and sexuality. However, it is as impossible to define (and thus contain) the heterogeneous and dark process of female bodily pleasure as the feminine practice of writing (in Leitch 2046).

The body

The French psychoanalyst and philosopher Luce Irigaray performs *écriture féminine*, straddling the boundary between theoretical and creative texts. Her poetic *and* philosophical texts explore "the way in which, within discourse, the feminine finds itself defined as lack, deficiency, or as imitation and negative image of the subject" (qtd. in Mary Eagleton 318). Irigaray takes the women's labia as a central metaphor in order to define *écriture féminine* by *privileging the sense of the touch, simultaneity and fluidity rather than masculine sight, linearity and fixity. Feminine texts do not privilege right or wrong, origins or endings, but resistance to dichotomies and to closure* (see Mary Eagleton 318-19).

Écriture feminine

The American academic Domna C. Stanton defends French feminists against the charge of critics who consider their "écriture feminine as too intellectual and elitist to be feminist" (qtd. in Mary Eagleton 335). Stanton argues that the French feminists dismantle reductive patriarchal myths and "practice what they preach by subverting the syntax, the semantics, and even the Cartesian logic of the Logos" (qtd. in Mary Eagleton 335). However, if woman is defined as the silenced and repressed Other of patriarchal speech, how can woman speak and assert her otherness or a feminist critic speak as a woman or for other women (Felman in Mary Eagleton 58)? The answer would be that patriarchal discourses are not monolithic and do not determine each and everything but contain gaps and contradictions that allow for alternative subject positions.

Lesbian and gay critics share the feminist rejection of the **heterosexual** or **heterosexist matrix** but go beyond the attempt to reconstruct the female position because lesbians and gays neither fit the category of femininity nor masculinity (see Wittig in Leitch 2012-24). In the so-called **post-feminist era** since the 1980s, **gender studies** have expanded the feminist perspective on woman as difference and femininity as an embodied experience and expression. Gender studies question the thesis that *woman* can be associated with a biological body and sex beyond culture. Gender studies are interested in differences within and between *women* as well as men, in the intersection of gender with race and class. They look at *the culture of gender and the gender of culture*. Teresa de Lauretis maintains that the heterosexual **construction of gender**, both masculine and feminine, is *a fundamental cultural technology that forms bodily and sexual experience, social relationships, knowledge, political and economic power* (1-3).

The question is whether individual men and women are determined by or can escape the gender system. Seyla Benhabib concedes that the individual is certainly constituted by social and discursive practices but maintains that the subject is not determined and incapacitated by them: as actors, we are not mere performers of cultural scripts but have the "chance to stop the performance for a while, to pull the curtain down, and only let it rise if one can have a say in the production of the play itself" (qtd. in Mary Eagleton 375). Judith Butler doubts whether gender is something like a role because a role implies that there is a substantial sexual self beyond culture. She claims that we enact gender in our everyday repetition of the gendered stylisation, gestures and movements of the body, our use of language and interaction, all of which "constitute the illusion of an abiding gendered self" (qtd. in RR 900). Thus, *identity does not precede performance but performance constitutes identity*: "if gender is the cultural significance that the sexed body assumes, and if that significance is codetermined through various acts and their cultural perception, then it would appear that from within the terms of culture it is not possible to know sex as distinct from gender" (qtd. in RR 904). The very fact that the

Performance

heterosexual gender system is not a natural given but a cultural construction based on multiple performative acts allows for different and subversive repetitions of arbitrary gender scripts.

Questions from feminism, gender theory, lesbian and gay perspectives

▶ How does heterosexual discourse construct femininity, masculinity and same-sex relationships? Which effects does it have on the identities, the experience, the social, economic and political positions of men and women?

▶ Do heterosexual, lesbian or gay writers adopt, transform or subvert the masculine conventions of writing and representing gender? How do particular characters in texts perform masculinity and/or femininity? What is the function of gaps, silence or contradictions in the texts under discussion?

▶ What is the position of female, lesbian or gay authors in the literary market?

▶ What is the role of women as buyers and readers of literature?

▶ How are female readers addressed by gendered texts and how do female readers respond to them?

For examples of gendered readings of literature, see Lorna Dee Cervantes' poem "The Body as Braille" (2.6 and appendix), Ernest Hemingway's "Banal Story" and Rose Tremain's story "My Wife is a White Russian" (3.5 and appendix).

The feminist questioning of the patriarchal agenda has been groundbreaking but has also weathered criticism. It has been argued that feminists run the danger of reiterating white patriarchal stereotypes by focusing on the difference from man, the female body and the subversion of masculine logic. The African American bell hooks reproaches white feminists for hypocrisy because talking about difference and Otherness, they

should incorporate the voices of the displaced, marginalized, exploited, and oppressed black people. It is sadly ironic that the contemporary discourse which talks the most about heterogeneity, the decentered subject, declaring breakthroughs that allow recognition of Otherness, still directs its critical voice primarily to a specialized audience that shares a common lan-

guage rooted in the very master narratives it claims to challenge.
(Qtd. in Mary Eagleton 282)

The American academic of Bengal descent, Gayatri Chakravorty
Spivak would agree to that argument but minimise the relevance
of the strife between French and Anglo-American versions of feminism in comparison to the difference between the few well-educat-
ed first-world feminists and the many illiterate third-world
women, divided by culture, class, language and access to communication. Spivak warns of turning third-world women into the subject of an ethnocentric analysis that is likely to repeat colonial
hegemony, and she invites Western critics to listen to their perspectives (see Mary Eagleton 61). Likewise, Chandra Talpade Mo-
hanty, an American feminist with Indian roots, rejects Western
feminist notions of privileging themselves as the ideal norm of the
modern emancipated woman and reducing third world women to
ignorant, poor, backward and exploited victims rather than acknowledging specific differences between and among women from
various cultures (see Mary Eagleton 392-393).

Postcolonialism and multiculturalism | 5.3.4

Since the 1960s, race and ethnicity have emerged as hot topics in
politics and the academia. The demise of the British Empire has
confronted Great Britain with a loss of its international power and
waves of immigration from its former colonies. The Civil Rights
Movement in the United States confronted white society with its
racial discrimination that belied its egalitarian and democratic
legacy. Postcolonial studies have been concerned with the impact
of colonialism and postcolonialism on both British cultures and
identities and those of the countries under and after the British
Empire. The concept of postcolonialism is an ambiguous umbrella
term, which signifies *the temporal and/or conceptual difference to colonialism in spite of the neocolonial conditions in many of the countries and
cultures subjected to global capitalism.* Postcolonial theory does research on the economic, political and cultural conditions and effects of colonial encounters and the postcolonial aftermath. The
historical slave-trade of Africans to America, mostly organised by
the colonial powers of Europe, is of mutual interest to African
American studies and postcolonial studies. Large-scale immigra-

tion to Great Britain, the Caribbean, Canada, Australia, South Africa and the United States of America has given rise to multicultural societies with great achievements and specific social, economic and political problems. Recent theories of multiculturalism attempt to leave the conceptual link of postcolonial theory to historical colonialism behind.

Postcolonial theory scrutinises the colonial representation of selves and others in connection with imperial practices, and the reverse postcolonial representation of selves and others under the influence of the colonial heritage. Postcolonial and (multi)cultural theory have dismantled the biological or genetic essence of **race** and defined it as *a significant social and cultural construction, which has been used to classify others as subordinate and legitimise social, economic and political practices, such as segregation, exploitation and disenfranchisement.* The alternative term **ethnicity** includes the language and culture of peoples, but has been *criticised as culturally racist* if used to define "others" simply by being deviant from "white" Western culture.

In his study *Orientalism*, the Palestinian thinker Edward W. Said explores how the Western nations have constructed a version of the exotic Orient as the other, an image that was primarily fed by Western fear (the threat of Islamic power) and desire (the promise of luxury and sensuality of the harem). Representing the repressed and the subconscious of the West, the Orient was both strange and familiar, always already known. The knowledge of the Orient, laid down in negative stereotypes in travel reports and academic studies, is closely related to the subjection of colonized oriental countries to Western justice and discipline, e.g. in schools and prisons (Said, *Orientalism* 40). The present discussion about the clash of civilisations between "enlightened" Western and "backward" Islamic cultures (among others), Said maintains, reiterates the **orientalist misrepresentation** of separate and opposite cultures, disregarding that "cultures are hybrid and heterogeneous and [. . .] are so interrelated and interdependent as to beggar any unitary or simply delineated description of their individuality" (*Orientalism* 347). Said has a point but he has also been criticised himself for continuing Orientalism because he tends to ignore works that portray the Orient in a more complex and balanced way.

Under the influence of Derrida, Homi Bhabha, a postcolonial theorist of Indian descent, developed a more ambivalent view of the construction of **identity** and **alterity** (Latin *alter: other*) than Said.

The Western binary opposition of self/other has subsumed those of white/black, mind/body, consciousness/subconscious, masculine/feminine, culture/nature, civilised/barbarian and progress/stasis. This binary discrimination of self and other establishes a clear hierarchy of values, which is undermined by hybridity on a conceptual level and mimicry on a social level. Bhabha uses the term **hybridity** to mark the *interdependent construction of post/colonial identities*, which combine and intersect binary oppositions in complex and ambiguous ways. Thus, the identities of coloniser and colonised are not clearly separate but "contaminated" with each other. In addition, the colonial or neocolonial other would be motivated to imitate (mimic) the codes of the dominant group, such as language, dress and manners. This form of **mimicry**, however, is very ambivalent since the imitators would never be quite accepted by the dominant group even if they embodied the standards in perfection (being more British than the British), and the "superiors" could never be sure whether the imitation was in earnest or mocking their ways: "The *menace* of mimicry is its *double* vision which in disclosing the ambivalence of colonial discourse also disrupts its authority" (Bhabha 126). The problems of hybridity and mimicry seem to be particularly visible in individuals of mixed ethnic descent, whose affiliations are expressed by doubling or hyphenation, such as Black British or Anglo-Indian, but are in no way restricted to these individuals. The postcolonial construction of British identity is also affected by the **diaspora** of immigrants. The migrant from the periphery of the former British Empire disturbs the British sense of a unified history and identity. The diasporic space "on the home turf" contests the cultural boundaries of Britishness and forms a supplement to the dominant culture that cannot be integrated (Bhabha 241). The novel *White Teeth* (2000) by the Black British Zadie Smith (1974-) presents multicultural hybridity and immigrant life in a very ironic and entertaining way, portraying the lives of two families over two generations, related by curious incidents and divided by differences of race, gender, sexual predilections, religious and political views.

The term hybridity has been criticised because it highlights differences between rather than within cultures. Gayatri Chakravorty Spivak demanded that scholars observe *the heterogeneous circumstances of race, class and gender within various cultural and historical contexts*. She claimed that the majority of the **subaltern** (underprivileged, lower class) post/colonial populations have hardly ever had the chance to articulate their positions in contrast to the post/colonial elites, who have been in close contact with Western cultures. Her postcolonial approach is informed by feminism and Marxism, asking to which extent the underprivileged can escape dominant social, cultural and economic structures.

Recently, it has been claimed that the paradigm of the colonial and postcolonial relationships between the West and the rest of the world is no longer adequate to understand contemporary societies in the postmodern process of globalization. Two dominant visions of contemporary intercultural developments and understanding rival each other: 1) **culturalists** argue that *cultures are ethnocentric, radically different and therefore basically inaccessible to each other.* They warn of a clash between cultures and call for mutual tolerance in a multicultural world; 2) **universalists** maintain that the *global economic exchange, mass media and mass migration tend to dissolve cultural boundaries, a process that leads to a transcultural and transnational fusion of elements by cosmopolitan individuals in a postmodern capitalist world.* The universalists argue that the difference between cultures is not as radical as to preclude any mutual understanding if the participants in the interaction are willing and able to adopt each others' perspectives and to move to a third place in-between their different cultures.

Both positions, if held in the extreme, should be qualified. While it is true that intercultural encounters over centuries have given evidence of colonial ignorance and the destruction of foreign cultures, the profitable economic and cultural exchange between different cultures is also well documented. The universalists' praise of the cosmopolitan migrant tends to diminish the importance of cultural boundaries and to ignore the very origins of migration and the diaspora, often owing to rigid *boundaries within* nation states, which exclude minorities from economic and political participation. Some universalists also underestimate the difficulties of moving between cultures. The following approaches argue for a third position between culturalists and universalists, which pays close attention to the various ways of negotiating multiple boundaries between and within cultures.

In **African American** studies, Paul Gilroy defies narrow views of a particular African ethnicity. Instead, he traces African American culture back to the complex and violent cultural "exchange" during the slave trade, in particular by (European) ships which brought Africans via "the middle passage" across the Atlantic to the Caribbean and America. *Roots in Africa and routes across the Atlantic are of equal importance to African American culture and identity* (Gilroy 190). Instead of an essentialist view of race, Gilroy favors a historical perspective, the chaotic and complex "structure of the transcultural, international formation" of what he calls "the black Atlantic" (4). Gilroy has been criticized for his concentration on the negative process of the forced African migration and diaspora. However, his take of *African American culture as a heterogeneous and fragmentary historical process* meets with contemporary interest in memory and narrative, as in Toni Morrison's (US, 1931-) postmodern historical novel *Beloved* (1987) about slaves who escaped from bondage but can hardly cope with their terrible past that surfaces in fragments of haunting memories.

The **Mexican American** theorist and writer Gloria Anzaldua takes the **borderlands** between Mexico and the United States as a *real and metaphorical barrier and contact zone* between cultures, which is reproduced within Mexican Americans. The Chicanos, people with Mexican ancestry (and/or *mestizo* descent, i.e. Indian and Spanish) in the United States, are *in-between languages and cultures*. They speak neither "real" Spanish nor English, feel at home neither north nor south of the border, can neither identify with Mexican culture nor with North American culture. "Chicanos straddle the borderlands" (qtd. in RR 1029), take part in both cultures but do not really belong to any. In addition, Anzaldua is very critical of the Hispanic *machismo* and the gendered division within Hispanic culture. Chicano and Chicana writing explores the divisions between and within these cultures, often mixing American English and Mexican Spanish. A sequence of stories and sketches, *The House on Mango Street* (1983) by the Chicana Sandra Cisneros (1954-), vividly presents the plight and fight of a poor Mexican American girl for independence in a Chicano neighbourhood in the United States.

The **Asian American** expert on culture, migration and globalisation, Lisa Lowe, takes a double position on Asians in America: 1) she is well aware of the *multiple differences between and within* Korean, Japanese, Chinese or Filipino cultures in America due to differences in cultural origins, generation, class and gender; 2) for political reasons she finds it useful to talk about *Asian Americans as a group*. Lowe suggests to "conceive of the making and practice of

Asian American cultures as nomadic, unsettled, taking place in the travel between cultural sites and in the multivocality of heterogeneous and conflicting positions" (qtd. in RR 1045). However, she would use the term Asian American as an ethnic category in order to fight discrimination against them in an act of **strategic essentialism**, using *specific features as ethnic markers for limited purposes, being aware of the changing and contradictory features within ethnic cultures.* Maxine Hong Kingston's (1940-) autobiographical fiction *The Woman Warrior* (1976) explores the difficult positions of Chinese women in America, who are torn between traditions and stories from the East and the role-models and demands of contemporary western society in the United States.

Postcolonial and multicultural questions

▶ Do the constructions of self and other endorse or undermine binary categories, stressing opposition, hierarchy, mutual interdependence or hybridity? How are differences between and within ethnic cultures or individuals portrayed? How do nationality, history, race, class and gender relate to each other? Do the texts stress homogeneity or heterogeneity in intercultural or transcultural relationships?

▶ How and for which reasons do Western, colonial or neocolonial representations construct selves and others in certain ways?

▶ Do the postcolonial or multicultural authors imitate, rewrite, appropriate, subvert or transcend Western concepts of the self and the other?

Example

Phillis Wheatley

Phillis Wheatley's poem reveals the difficulty and ambivalence of establishing an identity of one's own in a cultural discourse which would define her as an other. The speaker in the poem is ambiguous because she can be taken as the unique and gendered representation of Phillis Wheatley and/or the representative of all slaves. The speaker seems to ignore the economic and material conditions of slavery in order to avoid white readers' resentment but thereby also refuses to be identified as a slave. She replaces her bodily enslavement by spiritual liberation, appropriating Christianity in order to emancipate herself from being reduced to an "animal" under slavery. Moreover, she even assumes the pulpit of moral superiority by preaching to the reader against the Christian discrimination of Africans. Her message that African souls can be saved is juxtaposed by two sinister implications: white American Christians, favored by God like Abel, could be killed by their "black brothers", and white Christians with blackened souls could be punished by God. Thus, Christianity allows Wheatley to send the double message of African emancipation and revenge on white Americans. However, the Christian discourse of conversion denies any significance to African culture and identity other than a negative and obscure condition that has to be overcome. In other words, Phillis Wheatley is compelled to swap positions in order to become a self in a culture that denigrates her as an other. (Other poems of hers reveal hybrid features in imagery and tone, see Zapf, *Literaturgeschichte* 406. For a reading of multicultural literature, see Lorna Dee Cervantes' poem "The Body as Braille", see 2.6 and appendix).

Postcolonial and multicultural critics have researched the ethnic re-reading and rewriting of canonised literary and historical texts, the (difficult if not futile) recuperation of indigenous cultures as well as the construction of multicultural identities and literatures.

Reader 5.4

Reader-response theory (late 1960s-) refuses to accept the notion that a text contains meaning in itself since any analysis or interpretation depends upon the process of reading. Reader-oriented approaches are influenced by phenomenology, which

> The unread story is not a story; it is little black marks on wood pulp. The reader,
> reading it, makes it live: a live thing, a story.
> Ursula K. Le Guin, "Where Do You Get Your Ideas From?" (1989)

maintains that we have only access to something by experience of our consciousness (i.e. as phenomenon), and hermeneutics, which asserts that meaning is generated in a dialogue between the reader and the text, situated in historical circumstances (see also 1.2). Reader-oriented theories differ in the way they conceive the particular process of reading as (1) a self-less process dominated by the text, (2) a dialogue between text and reader, (3) a re-writing of the text and (4) a fundamental historical condition that already influences writing.

(1) The French phenomenologist Georges Poulet rejects the structuralist notion of the text as a system independent of its author: "there is no spider-web without a center which is the spider" (qtd. in Leitch 1331). Poulet conceives of reading as the **passive reception** of an author's ideas: "I surround myself with fictitious beings; I become the prey of language. Language surrounds me with its unreality [. . .] I am thinking the thoughts of another [. . .] as my very own" (qtd. in Leitch 1322). Adopting the perspective of the author transforms the reader's mind, who becomes an other as long as s/he identifies with the thinking subject presented to us in fiction. The problem of interpretation is to account for the transcendental subject we experience in the form of a literary object since "all subjective activity present in a literary work is not entirely explained by its relationship with forms and objects within the work" (qtd. in Leitch 1333). Poulet suggests *alternating between identification and detachment* in order to understand how the creative power is expressed in – but not contained by – particular literary forms.

(2) The German literary theorist Wolfgang Iser regards reading as a much more active process than Poulet. Iser argues that **the work** results from the **interaction** of text and reader: "the artistic pole is the author's text, and the aesthetic is the realization accomplished by the reader. In view of this polarity, it is clear that the work itself cannot be identical with the text or with its actualization but must be situated somewhere between the two" (qtd. in Leitch 1674). In order to explain reading, Iser refers to interpersonal communication: since we do not know how others experience us and vice versa, we continually have to make up for the information gap by imagining and interpreting their perspectives on the basis of what is revealed to us and what is concealed from to us. As in a conversation, the reader is "made to supply what is meant from what is not said. What is said only appears to take on significance as a reference to what is not said; it is the implications and not the statements that give shape and weight to the meaning" (qtd. in Leitch 1676). Iser discriminates between the **real reader** and the **implied read-**

er, which is the *virtual* role of the reader implied in the text, *actualised* in various forms by real readers. The text forms something like a fragmented script for constructing "the work" in the reader's mind, based on the interaction between explicit and implicit information. The **reader's wandering viewpoint** takes in individual segments of textual perspectives at a time. **Blanks** or **gaps** appear when the plot is interrupted, the point-of-view is shifting from one character to the next, a new chapter begins, etc., motivating the reader to anticipate developments and to connect perspectives. The present theme of a segment "becomes the background against which the next segment takes on its actuality, and so on" (qtd. in Leitch 1679). Thus, the past segments form a horizon, which prefigures the reader's understanding of the following segments and is continually changing with the intake of new information in a process that recalls the hermeneutic circle. The pleasure of reading depends upon a delicate balance between the confirmation and disappointment of expectations.

(3) The American Stanley Fish, who is influenced by post-structuralism, maintains that the "text" we discuss in the classroom is not the one written by the author and constituted by the words on the page. He calls for an explanation of the relative similarity of responses to a text among students in the classroom and of the different interpretations of the "same text" by the same reader over time. Fish does not believe in a pure act of reading as Poulet does: "interpretive strategies are not put into execution after reading [. . .] they give texts their shape, making them rather than, as it is usually assumed, arising from them" (qtd. in RR 218). Readers construct texts, using interpretive strategies "for writing texts, for constituting their properties and assigning their intentions" (qtd. in RR 219). Shared strategies of interpretation form **interpretive communities**: if we belong to the same interpretive community, we share ideas about "the same text", if we belong to different ones, we talk about "different texts". For example, readers can attribute different meanings to Daniel Defoe's *Robinson Crusoe* as a religious, a realist, a capitalist, a colonial or an adventure novel.

▶ What do you expect from the text in question?
▶ What is left unsaid in the text and how does it relate to what is told?
▶ How do you respond to the textual information and to the blanks?
▶ How do your perspectives and your anticipation change step by step?
▶ Why do you respond in a certain way? (Individual cognitive patterns and presuppositions or interpretive community).

Detective stories

Detective stories provide a good example since they redouble the reading of signs. Sherlock Holmes and Dr. Watson or Mrs. Marple and Mr. Stringer represent readers who have to fill gaps with the help of clues, which, however, may be red herrings and lead them on the wrong track. The real reader would be as surprised as Watson and Stringer about Holmes's and Marple's findings but probably feels superior to the companions of the protagonists. The text provides the role of a virtual reader somewhere in-between the protagonist and the helper, inviting real readers to decode signs without letting them in on the secret until the end of the story. If the interpretation of the evidence was too simple, there would be no suspense; if it was too complex, the reader would feel frustrated.

(4) The German literary scholar Hans Robert Jauß goes beyond studying the individual and subjective response to literature in his version of **reception theory** (*Rezeptions- und Wirkungsästhetik*). The reception of literature has a formative influence on writing itself because the literary text is written in response to, or anticipation of, the readers' **horizon of expectations**, constituted by models of reality and of art shared by the potential audience. A text follows, transforms or rejects the **paradigm**, the model of the text that defines the dominant conventions at a certain time. A text can introduce a new paradigm if it successfully challenges the prevailing models of writing. The new paradigm redefines the standards of expectations and of writing as well. A literary history of reception records the changing series of dominant and emerging paradigms in relationship to the readers' horizons of expectations. Ideal case studies in

reception history are provided by "works that evoke the reader's horizon of expectations, formed by a convention of genre, style, or form, only in order to destroy it step by step" (qtd. in Leitch 1555). For example, Angela Carter's short stories recall myths and fairy tales but give them a feminist twist, changing the narrative voice and focalisation from men to women and elevating women to protagonists of revised stories; the film *Shrek* (I) plays with fairy tales and popular television shows in an entertaining way, reiterating but ridiculing traditional plots, gender roles and romantic expectations. A literary history is completed if it represents systems of aesthetic paradigms in a historical sequence and its relationship to social history, for example "where the literary experience of the reader enters into the horizon of expectations of his lived praxis, preforms his understanding of the world, and thereby also has an effect on his social behaviour" (qtd. in Leitch 1564).

Questions of reception history

▶ How does the text relate to the readers' horizon of expectations concerning literature and culture?
▶ How does the text relate to the dominant paradigm of its particular genre?
▶ What is taken for granted in the text and what is foregrounded or explained?
▶ How did readers and critics actually respond to the text?
▶ How do the interpretations of the text change over time?

Examples

Initially, Phillis Wheatley's poems met with mixed responses not because she violated poetic norms but because she followed them. She was a slave and the first African American poet. Sceptical racist readers could not believe that an African could learn to read or even write accomplished poetry. These readers suspected that a white abolitionist had written the poems in order to support their case against slavery. Now her poems are widely acknowledged as the original paradigm of (feminine) African American poetry.

Beckett's absurd plays puzzled and frustrated spectators in the 1950s. *Waiting for Godot* and *Endgame* (see 4.2, 4.3, 4.4) do not present realistic characters and settings or a linear sequence of action. They do not make sense in a traditional way, and leave the spectator between laughter and empathy, producing an effect of alienation (Selden 130-32). However, the theatre of the absurd in the meantime has evolved into an important paradigm among dramatic genres.

Critics have remarked that reader-response theory is subjective and cannot directly access the process of reading in the mind. Retrospective reports of the reading experience shape the information according to preconceived notions of cognitive activity based on phenomenology, hermeneutics and psychology. In addition, it could be argued that the logic of reception history is flawed and circular because it derives the horizon of expectations from the text which is considered to be the answer to these expectations. However, reader-oriented approaches have been valuable in drawing attention to the target of texts, the particular ways in which texts appeal to readers and readers "realise" fictional worlds.

5.5 | Bibliography

PRIMARY SOURCES OF LITERATURE, CULTURE AND THEORY

Abrams, M. H. et al., eds. *The Norton Anthology of English Literature.* 7th ed. 2 vols. New York and London: Norton, 2000. (=NAEL 1 and 2).

*Ashcroft, B., Griffiths, G. and Tiffin, H., eds. *The Post-colonial Studies Reader.* 2nd ed. London and New York: Routledge, 2006. (Short passages of relevant theoretical texts concerning central questions of postcolonialism, such as language, representation and resistance, place, history, ethnicity, etc.).

Baym, Nina, et al., eds. *The Norton Anthology of American Literature.* 3rd ed. 2 vols. New York and London: Norton 1989. (=NAAL 1 and 2).

Bhabha, Homi. *The Location of Culture.* London and New York: Routledge, 1994.

Carter, Angela. *Burning Your Boats. The Collected Short Stories.* London: Penguin, 1997.

Cisneros, Sandra. *The House on Mango Street.* New York: Vintage, 1991.

Derrida, Jacques. *Of Grammatology.* Baltimore: Johns Hopkins UP, 1976.

*Davis, Robert Con, and Ronald Schleifer, eds. *Contemporary Literary Criticism: Literary and Cultural Studies.* 4th ed. New York and London: Longman, 1998. (Excellent collection of major theoretical texts with brief critical introductions and discussions of their concepts.)

Defoe, Daniel. *Robinson Crusoe.* Ed. Angus Rose. London: Penguin, 1985.

*Eagleton, Mary, ed. *Feminist Literary Theory. A Reader*. 2nd ed. Malden, Oxford, Victoria: Blackwell, 1996. (Very comprehensive compilation of texts; sometimes excerpts very short).

Foucault, Michel. *Die Ordnung des Diskurses*. Tr. Walter Seitter. Frankfurt: Fischer, 1992.

Foucault, Michel. *Der Wille zum Wissen*. Sexualität und Wahrheit 1. 6th ed. Tr. Ulrich Raulff and Walter Seitter. Frankfurt: Suhrkamp, 1994.

Foucault, Michel. *Überwachen und Strafen*. Die Geburt des Gefängnisses. Tr. Walter Seitter. Frankfurt: Suhrkamp, 1994.

Gilroy, Paul. *The Black Atlantic. Modernity and Double Consciousness*. Cambridge: Harvard University Press. 1993.

Goldberg, David Theo, ed., *Multiculturalism. A Critical Reader*. Oxford: Oxford University Press, 1997. (Collection of essays on the significance of knowledge, power, self and other, history, and representation within and between cultures).

Gordon, Avery F., and Christopher Newfield, eds. *Mapping Multiculturalism*. Minneapolis and London: University of Minnesota Press, 1996. (Collection of essays on the concept of multiculturalism and its effect on politics, the subject, narratives, capitalism and communication).

Greenblatt, Stephen. *Shakespearean Negotiations. The Circulation of Social Energy in Renaissance England*. Regents of the University of California: 1988.

Hawthorne, Nathaniel. *The Scarlet Letter and Selected Tales*. Rpt. Harmondsworth: Penguin, 1979.

Iser, Wolfgang. *Die Appellstruktur der Texte: Unbestimmtheit als Wirkungsbedingung literarischer Prosa*. Konstanz: Universitätsverlag, 1970.

Iser, Wolfgang. *Der implizite Leser*. München: Fink, 1972.

Iser, Wolfgang. *Das Fiktive und das Imaginäre. Perspektiven literarischer Hermeneutik*. 2nd ed. Frankfurt/Main: Suhrkamp, 2001.

Jauß, Hans Robert. *Literaturgeschichte als Provokation*. Frankfurt: Suhrkamp, 1970.

*Kimmich, Dorothee, Rolf Günter Renner, and Bernd Stiegler, eds. *Texte zur Literaturtheorie der Gegenwart*. Stuttgart: Reclam, 1997. (Good selection of key texts with readable introductions).

Kingston, Maxine Hong. *The Woman Warrior: Memoirs of a Girlhood Among Ghosts*. New York: Vintage, 1989.

Lauretis, Teresa de. *Technologies of Gender. Essays on Theory, Film and Fiction*. Bloomington: Indiana University Press, 1987.

*Leitch, Vincent B., ed. The Norton Anthology of Theory and Criticism. New York and London: Norton, 2001. (Very comprehensive: from antiquity to the present; excellent introductions; further reading).

Morrison, Toni. *Beloved*. New York: Vintage, 2004.

*Nischik, Reingard M., ed. *Short Short Stories Universal*. Stuttgart: Reclam, 1993.

*Rivkin, Julie, and Michael Ryan. *Literary Theory: an Anthology*. 2nd ed. Oxford: Blackwell, 2004. (RR; excellent selection of longer excerpts with brief introductions).

Said, Edward W. *Orientalism*. New York: Vintage, 1994.

Said, Edward W. *Culture and Imperialism*. New York: Vintage, 1994.

Shakespeare, William. *Macbeth*. Ed. Kenneth Muir. London and New York: Routledge, 1988.

Smith, Zadie. *White Teeth*. London: Penguin, 2001.

Stevenson, Robert Louis. *Dr. Jekyll and Mr. Hyde*. Stuttgart: Reclam, 1984.

Wellek, René, and Austin Warren. *Theory of Literature*. 3rd ed. New York: Harvest, 1970.

Wolfreys, Julian, ed. *Literary Theories. A Reader & Guide*. Edinburgh: Edinburgh University Press, 1999. (Comprehensive collection of texts with accessible introductions).

Woolf, Virginia. *A Room of One's Own*. London: Penguin, 2002.

INTRODUCTIONS TO THEORY

*Barry, Peter. *Beginning Theory. An Introduction to Literary and Cultural Theory*. 2nd ed. Manchester and New York: Manchester University Press, 2005. (Very clear and helpful; includes key questions and good examples of approaches).

Bertens, Hans. *Literary Theory. The Basics*. London and New York: Routledge, 2001. (Clear and readable introduction to thinkers and ideas).

Boehmer, Elleke. *Colonial and Postcolonial Literature. Migrant Metaphors*. Oxford and New York: Oxford University Press, 1995. (Very readable introduction to key problems of colonial and postcolonial literature in historical perspective, focus on the 19th and 20th century, incl. short discussions of many literary texts, chronology of events and publications, bibliography).

Broich, Ulrich, and Manfred Pfister, ed. *Intertextualität. Formen, Funktionen, anglistische Fallstudien*, Tübingen: Niemeyer, 1985.

Childs, Peter, Jean Jacques Weber, and Patrick Williams. *Post-Colonial Theories and Literatures. African, Caribbean, and South Asian*. Trier: WVT, 2006. (Thorough discussion of central concepts and good overviews of literary histories).

Culler, Jonathan. *Literary Theory. A Very Short Introduction*. 1997; Oxford: Oxford University Press, 2000. (Concise and entertaining).

Eagleton, Terry. *Literary Theory: An Introduction*. London: Blackwell, 2nd ed. 1996. (Fluent and vivid; critical survey of theory from left-wing perspective).

*Green, Keith, and Jill LeBihan. *Critical Theory and Practice: A Coursebook*. Rpt. London and New York: Routledge, 2002. (Very helpful combination of introductions to approaches, sample passages from theoretical and literary texts, many interesting exercises, glossaries of key terms and bibliographies for further reading).

*Guerin, Wilfred L. et al. *A Handbook of Critical Approaches to Literature*. 4th ed. New York and Oxford: Oxford University Press, 1999. (Very readable introduction to major approaches, all of which are applied with great insight to four texts, a poem, a play, a short story and a novel).

Gymnich, Marion, and Ansgar Nünning, eds. *Funktionen von Literatur: Theoretische Grundlagen und Modellinterpretationen*. Trier: WVT, 2005.

*Hopkins, Chris. *Thinking About Texts. An Introduction to English Studies*. Houndmills and New York: Palgrave, 2001. (Accessible approach to theories under the general topics of texts, authors, critics, genre, history and identities; numerous excerpts from theoretical and literary texts with accessible discussions).

Jacobs, Richard. *A Beginner's Guide to Critical Reading*. An Anthology of Literary Texts. Routledge: London and New York, 2001. (Provides excerpts from major literary texts and brief comments on useful approaches designed for undergraduate student readers).

Kramer, Jürgen. British *Cultural Studies*. München: Fink, 1997. (Useful discussion of the use of theories from Marxism to post-structuralism in cultural studies; includes introductions to several case studies).

Lausberg, Heinrich. *Elemente der literarischen Rhetorik: Eine Einführung für Studierende der klassischen, romanischen, englischen und deutschen Philologie*. München: Max Hueber, 2000.

Loomba, Ania. *Colonialism/Postcolonialism*. London: Routledge, 1998. (Excellent and easily accessible introduction to central questions and answers of postcolonial theory concerning texts, knowledge and power, race, class, gender, culture, nationalism and post-modernism; incl. very useful bibliography).

Ludwig, Hans-Werner. *Arbeitsbuch Lyrikanalyse*. 4th ed. Tübingen: Narr, 1994. (Includes discussion of poetics).

Meyer, Michael. *The Bedford Introduction to Literature. Reading, Thinking, and Writing*. 7th ed. Boston: Bedford/St. Martin's Press, 2005. (Combination of anthology of primary texts and hands-on guide to approaches in very readable form).

Selden, Raman, Peter Widdowson, and Peter Brooker. *A Reader's Guide to Contemporary Literary Theory*. 4th ed. New York and London: Prentice Hall and Harvester Wheatsheaf, 2001. (Introduction to 20th century theories from New Criticism to Lesbian and Queer Studies).

Selden, Raman. *Practising Theory and Reading Literature*. An Introduction. New York, et al.: Harlow: Pearson Education, 2000. (Very readable introduction to central questions of theories, brief examples of readings and a series of exercises).

Tyson, Lois. *Critical Theory Today. A User-Friendly Guide*. 2nd ed. New York: Routledge, 2006. (Comprehensively discusses principles of contemporary theories and significance for everyday life and literary analysis, presents helpful questions, advantages, and weaknesses of theories; applies all approaches to F. Scott Fitzgerald's *The Great Gatsby*).

Ueding, Gert, and Bernd Steinbrink. *Grundriß der Rhetorik*. 4th, updated ed. Stuttgart and Weimar: Metzler, 2005.

*Zapf, Hubert. *Kurze Geschichte der anglo-amerikanischen Literaturtheorie*. München: Fink, 1996. (Excellent critical introduction to major theorists from Plato to New Historicists).

REFERENCE WORKS

Ashcroft, Bill, Gareth Griffiths, and Helen Tiffin. *Postcolonial Studies*: The Key Concepts. London: Routledge, 2005. (Clear and comprehensive definitions).

Beck, R, H., and M. Kuester. *Terminologie der Literaturwissenschaft. Ein Handbuch für das Anglistikstudium*. Ismaning: Hueber, 1998. (Very helpful definitions and examples of technical terms).

Childers, Joseph, and Gary Hentzi. *The Columbia Dictionary of Modern Literary and Cultural Criticism*. New York: Columbia UP, 1995.

Groden, Michael and Martin Kreiswirth. *The Johns Hopkins Guide to Literary Theory & Criticism*. Baltimore and London: The Johns Hopkins University Press, 1994. (Longer articles on major theorists and critical approaches, few on individual terms).

Hawthorn, Jeremy. *A Glossary of Contemporary Literary Theory*. 4th ed. London: Arnold; New York: Oxford University Press, 2000. (Clear, sometimes too brief).

Lentricchia, Frank, and Thomas McLaughlin, eds. *Critical Terms for Literary Study*. 2nd ed. Chicago and London, 1995. (Fairly comprehensive articles on a few key concepts of literature and culture, such as discourse, gender, race, etc.).

*Makaryk, Irena R. *Encyclopedia of Contemporary Literary Theory, Approaches, Scholars, Terms*. Toronto: University of Toronto Press, 1993. (Comprehensive and reliable).

Murfin, Ross C., and Ray Supryia. *The Bedford Glossary of Critical and Literary Terms*. London: Macmillan. 1998.

Nöth, Winfried. *Handbuch der Semiotik*. 2nd, rev. and expanded ed. Stuttgart: Metzler, 2000.

*Nünning, Ansgar, ed. Metzler *Lexikon Literatur- und Kulturtheorie*. 3rd, updated ed. Stuttgart and Weimar: Metzler, 2004. (Excellent; best German encyclopedic dictionary in the field; for advanced students).

*Payne, Michael, ed. *A Dictionary of Cultural and Critical Theory*. Reprint Oxford: Blackwell, 1998. (Excellent contributions on authors, movements and concepts).

Renner, Rolf Günter, and Engelbert Habekost, eds. *Lexikon literaturtheoretischer Werke*. Stuttgart: Kröner, 1995. (Short summary of major theoretical works across history, includes brief assessment of relevance and reception).

*Strongly recommended."

Research papers, presentations and examinations

Contents

6.1	Academic standards	186
6.2	Getting organised	186
6.3	Writing a term paper	187
6.3.1	Defining topic, purpose and approach	187
6.3.2	Research for and use of secondary material	190
6.3.3	Writing the first draft	194
6.3.4	Revising the paper	195
6.3.5	Documentation	195
6.4	Presentation	198
6.5	Oral and written examinations	202
6.6	Bibliography	204

Abstract

In order to meet academic standards when writing papers or giving presentations, you are required to retrieve information systematically, to develop rational arguments and to present them as clearly as possible. Reading these suggestions carefully will help you to save time and to work more efficiently and successfully.

6.1 | Academic standards

> Knowledge is of two kinds. We know a subject our-
> selves, or we know where we can find information
> upon it.   Dr. Samuel Johnson (1775)

> Some books are to be tasted, others to be swal-
> lowed, and some few to be chewed and digested;
> that is, some books are to be read only in parts;
> others to be read, but not curiously; and some few
> to be read wholly, and with diligence and attention.
> Francis Bacon, "Of Studies" (1625)

In the beginning was the word, not Word® or other word-processing software. The skillful designing of a paper by computer is a means rather than an end. Philology (literally: the love of the word) or studying literature requires you to pay close attention to reading and writing. Sloppy wording, incoherent arguments, plagiarism and incomplete documentation are not acceptable. Papers and presentations offer an opportunity to reflect in depth on a topic of your interest, to develop new points of view and to share your insight with an interested audience. Doing research can be stimulating, but you need to know about its strategies and rules in order to make academic writing, presentation and discussion a rewarding experience. Studying offers the opportunity to practise retrieving information, developing arguments, presenting results and managing discussions, all of them central skills required in our information age. These standards serve as guidelines for academic work and its assessment:

Standards for academic work

▶ Well-defined purpose and relevance of topic
▶ Systematic approach and precise definition of terms of analysis
▶ Clear and understandable presentation of individual
  questions and answers supported by evidence
▶ Consistent and coherent argumentation
▶ Critical discussion and precise documentation of secondary
  material

6.2 | Getting organised

Plan and time your work well. Do not submit a panicky last-minute paper without an introduction, a conclusion and proofreading because you finish at five o'clock in the morning on the day of your deadline. Do not hand in a "cut-and-paste paper", which contains everything that you could find about your topic but does not contribute to your argument. Meet the deadline for your paper and make sure you observe the requirements, for example a research paper of 2000-3500 words within a given space of two weeks (workload: 90 hours or three credits) or a paper of 4500-6000 words within four weeks (workload: 150 hours or five credits).

Use about one third of your time for defining the topic and the approach selecting and reading primary and secondary sources, one third of your time for writing the first draft and one third for a careful revision of your text. Do not forget that interlibrary loans (*Fernleihen*) may take up to four weeks.

Time

Writing a term paper | 6.3

Defining topic, purpose and approach | 6.3.1

Fig. 6.1

Calvin and Hobbes on the art of academic writing.

Either a topic will be assigned to you or you will be free to pick a text and a topic of your choice. If you are given a topic, rephrase it into a question to guide your in-depth reading of the primary text. If not, take a text that you are interested in and find your own topic. Annotated editions, i.e. those by Norton and Bedford St. Martin's Press, can help you in two important ways: their introductions and notes will allow you to understand contemporary references or contexts, and their authoritative texts as well as selected criticism will provide you with a reliable and comprehensive basis for your own research. Read the text closely, mark interesting passages and take notes of problems, questions and points of interest; record the references with page numbers for quick access to relevant passages

Finding your topic

for your subsequent analysis. Summarise and arrange your findings systematically and try to draw preliminary conclusions in writing. Select a topic with one to three central questions for further discussion in your paper and make sure you pay attention to the following points:

▶ In the first sketch of your introduction, which you should write as soon as possible after your close reading of the primary text, *explain* **what** *your topic is,* **why** *it is important and* **how** *you will approach it.*

▶ Repress your desire to fill a couple of pages with the author's biography and a summary of the text, which are irrelevant unless they support a particular argument. Your instructor and reader will be familiar with the author's life and work in most cases.

▶ *Reformulate your topic into a series of questions.* Decide which additional sources you need in order to give answers to these questions. The key to good research is:
Ask simple questions and question simple answers.

Example: topic

Avoid topics that are too general, such as "Shakespeare's *Romeo and Juliet*", and superficial statements about everything in the play, or topics that are too specific, such as "Herbal Medicine in *Romeo and Juliet*", to avoid limiting your perspective to details. "Love in Shakespeare's tragedy *Romeo and Juliet*" would be a topic that can be handled within the confines of a term paper (in four weeks). The title can be transformed into various questions: What is love or rather, what does love mean in Shakespeare's time? What is a tragedy and which function does love fulfil in a tragic plot? What does love mean, especially to the characters of Romeo and Juliet? A careful reading of the play would draw your attention to the fact that love is a broad term defining relationships between men and women, men and men, women and women, parents and children, masters and servants, and that love takes on a spiritual, emotional or sexual quality for various characters in different situations, leading to conflicts between and within characters.

► In order to *specify your approach and terms of analysis* against existing criticism, read a general article on your topic, such as a comprehensive introduction to your primary text, an article in a *companion* or a *handbook*. Also read an overview of the writer's central concerns in a literary history and check relevant chapters in books specialised in analysing poetic, dramatic or narrative texts.

Example: approach and concepts

Ina Schabert's *Shakespeare-Handbuch* and her *Englische Literaturgeschichte aus der Sicht der Geschlechterforschung* provide a historical framework of gender constructions and titles for further reading, which help to assess the representation of love in *Romeo and Juliet*. In addition, the chapters on communication, character and action in a book on drama (e.g. Pfister or Fielitz) help to specify the analysis of the characters' opinions and positions in a structure of perspectives, actions and events.

► Write a *preliminary outline* to develop the structure of the paper either by means of topics or full sentence arguments (*thesis statements*). Arguments can follow various patterns, e.g. (1) a *temporal order* (from the beginning to the turning point and the resolution of a conflict), (2) a *logical order* (a statement about a fact, its causes and its consequences; contradiction and resolution or synthesis), (3) a *hermeneutic circle* (from the understanding of a general principle to that of specific passages or aspects, which in turn qualifies and deepens the general insight), or (4) a *rhetorical order* (from general to specific aspects or vice versa, from the familiar to the unfamiliar or from simple to complex issues).

Example: topic outline

The paper "Love in Shakespeare's tragedy *Romeo and Juliet*" may have the following topic outline:
1.   Introduction
2.   Love and gender in Shakespeare's age
3.   Love in *Romeo and Juliet*
3.1   Contradictory constructions of love due to gender, generation and class

3.2   Love and dramatic conflicts
3.2.1   The comedy of love
3.2.2   The tragedy of love
3.2.2.1 Fate or chance
3.2.2.2 Love and death
4.   Conclusion
List of works cited (or Bibliography – includes more than the works cited)

6.3.2 | Research for and use of secondary material

How to use secondary literature

Usually, academic studies combine the researcher's own observations with results from research by others. At first glance, reading secondary material before finding arguments of your own seems to save time and effort. On second thought, the sheer quantity of ideas by others may frustrate your search for your own ideas. Therefore, closely read the primary text with the help of your specific questions for three important reasons: (1) developing your own arguments is stimulating, (2) helps you to find your own position in criticism, and (3) facilitates your selection of statements to support your own ideas. *Do not follow others' opinions blindly but discuss them critically.* More often than you would think, publications do not fulfil the academic standards of consistent arguments and new insights. At best, secondary material improves your understanding of the subject and offers you the chance to rephrase your own questions and statements.

Fig. 6.2 |

Illustration by Sepp Buchegger. If you do not systematically select secondary material, you will suffer from information overkill.

Your central questions and arguments serve as guidelines for further research of secondary material. Checking the world wide web for information seems to be fast and easy but the problems involved are obvious: (1) frequently, the high number of references to web sites makes the adequate selection of information difficult or even impossible. Researching and selecting take an enormous amount of time, and (2) web sites offer much that is neither up-to-date nor reliable, let alone innovative or scientifically valuable (the endings of ".ac" in addresses of academic web sites in Great Britain and ".edu" in the United States form one criterion for selecting sources). The list of works at the end of this chapter includes several helpful web sites on literature and culture. University libraries store very useful and easily accessible information. They also offer brochures and guided tours, explaining how to find sources.

How to find secondary literature

The shortest path to important secondary material leads to the real or virtual **course-reader bookshelf** (*Semesterapparat*), which offers the general material picked for the particular course. This selection of books does not necessarily include the secondary literature on your specific topic, which you will find in bibliographies. **Current** (*laufende*) and **retrospective** (*abgeschlossene*) **bibliographies** *provide the most systematic, efficient and reliable sources of secondary material* (not the material itself, which you have to order from the library). Narrow down your search as much as possible in order to avoid an "information overkill". A simple name like Shakespeare generates hundreds of titles in the catalogue of the library, thousands of titles in a comprehensive bibliography or millions in the world wide web. The search for a title that ranks among the literary classics, such as *Romeo and Juliet*, will still yield dozens of hits in the library and hundreds in a large bibliography. Key words from your topic are a good idea to limit the search to a manageable number of titles.

Bibliographies

Retrospective bibliographies exist for most of the major authors and subjects. If annotated, they specify the topic, approach and arguments of a source, such as Michael O'Neill's *Literature of the Romantic Period: A Bibliographical Guide*. Many annotated and critical editions of primary works include a list of important secondary material, but depending on the year of publication, the editor's choice and your topic, that list might be outdated or of limited value.

Primary literature and highly selected secondary literature until 1965 can be found in the retrospective *New Cambridge Bibliography of English Literature 600-1950*, the *NCBEL*, which is being re-edited at present.

The most important current bibliography is the *International Bibliography of Books and Articles on Modern Languages and Literatures* (*MLA* or *MLAIB*), published by the Modern Language Association of America. It is available on CD-ROM or online in the university library. The current electronic *MLAIB* registers secondary material from 1963 until the present. If the title is not very specific, choose the subject terms, the subject headings or the full citation for the display of your search result in order to know more about the approach and the material covered in the source. The download of selected titles serves as a good basis for the bibliography of your paper.

Cross-check your findings with those in the electronic version (CD-ROM or online) of the *ABELL*, the *Annual Bibliography of English Language and Literature*, first published in 1920. The *ABELL* records primary as well as secondary literature and may list titles that you did not come across in the *MLA* even if it is not as up to date as its rival.

Bibliographies also record university theses. Particular collections of abstracts help you to assess their content. Abstracts of university theses can be found in the *Index of Theses with Abstracts* (GB), *Dissertation Abstracts International* (USA) and *English and American Studies in German. Summaries of Theses and Monographs* (Ger). In Germany, the university library of Göttingen probably holds the greatest number of academic theses in the form of copies on microfilm.

In addition, the *Year's Work in English Studies* presents a selective overview of the secondary material on important topics, including an assessment that helps you to decide whether a particular book deserves close study.

Fig. 6.3

Tullio Pericoli's Secondary Sources (1982) depicts the scholar's and the student's dream of efficient research.

How do you proceed?

▶ Find a recent, retrospective (and annotated) bibliography on the author or the era of your primary text as a starting point for research.

▶ Search the *MLA* for secondary material, cross-check the findings against those of the *ABELL* (if at hand), and combine the downloads in one list.

▶ Compare this list with your selection of titles from the retrospective bibliography, and add those you consider important to the download so as to create your preliminary electronic file of secondary texts.

▶ Add, if necessary, further material of interest from (hidden) bibliographies (*versteckte Bibliographien*) in secondary material. However, be as selective as you can in order to avoid drowning in too many texts.

▶ Select the most important works only. See which of them are available in your library and which have to be ordered via the interlibrary loan (allow four weeks for delivery). Narrow down your selection of secondary material to something between 10 and 15 articles and books for a paper that has to be delivered within two weeks, and to 15 to 25 in a paper you can spend four weeks on (unless specified otherwise). Before you order a book via the interlibrary loan, you may want to read a review of it. The *Internationale Bibliographie der Rezensionen wissenschaftlicher Literatur (IBR)* will help you to trace reviews.

▶ If you want to be up to date on secondary sources for a major thesis, check *Whitaker's Books in Print* (GB), *Bowker's Books in Print* (USA), the *Verzeichnis lieferbarer Bücher* (Ger) and the current journals that your university subscribes to or that the internet offers (see list below).

▶ Begin with one of the most recent of your selected texts, preferably one with a sound assessment of previous research, which supports your selection and your grasp of earlier material. Mark the most important titles in your preliminary bibliography.

▶ Obtain an overview of your material by closely reading the headline, introduction and conclusion of each text, and discard those texts which do not contribute any new and important argument.

▶ Scan the most important texts for relevant arguments; mark pertinent passages, take notes paraphrasing arguments in your own words, and quote important statements in full.

▶ Accurately document every paraphrase or quote in order to *avoid plagiarism* – and failing your paper – simply by recording the author and page of the reference in brackets in the body of the text (last name and page number: Gibaldi 204).

▶ Add notes to the titles in your bibliography or conveniently insert quotes at the appropriate place in the preliminary outline of your paper. In addition, an electronic database, the word-processing software or a mind-map (such as the MindManager®) are very useful for organising your findings.

6.3.3 | Writing the first draft

▶ Make sure that you have sufficient arguments that connect to your major topic statements, each of which should be illustrated by a reference to, or a quote from, the primary text.

▶ Check whether new insights from secondary material compel you to rephrase your questions, to qualify your statements or to revise your outline.

▶ Control the temporal, rhetorical and logical order of arguments in order to make sure that the arguments do not contradict but lead to each other.

▶ Examine whether comparisons account for *similarities and differences* between items of similar weight (a comparison between Juliet and her nurse would yield far less information than that between King Lear and his Fool). Draw your own conclusions.

▶ Begin your paragraphs with your topic sentence, which introduces the central idea.

▶ Keep the sentence structure simple (and elegant, if possible), use an elevated diction and avoid colloquialisms unless you want to make a particular point by using them.

▶ Provide links between the paragraphs and sections of your paper.

▶ Use images that enhance your arguments.

▶ Take great care to write a conclusion because it condenses your arguments and leaves a lasting impression on the reader. Explain why your approach has been useful in order to arrive at your results, and connect your insight into the primary text with its context. Summarise and evaluate your understanding in comparison to other sources.

▶ Once you are finished with the body of your text, rewrite the introduction, taking into account new ideas that occurred to you while writing.

Revising the paper | 6.3.4

Revise your paper and put it into the final form by reading it several times, focusing each time on different sources of possible errors:

▶ Read your paper aloud: as soon as you hesitate or get confused, you will probably detect a mistake in wording, syntax or argument.
▶ Eradicate contradictions, digressions and repetitions.
▶ Make sure that the quotes and examples prove your points.
▶ Take care to ensure smooth transitions between sentences, paragraphs and sections.

Check your use of prepositions, tenses, adverbs and adjectives, spelling and punctuation. Your quotes, references and list of works must be correct and complete; for example, put "direct quotes in quotation marks" but if

> a quotation runs to more than four lines in your paper, set it off from your text by beginning a new line, indenting one inch (or ten spaces if you are using a typewriter) from the left margin [...] without adding quotation marks. A colon generally introduces a quotation displayed in this way, though sometimes the context may require a different mark of punctuation or none at all. (Gibaldi 109; see section B of the bibliography).

Documentation | 6.3.5

Unless it is common knowledge, every idea obtained from someone else, whether paraphrased or quoted, has to be documented accurately. Various style sheets demand parenthetical references, footnotes or endnotes. The *parenthetical documentation* according to the *MLA Handbook for Writers of Research Papers* is fairly simple and widely accepted. According to this model, paraphrases or quotes should be referenced in parenthesis by the author's last name and the page number(s) of the borrowed information: (Gibaldi 204-205).

► If more than one text by the same author is to be documented, a
  shortened title has to be added: (Nünning, *Grundkurs* 10).
► If the author's name already appears next to the passage in
  question and can easily be related to the referenced information, the page number in brackets will suffice:
  Schabert argues that . . . (10-12).
► If what you quote or paraphrase is itself a quotation in another
  source, put the abbreviation „qtd. in" before the indirect source
  you cite in your parenthetical reference:
  Per Winther argues that in Ellison's novel *Invisible Man*, „the
  hero is rewarded for his labors; he has achieved that freedom
  which comes with the ability to give form to one's ideas, feelings, and experiences" (qtd. in Bourassa 3).
► Record further information that would hamper readability in a
  footnote, such as definitions of terms or references to more
  than two authors or sources.

The *parenthetical documentation* refers the reader to the complete
bibliographical information in the list of works cited or the bibliography at the end of the paper. References follow the subsequent
forms according to the conventions of the *MLA* (document information [in square brackets] only if available or if applicable):

Examples: bibliography

► A book is registered by the author's or editor's
  Last name, first name, [ed.] *Title*. [edition.] [volumes.] Place of
  publication: publisher, date.
  Gibaldi, Joseph. *MLA Handbook for Writers of Research Papers*. 6th ed.
  New York: The Modern Language Association of America, 2003.

► An online book [within a database]:
  Last name, first name. *Title*. [Trans./Ed. First name last name.]
  Place: publisher, year. [*Database*. Ed. First name last name. Version.
  Date of posting/revision.] Date of access. <online address>.
  Keats, John. *Poetical Works*. London: Macmillan, 1884. *Bartleby.com*.
  1999. Date of access: 1 November 2003. <www.bartleby.com/126/>.

► An article in a book:
  Last name, first name. "Title of the article." *Title of book*. [Trans./]

Ed. First name last name. Place: publisher, date. Page[s].
Neumann, Fritz-Wilhelm. "Anglistik im Internet." *Einführung in das Studium der Anglistik und Amerikanistik*. Eds. Uwe Böker and Christoph Houswitschka. München: C. H. Beck, 2000. 329-348.

▶ An article in a printed journal:
Last name, first name. "Title of article." *Title of journal* volume number. Issue number (date): page[s].
Jahn, Manfred, and Ansgar Nünning. "A Survey of Narratological Models." *Literatur in Wissenschaft und Unterricht* 27 (1994): 283-303.

▶ An article in an e-journal:
Last name, first name. "Title of article." *Title of e-journal* volume number. Issue number (year). Date of access. <online address>. (Add screenshot of web site if future access may be problematic).
Bourassa, Alan. „Affect, History, and Race and Ellison's *Invisible Man*." *Comparative Literature and Culture. A WWWeb Journal* 8.2 (2006). Date of access: 1 November 2007. <http://clcwebjournal. lib.purdue.edu/>.

▶ An article from a newspaper:
Last name, first name. "Title of article." *Title of newspaper* date: page[s].
Baldwin, Tom, Tony Helpin and Rosemary Bennett. "Universities must raise private cash." *The Times* 4 December 2003: 1.

▶ A part of an online publication:
Jahn, Manfred. "Narratology: A Guide to the Theory of Narrative." Part III of *Poems, Plays, and Prose. A Guide to the Theory of Literary Genres*. Version: 1.7. 28 July 2003. English Department, University of Cologne. Date of access: 1 November 2003. <http://www.uni-koeln.de /~ame02/pppn.htm>.

▶ A complete online scholarly project or database:
Title of the project/database. [Ed. first name last name.] Electronic publication information [incl. version number]. Date of publication or latest update. Institution or organisation. Date of access. <online address>.
Britannica Online. 2003. Encyclopaedia Britannica. Date of access:

1 Nov. 2003. <http://www.eb.com/>.
The WWW Virtual Library: Theater and Drama. Ed. Barry Russell. Updated daily. Date of access: 1 November 2003. <http://vl-theatre.com/>.

6.4 | Presentation

Presentations require sense in order to convey intelligent arguments and sensitivity to manage the social dimension of communication. Often, you will give a presentation and write your paper on the same topic, which allows you to prepare for both at the same time and to revise your paper after having received new input during the discussion of your topic in class. In spite of many similarities, a presentation and a paper address diverse audiences in different situations with the help of other media: think about the differences in goals, questions and proceedings. Your instructor and your peers usually differ in their expectations, knowledge and linguistic skills. In comparison to a paper, a presentation has to *limit the number and complexity of questions and answers* with regard to the academic standard of your peers. It may be required that you stimulate a discussion in the course rather than present an in-depth analysis and a conclusive opinion as in your written paper.

Finding out about your audience

Fig. 6.4 |

William Hogarth, The Lecture *(1736/37). Identify ten ways of passing your time while listening to a boring lecture.*

The presentation has to *take into account the listening comprehension skills and the limited attention span and memory of the audience.* The best arguments are of no use if you do not get them across to your audience for want of *a clear structure, an audible voice, a distinct articulation and understandable language*: "Think like a wise man but express yourself like the common people" (William Butler Yeats). Visual media can make up for the limitations of oral communication, but the visual information should support rather than replace speech.

It is difficult to give a perfect presentation because you have to pay attention to yourself, to your subject matter, its mediation and to your audience. Find out your three major strengths and maintain them. Try to identify your three major weaknesses and to improve on them over time.

Think about these issues before the presentation:

▶ Who is the audience, what do they know and what do they expect?
▶ What can you offer them for their benefit? Explain questions, points of interest and goals.
▶ Structure your presentation not only along logical but also along rhetorical and psychological lines in an explicit way: first present general and then more specific information, the familiar prior to the unfamiliar, the simple issues before the complex ones, use a particular instance or story in order to explain a general argument and repeat central arguments.
▶ Anticipate potential questions from your audience and prepare answers.
▶ How do you present your arguments? Try to practise speaking on the basis of key arguments on cards or transparencies only.
▶ How much time do you have and need for a good presentation? (Practise speaking and eye-contact in front of a mirror if you like.) Measure the time and take into account the handling of media. Check your voice by recording your presentation. Where and when does the presentation take place? Consider the size and acoustics of the room, the time of day and the duration of the presentation.
▶ Which media are to serve which purpose? *Less is more.*
▶ Are the transparencies designed appropriately? PowerPoint offers good templates. Take large-sized letters (at least 16 pt.) of one font, do not use more than 3 to 5 statements per page and

not more than 2 pages in 3 minutes.

▶ Does the audience need a handout and if so, when? The handout should include the outline, key definitions, arguments, quotes, tasks if needed and the works cited.

▶ Is the material arranged in a clear order to avoid confusion during the presentation?

▶ Are you motivated for the performance? Consider your own attitude towards yourself, your subject matter and your audience: develop a positive attitude by recalling your own good performances. Consider efficient ways of handling difficult questions, such as analysing these questions as a part of your response and returning those parts you cannot answer to the speaker or to the audience.

▶ Test your voice and your position in the room.

▶ Check the media and the technical equipment well before the presentation begins (microphone, overhead projector and screen, blackboard and chalk, flipchart and pens, television and video, laptop and projector, blinds).

Fig. 6.5

The art of using transparencies differs from that of shadow puppets.

During the presentation:

▶ Establish a positive relationship to your audience: stand upright but comfortably, look at your audience in a friendly way, introduce yourself and welcome your audience, keep up eye contact.

▶ Control your timing: put your watch on the desk next to your paper in order to check it without much ado every once in a while.

▶ Present your outline.

▶ Begin to speak slowly and distinctly in your normal voice in order to let you and your audience get used to your voice, then vary your vocal presentation by shifting the pitch, the volume and the speed of speaking in order to stress important points and to create a vivid atmosphere; leave pauses after important statements and at the end of sections to give your audience time to comprehend your arguments.

▶ Underline your speech with your (natural) body language.

▶ Repeat and paraphrase your key arguments, especially if you get the impression that the audience cannot follow your line of thought.

▶ What you say is what you show: the visual information should highlight the oral information.

▶ Present each transparency/poster/picture in 5 steps: announce what will be seen, show it, give the audience a moment to read or watch it, explain its function, remove the visual stimulus/switch off the OHP/insert a blank page in PowerPoint.

▶ Conclude your speech: summarise the key questions and arguments.

After the presentation:

▶ Ask your audience or your instructor for oral or written feedback.

▶ Take notes about the strong points and the weak points of your performance in order to improve your presentation skills.

▶ You may have to take questions or chair a discussion: remain standing upright in order not to lose momentum and not to miss anybody's reactions or remarks in the room.

▶ Take notes of questions and arguments raised by participants in order not to lose track of important comments.

▶ Respond both to the speakers and their arguments in a positive and constructive way (politely thank them for comments, hints and advice if possible; discuss their opinions).

▶ Try to relate statements to your presentation in order to create a coherent and comprehensive unit of both presentation and discussion.

▶ Impress your audience by using additional information and visual material that refer to aspects your presentation could not cover within the given time.

6.5 | Oral and written examinations

Contrary to widespread opinion, examinations are not intended to humiliate students or to reveal the extent of their ignorance under the eyes of embodied wisdom. Examinations give students the opportunity to show their knowledge and skills. Good performance pleases instructors for the student's sake and his/her own if taken as an indirect reflection of successful teaching. Since performance in examinations depends as much upon the questions as the answers, it is important to know the specific requirements and to try to meet them by appropriate preparation.

Types of examinations

A *written examination* at the end of a course tests the knowledge covered and skills practised in class unless otherwise specified. In addition to intensive studying, a look at previous examinations and paying close attention to the instructions before the beginning of the exam will pave the way towards a good grade.

The *"Prüfungsordnung"* and preparatory meetings or courses explain in detail the *requirements of the final written examination of your degree programme* or even let you practise by mock exams. Check the general proceedings, questions and demands by scrutinising previous examinations if available, by asking the examiner and students who passed. If you are given a range of topic areas to choose from in the examination, prepare for two areas in order to have an alternative if you find it difficult to handle the tasks given in one field.

Essay questions follow a similar procedure as written papers. The implications of the topic or questions have to be explained and dealt with in a systematic way. An outline with key questions and arguments or a mind-map to structure your essay should not take more than 25 percent of your time, the (legible!) writing 50 percent, and the final revision 25 percent.

In *oral examinations*, time is very limited. Therefore, it is essential to *present arguments* in concise statements, which show considerable knowledge and reflection, and which can be unfolded if time permits. In general, the preparation is very similar to that of written examinations, but instead of dealing with a single topic in depth, you should be prepared to connect texts, topics and contexts that are far apart. For example, you may be asked to compare Shakespeare's *Romeo and Juliet* with Beckett's *Waiting for Godot*, taking into account the uses of character, action, language, or the staging of the plays with respect to their cultural contexts.

Seven golden rules for exam preparations

▶ Know exactly what is expected from you.
▶ Time your studying.
▶ Carefully read primary material with the help of secondary sources.
▶ Retrieve relevant information; ask and answer questions in writing.
▶ Memorize important information, questions and arguments.
▶ If possible, practise mock exams with your peers or in preparatory courses.
▶ Try to relax in the hours before the examination instead of studying until the last minute: it is more important to be wide awake and able to concentrate than to be crammed to the brim with information.

Special hints for oral exams

▶ Listen carefully to the question, briefly reflect its direction and implications, and try to answer it precisely. Do not hesitate to ask for explanations if you do not know what the question aims at.
▶ Give a short overview of your arguments and begin with your most important answer before you unfold details. As a rule of thumb, talk as long as you are allowed to but talk wisely and avoid rambling.
▶ Pay attention to your examiner's signs of approval or disapproval. If the instructor rephrases and specifies his/her question, or points out shortcomings in your answer, you may have to give a better explanation for your opinion or to revise your arguments.

6.6 | Bibliography

This bibliography is restricted to a very small selection of helpful books under the following headings:

▶ A Anthologies and databases of literary texts 204
▶ B Beginning to study literature and culture: introductions 205
▶ C Cultural and literary theory and analysis: reference works 206
▶ D Dictionaries, encyclopaedias and websites of general interest 208
▶ E English and American literatures and cultures 210
  • International 210
  • Africa and the Caribbean 211
  • Asia 212
  • Australia and New Zealand 213
  • Canada 214
  • England, Ireland, Scotland and Wales 214
  • The United States of America 217
▶ F Bibliographies 219
▶ G Journals on literatures and cultures 221

The most accessible and important texts are marked by an asterisk*. For secondary sources on poetry, drama, narrative and literary theory, check the bibliographies of the previous sections. In general, titles are only annotated if they are very different from comparable sources. Sometimes, comprehensive sources of great interest are listed under more than one heading.

A ANTHOLOGIES AND DATABASES OF LITERARY TEXTS

Abrams, M. H. et al., eds. *The Norton Anthology of English Literature.* 8th ed. 2 vols. New York and London: Norton, 2006. (NAEL 1 and 2).

Alex Catalogue of Electronic Texts. Ed. Eric Lease Morgan. Date of access: 1 December 2007. <http://www.infomotions.com/alex/>. (1800 public domain e-texts of English and American literatures and philosophy).

Bartleby.com. Date of access: 1 December 2007. <http://www.bartleby.com>. (Good collection of texts and reference works).

Bibliomania. Date of access: 1 December 2007. <http://www.bibliomania.com/>. (Offers more than 2.000 e-texts in English, including reference books and study guides).

CETH - Center for Electronic Texts in the Humanities. 2005. Rutgers University. Date of access: 1 December 2007. <http://tabula.rutgers.edu/ceth/etext_directory/>. (Directory of electronic text centres mainly in the USA).

Electronic Text Center. University of Virginia. Date of access: 1 December 2007. <http://www.lib.virginia.edu/digital/collections/finding_digital.html>. (Provides more than 70.000 texts from the humanities in various languages and more than 350.000 pictures).

Gates, Henry Louis, ed. *The Norton Anthology of African American Literature*. 2nd ed. New York: Norton, 2004.

Gilbert, Sandra M., and Susan Gubar, eds. *The Norton Anthology of Literature by Women*. New York: Norton, 1985.

Gottesman, Ronald, Nina Baym, et al., eds. *The Norton Anthology of American Literature*. 6th ed. New York: Norton, 2003.

Humanities Text Initiative (HTI). University of Michigan. Date of access: 1 December 2007. <http://quod.lib.umich.edu/>. (Offers numerous links to databases of fictional and non-fictional texts, such as *American Verse Project, British Women Romantic Poets, The Medieval Review*, historical sources, etc.).

Lauter, Paul, ed. *The Heath Anthology of American Literature*. 4th ed. 2 vols. Boston: Houghton Mifflin, 2002. (Probably the most comprehensive anthology of literature in the United States in two volumes).

The Online Books Page. University of Pennsylvania. Date of access: 1 December 2007. <http://digital.library.upenn.edu/books/>. (More than 20.000 e-texts, including specialty archives, such as Black literature, children's literature, etc.).

An Online Library of Literature. Date of access: 1 December 2007. <http://www.literature.org/>. (Selection of 30 canonical authors, including great minds like Descartes and Darwin).

The Oxford Text Archive. 11 August 2006. Oxford University Press. Date of access: 1 December 2007. <http://ota.ahds.ac.uk/>. (Provides more than 2500 works of fiction as well as reference works in many languages).

ProQuest. Information and Learning. 2007. The Quorum. Cambridge. Date of access: 1 December 2007. <http://www.proquest.co.uk>. (Commercial provider of comprehensive databases of primary and secondary sources, in-

cluding dictionaries, bibliographies, and journals; free trials available).

Representative Poetry Online. Version 3.0 Ed. Combined Departments of English, University of Toronto. 16 October 2002. University of Toronto. Date of access: 1 December 2007. <http://rpo.library.utoronto.ca/display/index.cfm>. (Major anthology of poetry in English from the 16th to the early 20th century; six indexes).

Project Gutenberg. 1971-2002. Project Gutenberg & PROMO.NET. Date of access: 1 December 2007. <http://www.promo.net/pg/>. (More than 6.000 English e-texts of originals that were published before 1920).

Thieme, John, ed. *The Arnold Anthology of Post-colonial Literatures in English*. London: Arnold, 1996.

B BEGINNING TO STUDY LITERATURE AND CULTURE: INTRODUCTIONS

Ahrens, Rüdiger, Wolf-Dietrich Bald, and Werner Hüllen, eds. *Handbuch Englisch als Fremdsprache*. Berlin: E. Schmidt, 1995. (Provides general articles on teaching English as a foreign language, cultural and literary relationships between Germany, England and the USA, approaches to literature and an overview of postcolonial literatures).

Andermann, Ulrich, Martin Drees, and Frank Grätz. *Duden - Wie verfasst man wissenschaftliche Arbeiten?* 3rd, updated ed. Mannheim, Leipzig, Wien, Zürich: Dudenverlag, 2006.

Böker, Uwe, and Christoph Houswitschka, eds. *Einführung in das Studium der Anglistik und Amerikanistik*. München: C.H. Beck, 2008. (Comprehensive and sophisticated coverage of British and American cultural studies, linguistics, literary studies, teaching English as a foreign language, literature and media; internet resources; very long list of further reading).

Cottrell, Stella. *The Study Skills Handbook*. 3rd ed. Houndmills: Palgrave, 2006.

Fabian, Bernhard, ed. *Ein anglistischer Grundkurs: Einführung in die Literaturwissenschaft*. 9th ed. Berlin: Erich Schmidt Verlag, 2004. (Very systematic; chapters about using primary and secondary sources; stylistic, intertextual and historical approaches to texts more comprehensive than reading poetry, narrative and drama).

*Gibaldi, Joseph. *MLA Handbook for Writers of Research Papers*. 6th ed. New York, 2003. (Standard international reference source of how to research and document sources, incl. electronic media).

Highmore, Ben: *Everyday Life and Cultural Theory: An Introduction*. London: Routledge, 2002. (A very readable book that connects theory and practice).

*Korte, Barbara, Klaus Peter Müller, and Joseph Schmied. *Einführung in die Anglistik*. 2nd ed. Stuttgart and Weimar: Metzler, 2004. (Comprehensive overviews of cultural studies, linguistics, literary studies, teaching English as a foreign language and language practice; very readable and useful; incl. excellent annotated bibliography).

Kramer, Jürgen. *British Cultural Studies*. München: Fink, 1997. (Very readable study of historical development of cultural studies in Germany and Great Britain, central approaches and several examples).

Kranz, Dieter, and Paul Tiedemann. *Internet für Anglisten: Eine praxisorientierte Einführung*. Darmstadt: Primus/WBG, 2000.

Löffler, Arno, Rudolf Freiburg, Dieter Petzold, and Eberhard Späth. *Einführung in das Studium der englischen Literatur*. 6th ed. Tübingen and Basel: Francke, 2001. (Very useful introduction that offers case studies of individual texts).

Ludwig, Hans-Werner, and Thomas Rommel. *Studium Literaturwissenschaft. Arbeitstechniken und Neue Medien*. Tübingen: Francke, 2003. (Comprehensive, incl. online sources and presentation techniques).

Ogbue, Udoka. *Englischstudium & Internet*. Berlin: Cornelsen, 2001.

Reifegerste, E. Matthias. *Anglistik elektronisch in Freiburg: Eine Einführung in die elektronischen Informationsmittel für das Fach Anglistik*. Freiburg 2004. Date of access: 1 December 2007. <http://www.freidok.uni-freiburg.de/volltexte/222>. (The overview is not restricted to the university library in Freiburg but provides general information about reference works and links to international sources on the web).

Storey, John, ed. *What Is Cultural Studies? A Reader*. London: Arnold, 1996. (A collection of articles about central ideas and topics of cultural studies in GB, the USA and Australia).

Turner, Graeme. *British Cultural Studies: An Introduction*. 3rd ed. London and Boston: Routledge, 2002. (Helpful presentation of the history and concepts of cultural studies).

C CULTURAL AND LITERARY THEORY AND ANALYSIS: REFERENCE WORKS

*Abrams, M. H. *A Glossary of Literary Terms*. 8th ed. Fort Worth: Harcourt Brace College Publishers, 2005. (Very brief definitions and examples).

Ashcroft, Bill, Gareth Griffiths, and Helen Tiffin. *Postcolonial Studies: The Key Concepts*. 2nd ed. London: Routledge, 2005.

*Baldick, Chris. *The Concise Oxford Dictionary of Literary Terms*. 2nd ed. Oxford: Oxford University Press, 2004.

*Beck, Rudolf, Hildegard and Martin Kuester. *Terminologie der Literaturwissenschaft. Ein Handbuch für das Anglistikstudium*. Ismaning: Hueber, 1998. (Very clear definitions and examples).

Brydon, Diana, ed. *Postcolonialism. Critical Concepts in Literary and Cultural Studies*. 5 vols. London and New York: Routledge, 2000.

*Childers, Joseph, and Gary Hentzi, eds. *The Columbia Dictionary of Modern Literary and Cultural Criticism*. New York: Columbia University Press, 1995.

*Cuddon, J. A. *A Dictionary of Literary Terms and Literary Theory*. 4th ed. Rev. C. E. Preston. Oxford: Blackwell, 1998.

Davis, Robert Con, and Ronald Schleifer, eds. *Contemporary Literary Criticism: Literary and Cultural Studies*. 4th ed. New York and London: Longman, 1998. (Major anthology of approaches to literature and culture; incl. good introductions).

*Groden, Michael, and Martin Kreiswirth. *The Johns Hopkins Guide to Literary Theory & Criticism*. 2nd ed. Baltimore and London: The Johns Hopkins University Press, 2004. Date of access: 1 December 2007. <http://www.litguide.press.jhu.edu/>.

Guerin, Wilfred L. et al. *A Handbook of Critical Approaches to Literature*. 4th ed. Oxford: Oxford University Press, 1999.

Harmon, William, and C. Hugh Holman, eds. *A Handbook to Literature*. 9th ed. Upper Saddle River: Prentice, 2003.

*Hawthorn, Jeremy. *A Glossary of Contemporary Literary Theory*. 4th ed. London: Arnold; New York: Oxford University Press, 2001.

Hayward, Susan. *Key Concepts in Cinema Studies*. London and New York: Routledge, 2000.

Koebner, Thomas, ed. *Reclams Sachlexikon des Films*. 2nd, updated ed. Stuttgart: Reclam, 2007.

Kroll, Renate, ed. *Metzler Lexikon Gender Studies/Geschlechterforschung: Ansätze, Personen, Grundbegriffe*. Stuttgart: Metzler 2002.

*Makaryk, Irena R. *Encyclopedia of Contemporary Literary Theory, Approaches, Scholars, Terms*. Toronto: University of Toronto Press, 1993.

Murfin, Ross C., and Supryia M. Ray. *The Bedford Glossary of Critical and Literary Terms*. 2nd ed. Basingstoke: Palgrave Macmillan, 2003.

*Nünning, Ansgar, ed. *Metzler Lexikon Literatur- und Kulturtheorie*. 3rd, updated ed. Stuttgart and Weimar: Metzler, 2004. (Very comprehensive and sophisticated).

O'Sullivan, Tim, and John Hartley, eds. *Key Concepts in Communication and Cultural Studies*. 2nd ed. London: Routledge, 1994.

Payne, Michael, ed. *A Dictionary of Cultural and Critical Theory*. Oxford: Blackwell, 1997.

Preminger, Alex, and T. V. F. Brogan, eds. *The New Princeton Encyclopaedia of Poetry and Poetics*. 3rd ed. Princeton: Princeton University Press, 1993. (Comprehensive guide to history, techniques, genres and criticism of poetry).

Renner, Rolf Günter, and Engelbert Habekost, eds. *Lexikon literaturtheoretischer Werke*. Stuttgart: Kröner, 1995. (Short summary of major theoretical works across history, includes brief assessment of relevance and reception, some secondary sources).

Schweikle, Günther, and Irmgard Schweikle, eds. *Metzler Literatur Lexikon: Begriffe und Definitionen*. 2nd ed. Stuttgart: Metzler, 1990. (Short definitions of terms in literary criticism, international movements, genres, styles; lists of secondary material).

Taylor, Victor E., and Charles E. Winquist, eds. *Encyclopedia of Postmodernism*. London: Routledge, 2001.

Wilpert, Gero von. *Sachwörterbuch der Literatur.* 8th ed. Stuttgart: Kröner, 2001.

Wolfreys, Julian. *Critical Keywords in Literary and Cultural Theory.* Basingstoke: Palgrave Macmillan, 2004. (Presents key terms in comprehensive articles, including central quotes from theoretical studies, questions for additional consideration and further reading).

D DICTIONARIES, ENCYCLOPAEDIAS, AND WEBSITES OF GENERAL INTEREST

Anglistik Guide at the State and University Library at Göttingen. Date of access: 1 December 2007. <http://www.anglistikguide.de>. (Very helpful "subject gateway to scholarly relevant internet resources on Anglo-American language and literature"; resources are regularly updated, described and evaluated).

Bartlett, John. *Familiar Quotations: A Collection of Passages, Phrases and Proverbs Traced to Their Sources in Ancient and Modern Literatures.* 16th ed. Boston: Little, 1992. Date of access: 1 December 2007. <http://www.bartleby.com/100/>. (Large collection of quotes, complemented by additional collections on the website).

Brewer's Dictionary of Phrase and Fable. Ed. Adrian Room.16th ed London: Cassell, 2000. (Concise explanations of traditional words, names and phrases in cultural contexts).

Brewer's Dictionary of Modern Phrase and Fable. Eds. John Ayto and Ian Crofton. 2nd , updated ed. London: Weidenfeld & Nicolson, 2006. (Concise explanations of contemporary words, names and phrases in cultural contexts).

Die Brockhaus Enzyklopädie. 24 vols. 19th, rev. and updated ed. Leipzig and Mannheim: Brockhaus, 1986-1994.

Daemmrich, Horst S., and Ingrid Daemmrich: *Themen und Motive in der Literatur: Ein Handbuch.* 2nd ed. Tübingen: Francke, 1995.

Dictionary of Caribbean English Usage, with a French and Spanish Suppl. Ed. Richard and Jeannette Allsopp. Oxford: Oxford UP, 1996.

A Dictionary of Literary Symbols. Michael Ferber. Cambridge: Cambridge University Press, 1999.

Dictionary of Race and Ethnic Relations. Ed. Ernest Cashmore. 4th ed. London: Routledge, 1996.

A Dictionary of Slang and Unconventional English. Ed. Eric Partridge. 8th ed. Ed. Paul Beale. London: Routledge, 2002.

The Encyclopedia Americana. Grolier Educational Group. 1996. Date of access: 1 December 2007. <http://auth.grolier.com/login/go_login_page.html?bffs=N>. (Online access requires subscription).

Encyclopaedia Britannica. 32 vols. 15th ed. Ed. Daphne Daume. Chicago 2005. Also on CD-ROM. Date of access: 1 December 2007. <http://www.eb.com>. (Largest encyclopaedia in English: a wealth of knowledge).

Encylopedia.com. HighBeam Research. 2007. Date of access: 1 December 2007. <http://encyclopedia.com/>. (More than 57.000 frequently updated articles from the sixth edition of the *Columbia Encyclopedia*; incl. links to newspapers and journals).

EServer. Eserver.org. Iowa State University. 2004. Date of access: 1 December 2007. <http://eserver.org/>. (Offers more than 30.000 texts from the humanities and links to American studies sites).

Frenzel, Elisabeth. *Stoffe der Weltliteratur: Ein Lexikon dichtungsgeschichtlicher Längsschnitte.* 10th, updated ed. Stuttgart: Kröner, 2005. (Explores relationships between international literatures, for example the rewriting of Antigone, Don Juan, Faustus, etc.).

—. *Motive der Weltliteratur: Ein Lexikon dichtungsgeschichtlicher Längsschnitte.* 5th ed. Stuttgart: Kröner, 1999. (Supplement to *Stoffe der Weltliteratur*, on topics such as „incest", „the noble savage", etc.).

Hügli, Anton. *Philosophielexikon* 7th, updated ed. Hamburg: Rowohlt, 2007.

The Internet Public Library. School of Information. University of Michigan. Date of access: 1 December 2007. <http://www.ipl.org>. (Offers electronic texts and links about all cultural topics, such as business, classics, health, literature, newspapers, etc.).

Longman Dictionary of Contemporary English (DCE). 4th ed. Ed. Della Summers. Harlow and Munich: Langenscheidt-Longman, 2005. (Includes very useful copy on CD-ROM).

Longman Dictionary of English Language and Culture 2nd ed. Harlow: Longman, 2000. (Includes 15000 names, events, places and institutions of English-speaking cultures).

Mautner, Thomas. *A Dictionary of Philosophy.* Oxford: Blackwell, 1996.

Meyers Enzyklopädisches Lexikon. 25 vols. 9th, rev. and updated ed. Leipzig and Mannheim: Bibliographisches Institut, 1971-1992.

Microsoft Encarta Online Encyclopedia. Microsoft Corporation. 1997-2007. Date of access: 1 December 2007. <http://encarta.msn.com/artcenter_0/Encyclopedia_Articles.html#tcse/>.

New Dictionary of American Slang. Eds. Chapman, Robert L., Harold Wentworth, and Stuart B. Flexner. New York: Harper & Row, 1987.

The Oxford Companion to the Bible. Eds. Bruce M. Metzger and Michael D. Coogan. Oxford: Oxford University Press, 1993.

The Oxford Classical Dictionary. 3rd, rev. ed. Eds. Simon Hornblower and Antony Spawforth. Oxford: Oxford University Press, 2003.

The Oxford Companion to Classical Literature. 2nd ed. Ed. M. C. Howatson. Oxford and New York: Oxford University Press, 1997.

The Oxford Dictionary of Quotations. 6th ed. Ed. Elizabeth Knowles. Oxford University Press, 2004. (Complemented by the editor's *Oxford Dictionary of Modern Quotations.* 2nd, updated ed. Oxford: Oxford University Press, 2003).

The Oxford Dictionary of Slang. John Ayto. Oxford: Oxford UP, 1998.

Questia Media America 2007. Date of access: 1 December 2007. <www.questia.com>. (A commercial but affordable online library; thousands of very useful books and journal articles on many subjects in the humanities and social sciences, including up-to-date reference works from major publishers).

Die Religion in Geschichte und Gegenwart: Handwörterbuch für Theologie und Religionswissenschaft. Ed. Hans Dieter Betz. 4th, revised ed. Tübingen: Mohr, 1998.

The New Shorter Oxford English Dictionary on Historical Principles (SOED). 5th ed. Ed. Lesley Brown. Oxford: Clarendon Press, 2002.

Oxford Advanced Learner's Dictionary of Current English (OALD). 7th ed. Oxford: Oxford University Press: Cornelsen, 2006. (Includes very useful copy on CD-ROM).

The Oxford English Dictionary (OED). 2nd ed. Ed. J. A. Simpson and E.S.C. Weiner. 20 vols. Oxford: Clarendon-Oxford UP, 1989. CD-ROM, updated version 3.0, 2002. Date of access: 1 December 2007. <http://www.oed.com>. (The most comprehensive dictionary of the English language; particularly useful for historical meanings of words).

The Penguin Dictionary of Symbols. Chevalier, Jean, and Alain Gheerbrant. London: Penguin, 1996.

The Roland Collection of Films and Videos on Art. The Roland Collection & Pira Intl. 1998-2007. Date of access: 1 December 2007. <http://www.rolandcollection.com/>. (Videos of contemporary writers and philosophers).

Stanford Encyclopedia of Philosophy. Ed. Edward N. Zalta, et al. Metaphysics Research Lab at the Center for the Study of Language and Information. Stanford University. Regularly updated. Date of access: 1 December 2007. <http://plato.stanford.edu/contents.html>.

*Voice of the Shuttle: Web Page for Humanities Research. Ed. Alan Liu, et al. University of California, Santa Barbara, English Department. Date of access: 1 December 2007. <http://vos.ucsb.edu/>. (The most comprehensive and valuable meta-page on literatures in English in relationship to other fields, such as history, culture, the media etc.).

E ENGLISH AND AMERICAN LITERATURES AND CULTURES

In general, the following guides, handbooks, dictionaries and encyclopaedias provide information on major historical events and people, important literary and cultural movements, genres, works and literary characters. The literary histories usually present coherent overviews of cultural contexts in addition to the development of major genres and authors. For the sake of convenience, I inserted dictionaries of „englishes" used in various regions in the world in this section.

International

Benson, Eugene, and L. W. Connolly, eds. *Encyclopedia of Post-Colonial Literatures in English*. 2 vols. London: Routledge, 1994.

Blamires, Harry, ed. *A Guide to Twentieth Century Literature in English. Australia, Canada, the Caribbean, the Gambia, Ghana, India, Ireland, Kenya, New Zealand, Nigeria, Pakistan, Southern Africa, Sri Lanka, Uganda, United Kingdom*. London: Methuen, 1983.

Bondy, François, et al. *Harenbergs Lexikon der Weltliteratur: Autoren - Werke - Begriffe*. 5 vols. Dortmund: Harenberg, 1994.

Buck, Claire, ed. *The Bloomsbury Guide to Women's Literature*. New York: Prentice Hall, 1992.

*Contemporary Authors: A Bio-bibliographical Guide to Current Writers in Fiction, General Non-Fiction, Poetry, Journalism, Drama, Motion Pictures, Television, and Other Fields. Detroit: Gale, 1962ff. CD-ROM. Date of access: 1 December 2007. <http://www.galenet.com/servlet/GLD>. (Subscription required; the most comprehensive and up-to-date source on contemporary writers).

Contemporary Writers. Film and Literature Department of the British Council in association with BookTrust. Regularly updated. Date of access: 1 December 2007. <http://www.contemporarywriters.com>. (Brief biographies and lists of primary works of authors from GB und the Commonwealth).

*Dictionary of Literary Biography. Farmington Hills: Gale, 1978ff.
(Very useful and comprehensive, multivolume biographical encyclopaedia of international authors in print and online; illustrated essays on life and writings, complete lists of primary works, selective lists of secondary works).

Hall, Catherine, ed. *Cultures of Empire: Colonisers in Britain and the Empire in the Nineteenth and Twentieth Centuries. A Reader*. Manchester University Press, 2000.

Hawley, John C., ed. *Encyclopedia of Postcolonial States*. Westport: Greenwod Press, 2001.

International Who's Who of Authors and Writers 2004. 19th ed. London: Europa Publications, 2003.

Jansohn, Christa ed. *Companion to the New Literatures in English*. Berlin: Schmidt, 2002.

Jens, Walter, ed. *Kindlers Neues Literatur Lexikon*. 20 vols. München: Kindler, 1988-1992. (Summaries of international primary sources, brief evaluations, short lists of secondary sources; updated edition available on CD-ROM).

The Literary Encyclopedia and Literary Dictionary. Ed. Robert Clark, Emory Elliott and Janet Todd. The Literary Dictionary Company Limited. Date of access: 1 December 2007. <http://www.litencyc.com/>. (Subscription required; regularly updated and enlarged reference work, which also provides links to other websites about authors, books and topics).

Literary Resources on the Net. 15 June 2004. Ed. Jack Lynch. Rutgers University. Date of access: 1 December 2007. <http://andromeda.rutgers.edu:80/~jlynch/Lit/>. (Very useful meta-page that offers many valuable links to web sites on literatures in English).

Habicht, Werner, and Wolf-Dieter Lange, eds. *Der Literatur Brockhaus*. 3 vols. Mannheim: Brockhaus, 2003.

Marshall, P.J. *The Cambridge Illustrated History of the British Empire*. Cambridge: Cambridge University Press, 2001.

Murphy, Bruce, ed. *Benét's Reader's Encyclopedia*. 4th ed. New York: HarperCollins, 1996. (Comprehensive and international; features brief entries on literary movements, writers, genres, works, characters and terms of criticism).

Palmer, Alan. *Dictionary of the British Empire and Commonwealth*. London: Murray, 1996.

The Postcolonial Web. Ed. George P. Landow. Brown University and National University of Singapore. Date of access: 1 December 2007 <http://www.postcolonialweb.org/>. (Rich source of information on a wide variety of countries, topics, authors and secondary material in postcolonial studies).

ProQuest. Information and Learning. The Quorum. Cambridge. Date of access: 1 December 2007. <http://www.proquest.co.uk>. (Commercial provider of comprehensive databases of primary and secondary sources, including dictionaries, bibliographies and journals; free trials available to institutions).

Ross, Robert L., ed. *International Literature in English. Essays on the Major Writers*. Chicago: St. James Press, 1991. (Fairly comprehensive biographical and bibliographical essays on major writers from Africa, Asia, Australia, Canada, the Caribbean and New Zealand, including selected and annotated bibliographies).

Serafin, Steven R., ed. *Encyclopedia of World Literature in the 20th Century*. 4 vols. Farmington Hills: St. James, 2000.

Voice of the Shuttle: Web Page for Humanities Research. Ed. Alan Liu et al. University of California, Santa Barbara, English Department. Date of access :1 December 2007. <http://vos.ucsb.edu/>. (The most comprehensive and valuable meta-page on literatures in English in relationship to other fields, such as history, culture, the media, etc.).

Wagner, Hans-Peter. *A History of British, Irish, and American Literature*. Trier: Wissenschaftlicher Verlag Trier, 2003. (Very readable literary history; includes CD-ROM with complete text and numerous illustrations of authors, historical events and works of art).

Wilpert, Gero von, ed. *Lexikon der Weltliteratur*. 2 vols. 3rd, revised and updated ed. Stuttgart: Kröner, 2000. Incl. CD-ROM.

Africa and the Caribbean

Allsopp, Richard, ed. *Dictionary of Caribbean English Usage*. With a French and Spanish Supplement by Jeanette Allsopp. Oxford et al.: Oxford University Press, 1996.

Arnold, James A., ed. A *History of Literature in the Caribbean*. Vol. 2: *English- and Dutch-Speaking Regions*. Amsterdam: John Benjamins, 2001.

Benson, Eugene, and Leonard Conolly, eds. *Encyclopedia of Post-Colonial Literatures in English*. 2nd ed. London: Routledge, 2005.

Bute, Evangeline, and Harry Harmer. *The Black Handbook. The People, History and Politics of Africa and the African Diaspora*. London: Cassell, 1997.

Chapman, Michael. *Southern African Literatures*. 2nd ed. Scottsville: University of Natal Press: Longman, 2003.

Collison, Robert L., and Dalvan Coger. *Kenya*. Oxford: Oxford University Press, 1996.

Dabydeen, David, and Nana Wilson-Tagoe. A *Reader's Guide to West Indian and Black British Literature*. 2nd ed. London: Hansib Publications, 1997.

Dance, Daryl Cumber, ed. *Fifty Caribbean Writers. A Bio-Bibliographical Critical Sourcebook*. New York: Greenwood Press, 1986.

Gikandi, Simon, ed. *Encyclopedia of African Literature*. London and New York: Routledge, 2003.

Griffiths, Gareth. *African Literatures in English. East and West*. Harlow et al.: Longman, 2000.

Irele, F. Abiola, and Simon Gikandi, eds. *The Cambridge History of African and Caribbean Literature*. 2 vols. Cambridge: Cambridge University Press, 2004.

James, Louis. *Caribbean Literature in English*. London: Longman, 1999.

Killam, Douglas, ed. *The Companion to African Literatures*. Oxford: Currey, 2000.

King, Bruce, ed. *West Indian Literature*. 2nd, rev. ed. London: Macmillan, 1995.

Lindfors, Bernth, ed. *Twentieth Century Caribbean and Black African writers*. 3 vols. Detroit: Gale, 1992-1996.

Owomoyela, Oyekan, ed. *A History of Twentieth Century African Literatures*. Lincoln: University of Nebraska Press, 1993.

Page, James A., and Jae Min Roh. *Selected Black American, African, and Caribbean Authors. A Bio-Bibliography*. Rev. and expanded ed. Littleton, Colorado: Libraries Unlimited, 1985.

Parekh, Pushpa Naidu, and Siga Fatima Jagne, eds. *Postcolonial African Writers. A Bio-bibliographical Critical Sourcebook*. Chicago and London: Fitzroy Dearborn, 1998.

Silva, Penny, ed. *Dictionary of South African English on Historical Principles*. Oxford: Oxford University Press, 1996.

Taylor, Jeremy, ed. *Caribbean Handbook*. Antigua: FT Caribbean, 1991.

Asia

Barker, Amanda. *Bangladesh*. Oxford: Heinemann Library, 1994.

Brace, Steve. *Bangladesh*. Hove: Thomson Learning, 1995.

Datta, Amaresh, et al., eds. *Encyclopaedia of Indian Literature*. New Delhi: Sahitya, 1987–94.

Mehrotra, Arvind Krishna, ed. *A History of Indian Literature in English*. London: C. Hurst & Co, 2003.

Metcalf, Barbara D., and Thomas R. Metcalf. *A Concise History of India*. Cambridge: Cambridge University Press, 2003.

Mostow, Joshua, ed. *Columbia Companion to Modern East Asian Literature*. New York: Columbia University Press, 2003.

Myer, Hanna, ed. *India 2001: Reference Encyclopedia*. 3 vols. Bangalore: Indmark Publishing, 1995ff.

Naik, Madhukar K. *A History of Indian English Literature*. New Delhi: Sahitya, 1989.

Palling, Bruce, ed. *India: A Literary Companion*. London: John Murray, 1992.

Rahman, Tariq. *A History of English Literature in Pakistan*. Lahore et al.: Vanguard, 1991.

Robinson, Francis, ed. *The Cambridge Encyclopedia of India, Pakistan, Bangladesh, Sri Lanka, Nepal, Bhutan and the Maldives*. Cambridge: Cambridge University Press, 1989.

Silva, Chandra Richard de. *Sri Lanka: A History*. New Delhi: Vikas, 1992.

Walsh, William. *Indian Literature in English*. London et al.: Longman, 1990.

Australia and New Zealand

Bambrick, Susan, ed. *The Cambridge Encyclopedia of Australia*. Cambridge: Cambridge University Press, 1994.

Bassett, Jan. *The Oxford Illustrated Dictionary of Australian History*. Melbourne and New York: Oxford University Press, 1993.

Bennett, Bruce, Jennifer Strauss and Chris Wallace-Crabbe, eds. *The Oxford Literary History of Australia*. Oxford and Melbourne: Oxford University Press, 1999.

Bolton, Geoffrey, ed. *The Oxford History of Australia*. 5 vols. Oxford: Oxford University Press, 1996-2002.

Clarke, Francis G. *Australia: A Concise Political and Social History*. 2nd ed. Sydney: International Thomson Publishing, 1992.

Davison, Graeme, John Hirst and Stuart Macintyre, eds. *The Oxford Companion to Australian History*. Revised edition. Oxford: Oxford University Press, 2001.

Docherty, James C. *Historical Dictionary of Australia*. 3rd ed. Lanham: The Scarecrow Press, 2007.

Evans, Patrick: *The Penguin History of New Zealand Literature*. Auckland: Penguin Books, 1990.

Goodwin, Ken. *A History of Australian Literature*. London: Macmillan, 1986.

Hergenhan, Laurie ed. *The Penguin New Literary History of Australia*. Ringwood: Penguin Books, 1988.

Jackson, William Keith, and Alan McRobie. *Historical Dictionary of New Zealand*. 2nd ed. Lanham: The Scarecrow Press, 2005.

Jupp, James, ed. *The Australian People: An Encyclopedia of the Nation, Its People, and Their Origins*. Cambridge University Press, 2001.

Pierce, Peter, ed. *The Oxford Literary Guide to Australia*. Oxford: Oxford UP, 1988.

Ramsom, W. S., ed. *The Australian National Dictionary. A Dictionary of Australianisms on Historical Principles*. Melbourne: Oxford University Press, 1988.

Robinson, Roger, ed. *The Oxford Companion to New Zealand Literature*. Melbourne: Oxford University Press, 1998.

Shaw, John, ed. *Australian Encyclopedia*. Sydney: Collins 1985.

Sinclair, Keith, ed. *The Oxford Illustrated History of New Zealand*. Auckland: Oxford University Press, 1991.

Sturm, Terry, ed. *The Oxford History of New Zealand Literature in English*. 2nd ed. Auckland: Oxford University Press, 1998.

Webby, Elizabeth, ed. *The Cambridge Companion to Australian Literature*. Cambridge: Cambridge University Press, 2000.

Wilde, William H., Joy Hooton, and Barry Andrews. *The Oxford Companion to Australian Literature.* 2nd ed. Melbourne: Oxford University Press, 1994.

Canada

Benson, Eugene, ed. *The Oxford Companion to Canadian Literature.* 2nd ed. Toronto: Oxford University Press, 1999.

Braun, Hans, and Wolfgang Klooß, eds. *Kanada: Eine interdisziplinäre Einführung.* 2nd, rev. ed. Trier: WVT, 1994.

The Canadian Encyclopedia. Marsh, James H., ed. 2004. Historical Foundation of Canada. Date of access: 1 December 2007. <http://www.thecanadianencyclopedia.com/index.cfm?PgNm=Homepage&Params=A1>.

Hallowell, Gerald, ed. *The Oxford Companion to Canadian History.* Oxford: Oxford University Press, 2004.

Keith, William J. *Canadian Literature in English.* London: Longman, 1985.

Klinck, Carl F., ed. *Literary History of Canada. Canadian Literature in English.* 4 vols. 2nd ed. Toronto: University of Toronto Press, 1990.

Kröller, Eva-Marie, ed. *The Cambridge Companion to Canadian Literature.* Cambridge: Cambridge University Press, 2004.

Löschnigg, Maria and Martin. *Kurze Geschichte der kanadischen Literatur.* Stuttgart: Klett, 2001.

New, William Herbert, ed. *Encyclopedia of Literature in Canada.* Toronto: University of Toronto Press, 2002.

New, William H.: *A History of Canadian Literature.* 2nd ed. Montreal: McGill-Queen's University Press, 2003.

England, Ireland, Scotland and Wales

Alexander, Michael. *A History of English Literature.* Basingstoke: Palgrave Macmillan, 2000.

Bate, Jonathan, ed. *The Oxford English Literary History. 1960-2000: The Last of England?* Oxford: Oxford University Press, 2004. (Monumental work in progress; so far, volumes 2: 1350-1547 and 8: 1830-1880 have been published).

BBC. Updated daily. Date of access: 1 December 2007. <http://www.bbc.co.uk/>. (Offers an amazing range of up to date information on Great Britain and the world).

Borgmeier, Raimund, ed. *Die englische Literatur in Text und Darstellung.* 10 vols. Stuttgart: Reclam, 1982-1986. (A series of volumes by different editors, who wrote introductions to particular eras in literary history, which are complemented by anthologies of poems and excerpts from major texts).

Breuer, Rolf. *Irland. Eine Einführung in seine Geschichte, Literatur und Kultur.* München: Fink, 2003.

Briggs, Asa. A Social History of England. New ed. London: Penguin, 1999.

The British Council. 1 December 2007. <http://www.britishcouncil.org>. (Comprehensive jump page with numerous links to web sites that cover all aspects of British culture. The British Council, Germany, offers online-membership for a moderate fee with access to various comprehensive databases, including reference works, newspapers, etc.).

Brown, Alice, David McCrone, and Lindsay Paterson. *Politics and Society in Scotland.* London: Macmillan, 1996.

Cannadine, David, ed. *The Penguin History of Britain.* London: Penguin Books, 1996ff. (Work in progress in multiple volumes).

Carter, Ronald, and John McRae, eds. *The Routledge History of Literature in English. Britain and Ireland.* 2nd ed. New York and London: Routledge, 2001.

Caughie, John, and Kevin Rockett. *The Companion to British and Irish Cinema.* London: Continuum Press, 1996.

*Childs, Peter, and Michael Storry, eds. *Encyclopedia of Contemporary British Culture.* New York: Routledge, 1999.

Craig, Cairns, ed. *The History of Scottish Literature.* 4 vols. Aberdeen: Mercat Press, 1999.

Cunliffe, Barry, et al., eds. *The Penguin Illustrated History of Britain and Ireland.* From Earliest Times to the Present Day. Harmondsworth: Penguin, 2004.

Davies, Norman. *The Isles: A History.* London: Papermac, 2000.

Deane, Seamus. *A Short History of Irish Literature.* London: Hutchinson, 1986.

Dictionary of National Biography. 22 vols. London: Oxford University Press, 1967-68. (Comprehensive dictionary on British citizens, including colonial Americans; selection of entries in: *Concise DNB,* 1992; the complete reference work is being revised and will be published as the *Oxford Dictionary of National Biography*).

Directgov. E-Government Unit, Cabinet Office. London. Date of access: 1 December 2007. <http://www.direct.gov.uk/en/index.htm>. (Official up to date information on British politics, economics, education, environment and all services the British government provides).

Doyle, Brian. *English and Englishness.* London: Routledge, 1989.

*Drabble, Margaret, ed. *The Oxford Companion to English Literature.* 6th, rev. ed. New York: Oxford Univ. Press, 2006. (Brief information on movements, authors, works and genres; a shortened, updated and less expensive version was edited by Margaret Drabble, Jenny Stringer and Daniel Hahn. *The Concise Oxford Companion to English Literature.* 2nd ed. Oxford: Oxford University Press, 2003).

Erlebach, Peter, Bernhard Reitz, and Thomas M. Stein. *Geschichte der englischen Literatur.* Stuttgart: Reclam, 2007.

Fabian, Bernhard, and Willi Erzgräber, ed. *Die englische Literatur.* 2 vols. München: dtv, 2000. (The first volume presents extensive surveys of the historical context and the development of the genres; the second volume records authors' biographical and bibliographical information).

Foster, R. E., ed. *The Oxford Illustrated History of Ireland.* Oxford: Oxford University Press, 1995.

*Gardiner, Juliet, ed. *The Penguin Dictionary of British History.* London: Penguin, 2000.

Garlick, Raymond. *An Introduction to Anglo-Welsh Literature.* Cardiff: University of Wales Press, 1972.

*Gascoigne, Bamber. *Encyclopedia of Britain. The A-Z of Britain's Past and Present.* London: Macmillan, 1994.

Gelfert, Hans-Dieter. *Kleine Geschichte der englischen Literatur.* 2nd, updated ed. Munich: Beck, 2005.

German Web Portal to British Studies. British Council. 2004. Date of access: 1 December 2007. <http://www.britishstudies.de/index.htm>. (Offers bibliographies and numerous links to resources and institutions related to Great Britain).

Gifford, Douglas, Sarah Dunnigan, and Alan MacGillivray, eds. *Scottish Literature: in English and Scots.* Edinburgh: Edinburgh University Press, 2002.

Haigh, Christopher, ed. *The Cambridge Encyclopedia of Great Britain and Ireland.* Cambridge: Cambridge University Press, 1990.

Harvie, Christopher. *Scotland and Nationalism: Scottish Society and Politics, 1707–1994.* 2nd ed. London: Routledge, 1994.

Head, Dominic. *The Cambridge Guide to Literature in English.* 3rd ed. Cambridge: Cambridge University Press, 2006.

Hogan, Robert, ed. *Dictionary of Irish Literature.* 2 vols. Rev. and updated ed. Westport: Greenwood Press, 1996.

Innes, Catherine Lynette. *A History of Black and Asian Writing in Britain: 1700-2000.* Cambridge: Cambridge University Press, 2002.

Kamm, Jürgen, and Bernd Lenz. *Großbritannien verstehen.* Eds. Hans Kastendiek, Karl Rohe, and Angelika Volle. Darmstadt: Wissenschaftliche Buchgesellschaft, 2004.

Länderbericht Großbritannien. Geschichte. Politik. Wirtschaft. Gesellschaft. 3rd, rev. and updated ed. Bonn: Bundeszentrale für Politische Bildung, 2006.

Kiberd, Declan. *Inventing Ireland.* London: Harvard University Press, 1995.

Kosok, Heinz. *Geschichte der* angloirischen *Literatur.* Berlin: Schmidt, 1990.

Mathias, Roland. *Anglo-Welsh Literature: An Illustrated History.* 2nd ed. Bridgend: Seren 1992.

Maurer, Michael. *Kleine Geschichte Irlands.* Stuttgart: Reclam, 1998.

—. *Kleine Geschichte Englands.* Rev. and updated ed. Ditzingen: Reclam, 2007.

McCormack, W.J., ed. *The Blackwell Companion to Modern Irish Culture.* Oxford: Blackwell, 1999.

Moody, Theodore William, T. X. Martin, F.J. Byrne, et al., eds. *A New History of Ireland.* 9 Vols. Oxford University Press, 1976-2003.

*Morgan, Kenneth O., ed. *The Oxford Illustrated History of Britain.* Revised Ed. Oxford: Oxford University Press, 2001.

*Morley, David, and Kevin Robins, eds. *British Cultural Studies. Geography, Nationality, and Identity.* Oxford: Oxford University Press, 2001.

National Statistics Online. Updated regularly. Date of access: 1 December 2007. <http://www.statistics.gov.uk>. (Statistics on economics, environment, health, population, society, tourism, etc.).

Nünning, Ansgar, ed. *Eine andere Geschichte der Literatur. Epochen, Gattungen, und Teilgebiete im Überblick.* 3rd, expanded ed. Trier: WVT, 2004.

Nünning, Ansgar, and Eberhard Kreutzer, eds. *Metzler Lexikon englischsprachiger Autorinnen und Autoren.* Stuttgart and Weimar: Metzler, 2006.

Nünning, Vera, ed. *Kulturgeschichte der englischen Literatur: Von der Renaissance bis zur Gegenwart.* Tübingen: Francke, 2005.

*Oakland, John. *British Civilization.* 5th ed. London and New York: Routledge, 2002.

*O'Driscoll, James. *Britain: An Introduction.* 9th ed. Oxford University Press, 2002.

Owusu, Kwesi, ed. *Black British Culture and Society: A Text Reader.* London: Routledge, 2000.

*Rogers, Pat, ed. *The Oxford Illustrated History of English Literature.* Oxford: Oxford University Press, 2001.

Royle, Trevor. *The Mainstream Companion to Scottish Literature*. Edinburgh: Mainstream, 1993.

Sampson, George, ed. *The Concise Cambridge History of English Literature*. 3rd, rev. and updated ed. Cambridge: Cambridge University Press, 1990.

Samuel, Raphael, ed. *Patriotism: The Making and Unmaking of British National Identity*. Vol.2: *Minorities and Outsiders*. London: Routledge, 1989.

Sanders, Andrew. *The Short Oxford History of English Literature*. 3rd ed. Oxford: Oxford University Press, 2004. (Includes literature in English from Wales, Scotland and Ireland, as well as a selection of other postcolonial literatures).

Schabert, Ina. *Englische Literaturgeschichte. Eine neue Darstellung aus der Sicht der Geschlechterforschung*. Stuttgart: Kröner, 1997.

Schabert, Ina. *Englische Literaturgeschichte des 20. Jahrhunderts. Eine neue Darstellung aus der Sicht der Geschlechterforschung*. Stuttgart: Kröner 2006.

Schlueter, Paul, and June Schlueter, eds. *An Encyclopedia of British Women Writers*. *Rev. and expanded ed.* New Brunswick, NJ: Rutgers University Press, 1998.

*Seeber, Hans Ulrich, ed. *Englische Literaturgeschichte*. 4th, enlarged ed. Stuttgart and Weimar: Metzler, 2004.

Stephens, Meic, ed. *The Oxford Companion to the Literature of Wales*. Cardiff: University of Wales Press, 1998.

Storry, Mike, and Peter Childs, eds. *British Cultural Identities*. London: Routledge, 1997.

Stringer, Jenny, ed. *The Oxford Companion to Twentieth-Century Literature in English*. Oxford: Oxford University Press, 1996.

Thies, Henning, ed. *Hauptwerke der englischen Literatur. Einzeldarstellungen und Interpretationen*. 2 vols. München: Kindler, 1999.

Vance, Norman. *Irish Literature: A Social History. Tradition, Identity and Differences*. 2nd ed. Dublin: Four Courts, 1999.

*Welch, Robert, ed. *The Oxford Companion to Irish literature*. Oxford: Clarendon Press, 1996. (The editor also published a shorter version: *The Concise Oxford Companion to Irish Literature* in 2000).

Wynne-Davis, Marion, ed. *The Prentice-Hall Guide to English Literature*. New York, 1990. (Unique combination of 12 longer essays on literary history and a reference section on authors, genres, works and cultural contexts).

United States of America

Adams, Willi Paul, and Peter Lösche, eds. *Länderbericht USA. Detaillierter Überblick zur Geschichte, Politik, Geographie, Wirtschaft, Gesellschaft und Kultur der USA*. 4th, revised and updated ed. Bonn: Bundeszentrale für politische Bildung, 2004.

American National Biography. 24 vols. Eds. John A. Garraty and Mark C. Carnes. New York: Oxford University Press, 1999.

Andrews, William L., et al., eds. *The Oxford Companion to African American Literature*. New York: Oxford University Press, 1997.

Bercovitch, Sacvan, ed. *The Cambridge History of American Literature*. 8 vols. Cambridge: Cambridge University Press, 1994-2006. (Most comprehensive literary history of the US).

Campbell, Neil, and Kean, Alasdair. *American Cultural Studies. An Introduction to American Culture*. London: Routledge, 2004.

Cayton, Mary Kupiec, Elliott J. Gorn, and Peter W. Williams, eds. *Encyclopedia of American Social History*. 3 vols. New York: Scribner's, 1993.

*Conn, Peter. *Literature in America. An Illustrated History*. Cambridge: Cambridge University Press, 1989.

Davidson, Cathy N., and Linda Wagner-Martin. *The Oxford Companion to Women's Writing in the United States*. New York: Oxford University Press, 1995.

Elliott, Emory, ed. *The Columbia Literary History of the United States (CLHUS)*. New York: Columbia University Press, 1988.

*Engler, Bernd, and Kurt Müller, eds. *Metzler Lexikon amerikanischer Autoren*. Stuttgart: Metzler, 2000.

Gidley, Mick, ed. *Modern American Culture. An Introduction*. London: Longman, 1993.

*Gray, Richard J. *A History of American Literature*. Oxford: Blackwell, 2004.

Hart, James D., ed. *The Oxford Companion to American Literature*. 6th ed. New York: Oxford University Press, 1995.

Heideking, Jürgen, and Vera Nünning. *Einführung in die amerikanische Geschichte*. München: C. H. Beck, 1998. (Political, economic, social, ethnic, gender history; helpful information on further reading and research).

Hornung, Alfred. *Lexikon amerikanischer Literatur*. Mannheim: Meyers Lexikonverlag, 1992.

Mauk, David, and John Oakland. *American Civilization. An Introduction*. 4th ed. London: Routledge, 2005.

Morris, Richard B. *Encyclopedia of American History*. 7th ed. New York: Harper Collins, 1996.

Official US Executive Branch Web Sites. A Library of Congress Internet Resource Page. Date of access: 1 December 2007. <http://www.loc.gov/rr/news/fedgov.html>. (The site offers links to official and independent agencies dealing with topics like politics, commerce, education, justice, etc.).

Parini, Jay, ed. *The Oxford Encyclopedia of American Literature*. 4 vols. New York: Oxford University Press, 2004.

Perkins, George, ed. *HarperCollins Reader's Encyclopedia of American Literature*. 2nd ed. New York: HarperResource, 2002.

*Raeithel, Gert. *Geschichte der Nordamerikanischen Kultur*. 3 vols. 4th, revised and updated ed. Frankfurt: Zweitausendeins, 2002.

Ruland, Richard, and Malcolm Bradbury. *From Puritanism to Postmodernism: A History of American Literature*. London: Penguin, 1999.

Salzmann, Jack, ed. *The Cambridge Handbook of American Literature*. Cambridge: Cambridge University Press, 1990.

Speitkamp, Winfried. *Kleine Geschichte Afrikas*. Stuttgart: Reclam, 2007.

Thies, Henning, ed. *Hauptwerke der amerikanischen Literatur. Einzeldarstellungen und Interpretationen*. München: Kindler, 1995.

Webster's Third New International Dictionary of the English Language. Ed. Philip B. Gove. Springfield: Merriam-Webster, 1993. (Biggest etymological American dictionary, more than 450000 entries).

Webster's New International Comprehensive Dictionary of the English Language. Encyclopedic edition. Köln: Müller, 2004.

Wersich, Rüdiger, ed. *USA Lexikon. Schlüsselbegriffe zu Politik, Wirtschaft, Gesellschaft, Kultur, Geschichte und zu den deutsch-amerikanischen Beziehungen*. Berlin: Schmidt, 1999.

*Zapf, Hubert, ed. *Amerikanische Literaturgeschichte*. 2nd, updated ed. Stuttgart and Weimar: Metzler, 2004.

F BIBLIOGRAPHIES

Anglistik Guide at the State and University Library at Göttingen. Date of access: 1 December 2007. <http://www.anglistikguide.de>. (Very helpful „subject gateway to scholarly relevant internet resources on Anglo-American language and literature"; resources are regularly updated, described and evaluated).

Annual Bibliography of English Language and Literature (*ABELL* or *MHRA Bibliography*). Leeds: Maney for Modern Humanities Research Association, 1920- . Date of access: 1 December 2007. <http://collections.chadwyck.com/marketing/index.jsp>. (Subscription required; free trial available; comprehensive international bibliography of literature and secondary material in English, which can be searched by keyword, title keyword, author, publication details and date; includes book reviews; listings considerably predate the *MLAIB* database, which begins in 1963 but covers more up-to-date material than the *ABELL* after 1980).

British Studies Bibliography. British Council. 1999. Date of access: 1 December 2007. <http://www.britishcouncil.org/studies/bibliography/index.htm>. (Comprehensive, if not quite up-to-date, database, which can be searched by subject, author and title).

British National Bibliography (BNB). The British Library. Date of access: 1 December 2007. <http://www.bl.uk/services/bibliographic/natbib.html>. (Lists everything published in the United Kingdom).

The British Library. Date of access: 1 December 2007. <http://www.bl.uk/>. (Offers a number of online catalogues, which register millions of books, newspapers, journals, maps, images, recordings, etc.; search in individual catalogues or in integrated catalogue).

*Copac. Manchester Computing, Manchester University. Date of access: 1 December 2007. <http://copac.ac.uk/>. (Offers access to the merged online catalogues of 24 university research libraries in the UK and Ireland, the British Library and the National Library of Scotland).

Dissertation Abstracts International. (Summaries of university theses of the USA since 1980; lists North American theses since 1861 and British theses since 1988; also online: Thomson Dialog. Updated monthly. Date of access: 1 December 2007. <http://library.dialog.com/bluesheets/html/bl0035.html>).

Elektronische Zeitschriftenbibliothek (EZB). Date of access: 1 December 2007. <http://rzblx1.uni-regensburg.de/ezeit/>. (Offers numerous e-journals; some journals offer table of contents only, others full texts for free).

The English Short Title Catalogue 1473-1800 (ESTC) on CD-ROM. (List of publications in GB and its colonies until 1800).

English and American Studies in German. Summaries of Theses and Monographs. Ed. Horst Weinstock. Tübingen: Niemeyer, 1968ff. (Abstracts of German university theses).

Fachbibliographien und Online-Datenbanken Anglistik, Amerikanistik (FabiO). Bibliotheksservice-Zentrum Baden-Württemberg. University of Konstanz. Date of access: 1 December 2007. <http://www2.bsz-bw.de/cms/recherche/links/fabio/fabioANG.html>. (Offers many links to international websites and databases on English and American studies; search by nationality, genre or topic).

Gender Inn. English department of Cologne university. Date of access: 1 December 2007. <http://www.uni-koeln.de/phil-fak/englisch/datenbank>. (Offers bibliographies of gender studies and links to webpages that focus on gender studies).

Global Books in Print. Bowker. Updated regularly. Date of access: 1 December 2007. <http://www.globalbooksinprint.com/bip/>. (Useful for search of recent publications on particular authors or topics).

*Harner, James L. *Literary Research Guide. An Annotated Listing of Reference Sources in English Literary Studies*. 4th ed. New York: MLA, 2002. (Enormously helpful annotated bibliography of fundamental reference works, such as bibliographies, dictionaries, encyclopaedias, handbooks, histories, etc.).

Index to Theses with Abstracts. 1 December 2007. <http://www.theses.com/>. (Subscription required; comprehensive listing of British and Irish university theses with summaries since 1716).

Internationale Bibliographie der geistes- und sozialwissenschaftlichen Zeitschriftenliteratur/ International Bibliography of Periodical Literature. 1896ff. Saur Verlag. CD-ROM and *online*, 1983ff. Thomson. <http://gso.gbv.de/DB=2.4/LNG=DU/LNG=EN/>. (Subscription required; comprehensive international bibliography of articles in periodicals that cover the humanities and social sciences).

Karlsruher Virtueller Katalog (KVK). Date of access: 1 December 2007. <http://www.ubka.uni-karlsruhe.de/kvk.html>. (Offers access to many German and international online library catalogues).

Krikos, Linda A., and Cindy Ingold. *Women's Studies: A Recommended Bibliography*. 3rd ed. Westport and London: Libraries Unlimited, 2004.

The Library of Congress Online Catalogue. The Library of Congress. Date of access: 1 December 2007. <http://catalog.loc.gov/>. (The Library of Congress holds a collection of more than 126 million items, including books, recordings and manuscripts).

MLA International Bibliography of Books and Articles on the Modern Languages and Literatures (MLAIB or PMLA Bibliography). New York: MLA, 1922ff. CD-ROM. Date of access: 1 December 2007. <http://www.mla.org>. (The CD-ROM and the online version provide an extensive, very useful and current bibliography that allow very quick and specific searches for secondary literature between 1963 and today; findings should be cross-checked with those in the *ABELL*).

The New Cambridge Bibliography of English Literature 600-1950 (NCBEL). 2nd ed. Eds. George Watson and I.R. Willison. Cambridge: Cambridge University Press, 1969-1987. (Records primary literature of Great Britain and highly selective secondary material from the year 600 to the mid 1980s. Useful for research on minor authors and selective historical criticism).

OPAC der Zeitschriftendatenbank, Date of access: 1 December 2007. <http://dispatch.opac.d-nb.de/DB=1.1/>. (Lists more than 1 million titles of journals and thousands of libraries where you can find and order them).

Periodicals Content Index (PCI). ProQuest 2004. Date of access: 1 December 2007. <http://pio.chadwyck.com/marketing.do>. (Campus licence required; free trial available; covers journals from the humanities and social sciences).

Research Libraries Group. Date of access: 1 December 2007. <http://www.oclc.org/>. (Offers links to collections in libraries, archives and museums).

*Virtuelle Bibliothek der Universitäts- und Landesbibliothek Düsseldorf für den Bereich Anglistik/Amerikanistik: Date of access: 1 December 2007 <http://www.ub.uni-duesseldorf.de/home/ebib/fachinfo/faecher/ang/dvb>. (Offers a great number of links to websites concerning English and American studies).

Verzeichnis lieferbarer Bücher (VLB). München: Saur, 1971ff. Online <http://www.vlb.de/portal.htm> or <http://www.buchhandel.de/>. (Lists all titles currently available in Germany).

The Year's Work in Critical and Cultural Theory. Ed. Kate McGowan. Oxford: Oxford University Press, 1991 ff. (Companion volume to YWES, see below; summarises and comments on relevant books in critical and cultural studies, for example on gender, ethnicity, film, etc.).

The Year's Work in English Studies (YWES). Eds. William Baker and Kenneth Womack. 1920ff. Oxford: Oxford University Press. (Summarises and evaluates selected secondary sources in major fields of literary research).

G Journals on literatures and cultures

Take a look at the latest copies of journals for recent research on topics of your interest. Some of the websites quoted here are free of charge but may only give the table of contents, the abstracts of articles or older volumes of the journals. Check whether your university holds campus licences for commercial databases, which you can find in the digital library.

Anglia: Zeitschrift für Englische Philologie.

anglistik & englischunterricht.

Arbeiten aus Anglistik und Amerikanistik (AAA).

Archiv für das Studium der Neueren Sprachen und Literaturen Date of access: 1 December 2007. <http://esv.info/z/ARCHIV/Zeitschriften.html>.

Ariel: A Review of International English Literature. Date of access: 1 December 2007. <http://jcl.sagepub.com/cgi/content/citation/19/2/147?ck=nck>.

Australian Journal of Cultural Studies. Date of access: 1 December 2007. <http://wwwmcc.murdoch.edu.au/ReadingRoom/serial/AJCS/AJCSindex.html>.

Cercles. Revue pluridisciplinaire du monde anglophone. Date of access: 1 December 2007. <http://www.cercles.com/>.

Comparative Literature and Culture. Date of access: 1 December 2007. <http://clcwebjournal.lib.purdue.edu>.

Critical Inquiry. Date of access: 1 December 2007. <http://www.journals.uchicago.edu/CI/loi/ci>.

Critical Quarterly. Date of access: 1 December 2007. <http://www.criticalquarterly.com>.

Cultural Critique. Date of access: 1 December 2007. <http://muse.jhu.edu/journals/cultural_critique>.

Cultural Studies. (Also online; subscription required; date of access: 1 December 2007. <http://www.tandf.co.uk/journals/routledge/09502386.htm>).

Cultural Studies <-> Critical Methodologies. (Also online; subscription required; date of access: 1 December 2007. <http://www.sagepub.com/journalsProdDesc.nav?prodId=Journal201379>).

Culture, Theory and Critique. (Also online; subscription required; date of access: 1 December 2007. <http://www.tandf.co.uk/journals/routledge/14735784.html>).

Differences: A Journal of Feminist Cultural Studies. Date of access: 1 December 2007. <http://muse.jhu.edu/journals/differences/>.

Eighteenth-Century Studies. (Also online; subscription required; date of access: 1 December 2007. <http://www.jstor.org/journals/00132586.html>).

Enculturation: An Electronic Journal for Cultural Studies and Theory. Date of access: 1 December 2007. <http://enculturation.gmu.edu/index.html>.

English Studies: A Journal of English Language and Literature. Date of access: 1 December 2007. <http://www.tandf.co.uk/journals/titles/0013838X.asp>.

Erfurt Electronic Studies in English. EESE. Date of access: 1 December 2007. <http://webdoc.gwdg.de/edoc/ia/eese/eese.html>.

European Journal of Cultural Studies. Date of access: 1 December 2007. <http://ecs.sagepub.com/>.

ELH: A Journal of English Literary History. (Also online; subscription required; date of access: 1 December 2007. <http://www.jstor.org/journals/00138304.html>).

Forum: Qualitative Social Research. Date of access: 1 December 2007. <http://www.qualitative-research.net/fqs/fqs-eng.htm>.

gender forum. Date of access: 1 December 2007. <http://www.genderforum.uni-koeln.de/>.

International Journal of Cultural Studies. Date of access: 1 December 2007. <http://ics.sagepub.com/>.

Journal of American Studies. Date of access: 1 December 2007. <http://journals.cambridge.org/action/displayJournal?jid=AMS>.

Journal of British Studies. Date of access: 1 December 2007. <http://www.journals.uchicago.edu/loi/jbs>. (Table of contents online).

Journal of Caribbean Studies. Date of access: 1 December 2007. <http://www.tandf.co.uk/journals/titles/17442222.asp>.

Journal of Commonwealth Literature. (Table of contents online; subscription required; date of access: 1 December 2007. <http://jcl.sagepub.com>).

A Journal of English Literary History (ELH). Date of access: 1 December 2007. <http://muse.jhu.edu/journals/elh/>. (Subscription required).

Journal for the Study of British Cultures. Date of access: 1 December 2007. <http://www.jsbc.de>. (Table of contents online).

Journal of Popular Culture. Date of access: 1 December 2007. <http://www.blackwellpublishing.com/journal.asp?ref=0022-3840>.

Journal of Postcolonial Writing. (Formerly *World Literature Written in English*; also online; subscription required; date of access: 1 December 2007. <http://www.tandf.co.uk/journals/titles/17449855.asp>).

KulturPoetik: Zeitschrift für kulturgeschichtliche Literaturwissenschaft. Date of access: 1 December 2007. <http://www.kulturpoetik.de>. (Only abstracts and selection of articles online; incl. bibliography of cultural studies).

Literatur in Wissenschaft und Unterricht (LWU). Date of access: 1 December 2007. <http://www.anglistik.uni-kiel.de/LWU/default.html>.

Modern Drama. Date of access: 1 December 2007. <http://muse.jhu.edu/journals/modern_drama/>. (Subscription required).

Modern Fiction Studies (MFS). (Also online; excerpts available; access to full texts restricted to subscribers; date of access: 1 December 2007. <http://muse.jhu.edu/journals/modern_fiction_studies/>).

Modern Language Notes (MLN). (Also online; subscription required; date of access: 1 December 2007. <http://www.jstor.org/journals/01496611.html>).

Modern Language Review (MLR). (Also online; subscription required; date of access: 1 December 2007). <http://www.mhra.org.uk/Publications/ Journals/mlr.html>.

New Literary History (NLH). Date of access: 1 December 2007. <http://muse.jhu.edu/journals/new_literary_h istory/>. (Subscription required)

Nineteenth-Century Literature. (Also online; subscription required; date of access: 1 December 2007. <http://www.jstor.org/journals/08919356.html>).

NLH: New Literary History. (Also online; subscription required; date of access: 1 December 2007. <http://www.jstor.org/journals/00286087.html>).

Philological Quarterly. Date of access: 1 December 2007. <http://vnweb.hwwilsonweb.com/hww/Journals/getIssues.jhtml?sid=HWW:OMNIS&issn= 0031-7977>.

Poetica: Zeitschrift für Sprach- und Literaturwissenschaft

Postmodern Culture. Date of access: 1 December 2007. <http://www3.iath.virginia.edu/pmc/contents. all.html>. (Free access to many articles).

Prose Studies. Date of access: 1 December 2007. <http://www.tandf.co.uk/journals/titles/ 01440357.asp>.

Public Culture: Bulletin of the Centre for Transnational Cultural Studies. Date of access: 1 December 2007. <http://muse.jhu.edu/journals/public_culture/>. (Abstracts online for free; access to full texts restricted to subscribers).

Publications of the Modern Language Association of America (PMLA). (Also online; subscription required; date of access: 1 December 2007. <http://www.jstor.org/journals/00308129.html>).

Representations. (Also online; subscription required; date of access: 1 December 2007. <http://www.representations.org/>).

Rhizomes Net: Cultural Studies in Emerging Knowledge. Date of access: 1 December 2007. <http://www.rhizomes.net>.

Scottish Affairs. Date of access: 1 December 2007. <http://www.scottishaffairs.org/>.

Shakespeare-Jahrbuch. (Also online; subscription required; date of access: 1 December 2007. <http://www.digizeitschriften.de/ index.php?id=loader&tx_jkDigiTools_pi1 [IDDOC]=38555>).

Shakespeare Quarterly. (Also online; subscription required; date of access: 1 December 2007. <http://www.jstor.org/journals/00373222.html>; excerpts available without subscription:<http://muse.jhu.edu/journals/shakespeare_quarterly/>).

Shakespeare Survey. Date of access: 1 December 2007. <http://www.cambridge.org/uk/ literature/shakespearesurvey/>.

Sport in Society. (Also online; subscription required; date of access: 1 December 2007. <http://www.tandf.co.uk/journals/titles/14610981.asp>.

Studies in English Literature 1500-1900. (Also online; subscription required; date of access: 1 December 2007. <http://www.jstor.org/journals/00393657.html>; excerpts available: <http://muse.jhu.edu/journals/studies_in_english_literature/>).

Studies in Philology. Date of access: 1 December 2007. <http://muse.jhu.edu/journals/studies_in_philology/>. (Subscription required).

Studies in Romanticism. Date of access :
1 December 2007. <http://www.enotes.
com/studies-romanticism-journals>.

Theory, Culture & Society. (Abstracts online;
date of access: 1 December 2007.
<http://www.sagepub.net/tcs/>).

*TRANS: Internet-Zeitschrift für Kulturwis-
senschaften.* Date of access: 1 December 2007.
<http://www.inst.at/trans/>.

Twentieth-Century Literature. (Also online;
subscription required; date of access:
1 December 2007. <http://www.jstor.org/jour-
nals/0041462X.html>).

Victorian Studies. (Also online; abstracts
available; subscription required for access to
full texts; date of access: 1 December 2007.
<http://muse.jhu.edu/journals/victorian_
studies/>).

Wasafiri. (Also online; subscription required;
date of access: 1 December 2007.
<http://www.wasafiri.org/>).

Women: A Cultural Review. (Also online;
subscription required; date of access:
1 December 2007.
<http://www.tandf.co.uk/journals/
titles/09574042.asp>).

*Zeitschrift für Anglistik und Amerikanistik
(ZAA).*

The number of online journals is quickly
growing. Check the databases given below
and the meta-pages recorded in section
D for current listings of electronic journals.

Elektronische Zeitschriftenbibliothek. Univer-
sitätsbibliothek Regensburg. Date of access:
1 December 2007. <http://rzblx1.uni-regens-
burg.de/ezeit/fl.phtml?bibid=UBB&colors=7>.
(Access depends upon policy of individual
journal and campus licence).

Journal Storage. The Scholarly Journal Archive.
Date of access: 1 December 2007.
<http://www.jstor.org>. (Campus licence or
individual membership required).

Project Muse. Scholarly Journals Online. Date
of access: 1 December 2007.
<http://muse.jhu.edu/>. (Campus licence or
individual membership required).

Appendix | 7

Contents

7.1	Analyses	226
7.2	Index	232
7.3	Acknowledgements	241

Abstract

The analyses given below suggest readings which are by no means comprehensive or complete. They point to approaches that can be productively applied to these texts.

7.1 | Analyses

Chapter 2: Poetry

Exercise 1. Henry Wadsworth Longfellow's poem "Nature" (pp. 54-55).

(D+C+B) The poem is an Italian sonnet with two quatrains and two tercets (abba abba cde cde) in iambic pentameter. The poetic division into two parts parallels the rhetorical one between the vehicle of the simile, the mother, who brings her child to bed at night, and the tenor, Nature, who leads human beings to death at the end of their lives. The key terms "playthings", "leads", and "by the hand" are repeated in the second part in order to stress the parallel between child and the adult. Caesuras in line one, three and eight to eleven, and the shift of stress towards "more splendid" and "not please" (line 8) stress the child's hesitation. The discomforts of ageing and the fear of death are toned down by figurative language. Mother Nature is a comforting figure, who takes care of human beings as if they were her own children. The metaphor "playthings" signifies the activities we like to do but have to give up in old age. Being gently led to rest embellishes the process of ageing and dying. The metaphor of sleep, which clouds our understanding, points at the growing mental limitations of the elderly.

(A+B) The speaker includes everybody in the plural pronouns "we" and "us". The mood is calm and the tone contemplative. Content, rhetoric and poetic form are harmoniously intertwined. The simile dispels any fear of death by safely putting humanity into the hands of Mother Nature, creating a Romantic contrast to the 19th century notions of evolution and progress through the enlightened mastery over nature

Exercise 2. "The Body as Braille" by Lorna Dee Cervantes (pp. 55-56).

(A+B+C) The simile of the title implies that the body is a system of signs that can be read by the blind with their hands, provided that they have learned how to read it. The lyrical poem is rather unusual because the female persona quotes three other utterances and positions herself in an ambiguous relationship to them. The speaker talks to herself rather than to her lover, marking the difference between physical and verbal communication. She conceals her thoughts from him but the author allows the reader into her private thoughts. The speaker calmly reflects on how to define her passion rather than indulging in an immediate expression of emotion.

His reading of her back with his hand results in an interpretation which is flattering but superficial in comparison to her expression of emotions and insights. His paying attention to her back rather than to her face corresponds to her reticence. They are together in a physical sense but apart in a mental and cultural sense. Her own vision of her passion takes the form of an ambivalent simile, which blends heat and coldness. The moon, which waxes and wanes, is a traditional symbol of female changeability and fertility. The white ring can be seen from two perspectives. The quote of the metaphor from her Latino grandmother ("dijo mi abuela") invokes a magic and supernatural quality of love. The utterance of (male American) scholars provide a contrasting "natural" explanation of love as a reflection of light, in metaphoric terms as a female response (moon) to male appreciation (sun). She combines and transforms both perspectives in the conceit of "a storm brewing in the cauldron / of the sky." The brewing cauldron is associated with heat and witches, the beginning storm in the sky with coldness and power, images that convey the impression of the dangerous dynamics of her love. The speaker leaves her lover in the dark about her love, whether it has a future of whatever kind or whether he will be in for a cold shock.

The title introduces an alliteration, which the body of the text (about the text of the body) continues: "body", "braille", "back", "beautiful", "burning", "brewing". The lover characterises her with the general term "beautiful" but does not realise her passion. The alliteration of "crystals" and "cauldron" supports the paradoxical combination of coldness and heat, which describe her love. The repetitions of "moon" and "ice" give more weight to the cool and changeable side of her. (D+E)

The graphic design suggests a rise and fall in the growing and waning of the lengths of lines, supporting the image of the moon and changeability. The gradual reduction of the last seven lines from seven to two words mirror the difference between her reflection on the relationship and the reticent communication with her lover. The male perspectives on the external beauty of the body and natural phenomena are juxtaposed with the female and multicultural vision, which transcend what is palpable and suggest a powerful dynamics beyond his reach.

Chapter 3: Narrative

Exercise 1. Ernest Hemingway's "Banal Story" (p. 89).

The title raises curiosity because the banal story must be of some interest in order to be written and read. The covert heterodiegetic narrator mediates the nameless male character's perspective in fixed internal focalisation. The story begins *in medias res*, indicated by the initial "So", as if the man at the desk decided to take his time ("slowly") to eat an orange because he had difficulties with writing. The wintry turn outside and the lack of heat inside the room create an uncomfortable atmosphere. The man's thoughts (in free indirect discourse) imply that he was freezing, and is relieved upon feeling the heat of the stove, which gives life in a very basic sense. His reaching for another orange without eating it reveals either that he has time or that his attention is drawn to the news in the paper he reads. Apparently, he is primarily interested in sensations, male sports and far away places, which promise adventurous romance or "Life" as opposed to his "life" in a rather dreary place. The fact that his situation seems to be rather boring and unpleasant motivates his escapist desire for heroic action elsewhere. On the other hand, the man is also interested in the arts and in writing, fields which refer back to his place at the writing-table and suggest his profession. The nameless man is a writer but also the general representative of autonomous masculinity, revealed in his detachment from any personal relationships and in the split between his own "life" and the "Life" he is fascinated by. The combination of the heterodiegetic narrator and the internal focalisation mirror the division between the man's external and internal life. The story explores the banal but important difference between life, Life, and the vicarious experience of romance via reading. In a way, the story is all about Hemingway's own obsession with masculinity, adventure, sports, exotic places and the need to retreat in order to write fiction.

Exercise 2. Rose Tremain's story "My Wife is a White Russian" (p. 90).

The autodiegetic narrator betrays no critical distance towards himself but rather presents his current thoughts and perceptions. The choice of the autodiegetic narrator corresponds to the character's egocentric view of the world, which is indicated by the anaphoric repetition of "I" in the first four sentences, and his cold erotic obsession with talking about what he owns. His autoeroticism dominates his view of human and heterosexual relationships. The rich location symbolically supports his social status but also becomes the place of his public embarassment. He seems to have a problem with the young, apparently healthy, and courteous Australians because he himself cannot accept his speech impediment, which is probably the result of a stroke. His handicap counteracts his pride and power. Instead of stimulating him, uttering the "hard" word "*Diamonds*!" turns into a grotesque performance. The rich and hard-hearted man is reduced to a pathetic spectacle. His beautiful wife's smile is extremely ambiguous. Now he, who was so powerful, would be helpless without his wife. This new dependency creates a tension, which prefigures conflicts within and between characters.

Hemingway's and Tremain's male figures have a limited, narrow perspective on life in these stories. They are egocentric and interested in autonomy and performance, whether in sports or in business, rather than in relationships. Their concept of romance focuses on male rivalry but seems to be emptied of love. However, Tremain's rich man has an inkling that the use of his wife as a decorative object is closely related to her lack of love for him.

Chapter 4: Drama

Exercise 1. Arthur Miller's *Death of a Salesman* (p. 124).

The author describes the music, place, time, props, the protagonist's name, age, clothes, behaviour, psychological disposition and the particular nature of the utterance in order to define the character in context. The ordinary first name Willy generalises the character and the telling name Loman suggests that he is low in money and in spirit. The fine melody is associated with dreams of freedom and space, which contrast with the buildings looming up around his small house. The number and large size of his suit-cases, his exhausted behaviour, and his sigh show the old and humble salesman's suffering and disillusionment. He can rely on his cheerful and loving wife, who would never express her dislike of his temper. Both direct and indirect characterisation draw a difficult, unrealistic, unstable and divided character.

The wall of fog outside at night is an objective correlative of the mother's morphine addiction, as Edmund realises, but both father and son do not see their drinking and their intention to ignore Mary coming down the stairway have the same effect. The fog horn, which warns ships not to founder on the coast, might serve as a reminder to help Mary but neither father nor son try to get through to her. Their mechanical way of playing cards highlights the lack of light-hearted playfulness between them, as opposed to the game of mutual accusation, which time and again disrupts their underlying feeling of attachment to each other. Whereas the father represses his responsibility for his wife's present situation by putting the blame on the drug, Edmund tries to pierce Tyrone's wall of fog by blaming him of being guilty of her addiction. In turn, the father blames Edmund for having been born, using the ultimate insult and repressing his own responsibility for the present situation. Father and son are caught in a bond of love and hate, which materialises in a vicious circle of accusation and denial. They *talk* instead of acting to change their situation or help Mary, and they speak *about* her rather than to her, a fact that betrays their helplessness and resignation. Their drinking in the dimly lit home at midnight raises the ghosts of the past, which are haunting the disintegrating family.

Chapter 5: Literary Theory

The limerick "Three blind mice" can be interpreted as a condensation of the Oedipus complex and castration anxiety. The blindness of the mice, if taken to represent boys, indicates that they are oblivious of their desire for the mother in the farmer's wife. The farmer's absence seems to allow the boys to fulfill their Oedipal desire but the wife enforces the patriarchal law by castrating the boys with the knife, which symbolises the father's phallus. The anonymous verse can be read as a complex image of subconscious male desire and anxiety. Psychoanalytically oriented feminists could read the limerick as the woman's endorsement of patriarchal rules, or, what is more likely, as a form of empowerment that curtails male domination.

Structuralist analysis of Phillis Wheatley's poem "On being brought from Africa to America" (p. 37).

The poem parallels the following binary oppositions: Africa/America, past/present, (justice)/mercy, heathen/Christian, night/day, ignorance/knowledge, black/white, (damnation)/redemption, devil/God, Negroes/Christians, Cain/Abel, devil/angel, (uneducated)/refined. The poem shows a very symmetric and regular structure in terms of metre and rhyme. The iambic pentameter is only inverted thrice, marking "taught" in the second line (in alliteration with "T'was"), and the chiasmic equivalence of the rhymes "I"/"eye", "knew"/"view" in the two central lines of the poem. The opposition between "I" and "Some", past and present, simple ignorance and discriminating "knowledge", and the equivalent alliteration of "sought"/"scornful" suggest an analogy between the speakers past blindness and the white American's present ignorance. This doubling of opposition and equivalence disturbs the prevalent binary opposition between black and white, as does that between her past and the present, and her past conversion and the possible future of Africans. This doubling suggests that "Some", who discriminate Africans, could change their views of Africans as these could change their views of God. The individual movement from Africa to America and the conversion from paganism to Christianity can be read as a general model for enslaved African-Americans.

The poem uses the regular conventions of English poetry and partly endorses the binary system of Christian values. It reiterates the binary system of the (white Puritan) American dream of spiritual liberation from bondage in the Old World and of regeneration in the Promised Land of the New World. The transfer of these structures to African-Americans, however, transgresses the system of North American slavery, which is partly built upon the racist Christian denigration of African "heathens", identifying them as "diabolic" and as descendants from the jealous murderer Cain. The potential conversion of all African-Americans claims their redemption and integration into the Christian system of values in opposition to their present exclusion from it or rather their reduction to its negative other (for a more critical interpretation, see 5.3.4 Postcolonialism).

7.2 | Index

The index records technical terms, movements, theories, periods, authors and titles. Definitions and central explanations of technical terms are given on the pages that are highlighted **in bold letters** in the index instead of being repeated in a glossary. The German term is only mentioned if it differs significantly from the English expression.

absence 141, 150, 165
absurd, drama and theatre **101-102, 113,** 118-119, 179-180
Abweichung(sästhetik) **146**
Achebe, Chinua ("Dead Man's Path") 74-75
achronic/*Achronie* 120
action 63, **81-**83, 103-108, 112-115, 119-120
addressee/*Adressat* . . .8, **26,** 29-30, **62,** 102, 146
ad spectators 105
aesthetic experience/*ästhetische Erfahrung* **5, 13,** 24
aesthetic object **6-7,** 143
aesthetic structure **81**
affective fallacy **143**
African American studies 168-69, 172-173, 178-180
agent **83,** 100, 113
Alice's Adventures in Wonderland (Lewis Carroll) 13
alienation 85, 100-101, 180
Allegorie/allegory .27, **34**
alliteration **45,** 102, 148
allwissend (Erzähler) **67**
alternate rhyme **46**
alter, alter ego, alterity (see also other) **140, 170**
Althusser, Louis 156
Ambiguität/ambiguity/ambiguous **9,** 13, 27, 35, 63, 84-85, 104, 143
anachronic/*Anachronie* **78**
analepsis **78**
Analyse/analysis **3, 11-**12, 26, 52-53, 63, 81, 83, 85-86, 98, 145, 175
Anapäst/anapaest/ic **42**

Anapher/anaphora 38
"Annabel Lee" (Edgar Allan Poe) 47-48
annotated edition **10**
antagonist 103, **112**
anti-illusionist postmodernist fiction **84-**85
Antithese/antithesis 48
Anzaldua, Gloria 173
approach **2-3,** 53, 63, 86, **133-135,** 139, 142-145, 154-155, 157, 165, 172, 180
apron stage **116**
arbiträr/arbitrary 142, **145,** 151, 153-155
Aristotelian drama/*aristotelisches Drama* **103-104**
Aristotle 4, 7, 106-108
Arnold, Matthew ("Dover Beach") 40
art for art's sake 6
Ashbery, John ("Our Youth") 51-52
Asian American 173
aside **104-105,** 121
assonance/*Assonanz* **45**
asyndeton **39-40**
As You Like It (William Shakespeare) 96, 98, 108
atmosphere 70, 75, 80
Augenreim **45**
auktorialer Erzähler **63**
Auslassung **77**
aut delectare aut prodesse **5**
author 4, **6-**10, 14-15, 17, **26-**27, **29-**30, **62, 66,** 69, **84-85,** 96, **135-137,** 139, 143, 145, 153, 164, 176
- implied **62**
- real 26, **62,** 66
authorial narrative/narrator **63, 66-67,** 69
autodiegetic narrator **69-**70, 77

"To Autumn" (John Keats) 50

"The Baby" (Donald Barthelme) 71-72,
                                   142, 162-163
Bachtin, Michael/Bakhtin, Michail 157
ballad **46-47**
   - folk- **46**
   - *Volks-* **46**
ballad stanza/*Balladenstrophe*..............**46**
"Banal Story" (Ernest Hemingway) 89
Barnes, Julian (*Talking It Over*) 72, 78
Barth, John ("Life Story") 84, 96
Barthelme, Donald ("The Baby") 71-72,
                                   142, 162-163
Barthes, Roland 149, 153
base/*Basis* **155**
Beauvoir, Simone de 164
Beckett, Samuel 101-102, 113,
                                 118, 179-180
   - *Endgame* 101, 118
   - *Waiting for Godot* 102, 113
Behn, Aphra (*Oroonoko, or the Royal Slave*) ...65
bell hooks 168
Benhabib, Seyla 167
Beiseite-Sprechen **104**
Bericht **104**
Beschönigung 37
Betonung **37, 111**
Bhabha, Homi 170-171
Bildempfänger (of metaphor) **32**
Bildspender (of metaphor) **32**
binary opposition **146**, 148, 150, 171
Binnenerzählung **70**
Binnenreim **45**
biographical approach **135**
Black Comedy (Peter Shaffer) **115**
Blake, William ("The Tyger") 39
blank verse 99
"The Body as Braille" (Lorna Dee
   Cervantes) 55, 168, 175
Bond, James.............................86
Brave New World (Aldous Huxley) 6
Briefroman **66**
"British Museum Reading Room"
   (Louis MacNeice) 31
Brontë, Charlotte (*Jane Eyre*) 79-80, 82
bürgerliches Trauerspiel/domestic tragedy ...108
Bunyan, John (*Pilgrim's Progress*) 5
Butler, Judith 167

caesura **42**-43
canon 2-**3, 14**
Carroll, Lewis (*Alice's Adventures
   in Wonderland*) 13
Carter, Angela ("Little Red Riding Hood") 82
The Castle of Otranto (Horace Walpole) 14
catastrophe 113
catharsis **107**

Cervantes, Lorna Dee ("The Body
   as Braille" 55, 226
Cervantes, Miguel (*Don Quixote*) 5
character 5,7, 29, 62-63, 66-69,
      73-75, **80-81**, 83-84, 96-**106, 111**-113, 117
characterisation, direct and indirect 88
chiasmus **38**
"Chicago" (Carl Sandburg) 39
Childress, Alice ("Health Card") 60-62
chorus 104
Cisneros, Sandra (*The House on
   Mango Street*) 173
Cixous, Hélène 166
climax 113
closed character 81, 106
closed form (of drama) **113**
close reading 26, 105, **144**
closure (of a narrative) **82**
code **9**-10, 112
Collins, Wilkie (*The Woman in White*) 72
combination (syntagmatic) **146**, 148
comedy 98, **108-109**, 114
   - farcical/farce 115
   - of humours **109**
   - of manners 100, **109**-110
   - romantic **108-109**
   - satiric **109**, 114
"The Company of Wolves"
   (Sara Maitland) 82
complication 61, **113**
composition 11-12, 26-27, 51
conceit **31**
conception of figures **106**
concordia discors **12**
condensation **139**
configuration **111**
conflict 61, 82, 108, **112**-113, 125
connotation 17, **141**
consonance **45**
constellation of characters **81, 111**
context/ual 3, 9-10, 12-15, 52-53,
                     71, 86, 108, **155**-159
Copernican revolutions 132
Copernicus 132
couplet 8, 27, **45-46**, 48
covert narrator **69**
critical apparatus **10**
critical edition **10**
criticism 3
   - literary **10-13**
   - and theory 2-3, 135-169
cultural materialism **159**-160
cultural turn **133**

dactyl/*Daktylus* **42**-43
"Daffodils" (William Words-
   worth) 34-35, 42, 48
Darwin, Charles 133

"Dead Man's Path" (Chinua Achebe) 74
Death of a Salesman (Arthur Miller) 120, 124
deconstruction, deconstructivism, deconstructivist 150, 155
defamiliarisation **147**
A Defence of Poetry (Percy Bysshe Shelley) . . .22
Defoe, Daniel (*Robinson Crusoe*) 64
denotation **141,** 144
dénouement 113-114
Derrida, Jacques 150-151, 153, 170
detachment (aesthetic) **13,** 107
deviation 43, **146-**147
dialogic/al **157**-158
dialogue **13,** 29, 46, 67, 96,
                                   99-103, 110, 175-176
diaspora 171
Dickens, Charles 82
  - *Hard Times* 5-6
  - *Great Expectations* 82
Dickinson, Emily 42
différance **150-151**
difference **145,** 150
direct characterisation 88
direct discourse/*direkte Rede* 73-74
discourse (cultural) **162**-163
  - authoritative **157**
  - double-voiced **158**-159
  - narrative **60, 64-69,** 73-75
  - persuasive **157**
discourse time **77**
displacement **139**
domestic tragedy/*bürgerliches Trauerspiel* . . .108
Donne, John
  - "Song" 42
  - "The Sun Rising" .38
Don Quixote (Miguel Cervantes) 5
"Dover Beach" (Matthew Arnold) 40
Dr. Jekyll and Mr. Hyde
  (Robert Louis Stevenson) 140
Dracula (Bram Stoker) 13
drama (see also comedy, morality play,
tragedy) 7, 67, **96,** 104-106, 113-114, 119
  - absurd **101, 113**
  -Aristotelian **103-104**
  - epic **103-104**
dramatic communication **96**
dramatic irony **98**
dramatic language **99**
dramatic monologue **29**
dramatis personae **111**
Drayton, Michael (English sonnet) 27-28
Dreiheber **42**
dupe **108**
duration (of a narrative) **77**
duration (of a performance) 8, **119**

Eagleton, Terry 149
écriture feminine **165**-166

editing/edition 9-10
ego (*Ich*, psychoanalysis) **137,** 140, 142
eigentliche Sprache **30**
Einleitung **113**
elegy 7
Eliot, Thomas Stearns ("The Love
  Song of J. R. Prufrock") 29-31, 43
ellipsis **77**
embedded narrative .70
Empfindsamkeit/Empfindung 66
emphasis **37-**39, 41, 111
Endgame (Samuel Beckett) 101, 118-119,
                                        179-180
end rhyme **45-**46
end-stopped line **42**
English sonnet **27, 48-**49
Enjambement **42**
epic drama **103-**104
epic narrator (in drama) **104-**105
epic poetry 24
epilogue **104**
Epipher/epiphora **38**
epistolary novel 66
equivalence 148, 153
erlebendes Ich **64**
erlebte Rede **73-**75
Erwartungshorizont **178**
Erzähldauer **77**
erzählendes Ich **64**
Erzählerbericht **74**
Erzählsituation **63, 67**
erzählte Zeit **77**
Erzählung **60**
Erzählweise **60**
Erzählzeit **77**
An Essay on Criticism (Alexander Pope) 25
essentialism/essentialist 153, 173, 174
Etherege, George (*The Man of* Mode) . .100, 109
ethnic/ity **170**
euphemism **37**
ex parte **104-105**
experiencing **64**
experimental theatre **110**
expliziter Erzähler **69**
exposition 105, **113**
external communication 26, **96-98**
external focalisation **72**
extradiegetic narrator **71**
extrinsic approach **4, 86**
eye-rhyme 45

fall (action in drama) **113-114**
farce 115
feminine rhyme 45
feminism **164-169**
fiction 4-5, 71, 80, **84-85**
fictional character **80-**81, 83, 99, 105-**106**
fictional discourse **62**

fictional story . . . .**.62,** 85
fictional time (of a drama) **115, 119**
Field (Vincent van Gogh) 11
figural narrative situation . . . .**.63, 67**
figurative language/*figurative Sprache*
   (see also: ambiguity, antithesis, conceit,
   epic simile, hyperbole, irony, metaphor,
   metonymy, oxymoron, paradox, pun,
   symbol, understatement) . . . .**.30-31,** 41
first-person narrative/narrator . . . .**.62-69**
Fish, Stanley 177
fixed focalisation/*fixierte Fokalisation* **72**
flashback . . . .**.78**
flashforward . . . .**.78**
flat character/type . . . .**.81,** 106, 108
focalisation/*Fokalisierung* 69, **72,** 74, **81,** 106,
                                            108, 148, 179
folk ballad . . . .**.46**
foot/feet (in metre) . . . .**.42**
foreground/ing (aesthetic) 30, 33, 67, 74,
                                       85, **146-149**
Formalism **145-147**
Foucault, Michel 162
fourth wall 117
frame narrative . . . .**.76**
free indirect discourse/*freie indirekte*
   Rede . . . .**.73-75**
free verse . . . .**.43-45**
frequency . . . .**.78**
Freud, Sigmund **137-140**
Fünfheber . . . .**.42**
Füssli, Johann Heinrich
   (*King Lear*) 102-103, 107

Gadamer, Hans-Georg (see also
   hermeneutics) 11
gap (*Lücke, Leerstelle;*
   deconstructivism) 150, 165, 167
   - (reader response) **176-178**
Gedankenwiedergabe, indirekte 76
Gemeintes (metaphor) 32
Geminatio 38
gender, ~ studies 164, **167-168**
genre . . . .**.7-8, 13-15**
Geschichte . . . .**.60, 113**
geschlossene Form (Drama) **113**
geschlossenes Ende . . . .**.82**
Gesichtspunkt . . . .**.69**
Gilman, Charlotte Perkins
   ("The Yellow Wallpaper") 70-71
Gilroy, Paul 172
Gogh, Vincent van (*Field*) 11-12
Gothic novel 14
Great Expectations (Charles Dickens) 82
Greenblatt, Stephen 163
Guckkastenbühne **117**
gynocriticism **164**

Halbreim/half-rhyme . . . .**.45**
haiku . . . .**.46**
Haltung . . . .**.26**
Handlungsstrang . . . .**.63**
Handlungsstruktur . . . .**.60, 81**
Hard Times (Charles Dickens) 5-6
Harry Potter (J. K. Rowling) 5
Hauptfigur **112**
Haupthandlung **114**
Haupttext . . . .**.96**
Hawthorne, Nathaniel
   (*The Scarlet Letter*) 70, 158
"Health Card" (Alice Childress) 60-62
The Heidi Chronicles (Wendy
   Wasserstein) 120
Hemingway, Ernest ("Banal Story") . .89-90, 228
hermeneutic circle 13
hermeneutics **11-13, 136-137**
hero/heroine 82, 107
heroic couplet . . . .**.46**
heterodiegetic narrator **69**-70, 74
heteroglossia/heterglot **157**
Hirsch,Jr., E. D. 136
Höhepunkt **113**
Holmes, Sherlock 178
homodiegetic narrator **69-70**
Horace/*Horaz* . . . .**.5,** 77
horizon of expectations 178
Howard, Henry, Earl of Surrey 48
"Humpty Dumpty" 22, 43
Huxley, Aldous (*Brave New World*) 6
hybrid/ity 170-**171**
Hyperbel/hyperbole . . . .**.37**

iamb/ic **42**-43, 46, 99
I-as-protagonist . . . .**.65**
I-as-witness . . . .**.65**
Ich (ego, psychoanalysis) **136**
Ich-Erzähler/Erzählsituation **63-66**
Id (psychoanalysis) **136**
identical rhyme . . . .**.45**
identity 133, 137-138, 141, 143,
                          150, 164-165, **167, 170**
ideological, ~ apparatus, ideology **155**-157
illusion 66-68, **84,** 104-105, 114, 117-118
illusionist theatre 110
imagist/*isch* . . . .**.24**
imitation 4, 7, 67
implied author . . . .**.62**
implied fictional communication . . . .**.62**
implied reader . . . .**.62, 176-177**
The Importance of Being Earnest
   (Oscar Wilde) .112-113
impure rhyme . . . .**.45**
"In a Station of the Metro"
   (Ezra Pound) 23-24, 30, 32
in medias res **77,** 120
indeterminacy, indeterminate 51, 153-155

indirect characterisation/*Charakterisierung* . . .88
indirect discourse/*indirekte Rede* **73-75**
indoor theatre **116**
innerer Monolog/interior monologue **73, 76**
intentional fallacy/*intentionaler*
    Trugschluss 136, **137**, 143
intercultural 172
internal communication 26, **96-98**
internal focalisation **72**
internal rhyme **45**
interpretation . . . **3**, 10-13, 52, 78, 119, 136-140
interpretive community **177**
intertextual/ity **153-154**
intradiegetic narrator **70**
intrinsic **4**, 6, 52
intrinsic approach **143**
intrusive narrator **66**
inversion **53**
Irigaray, Luce 166
ironic/irony 29, **37**-38, 52, 61,
    74, 79, 82, 84, **98**, 102, 104, 113,
    115, 119, 158-159
Iser, Wolfgang 176-77
Italian sonnet/*italienisches Sonett* **48-49**

Jakobson, Roman .147-148
Jambus **42**
Jane Eyre (Charlotte Brontë) 79-80, 82
Jauß, Hans Robert 178
Jonson, Ben (*Volpone*) 109, 114, 158
Joyce, James 68
  - *A Portrait of the Artist as a*
    Young Man .68, 75-76
  - *Ulysses* 76

Kanon 2-**3**, 14
Kant, Immanuel 133
Katastrophe 113
Katharsis **107**
Keats, John ("To Autumn") 50
Kinderreim **22**
King Lear (William Shakespeare) . .102-103, 107
Kingston, Maxine Hong
    (*The Woman Warrior*) 174
Klimax 113
kommentierte Ausgabe **10**
Konfiguration **111**
Kreuzreim **46**
Kristeva, Julia 165
Kunstballade **47-48**

Lacan, Jacques **141-143**
language, communicative
    functions of **147-148**
langue **145-146**
laughter 109
Lauretis, Teresa de 167

Leser
  - *impliziter*/implied **62**
  - *realer*/real .26, 62
libido 138
"Life Story" (John Barth) 84, 96
limerick 148
line (of verse) **22**
line-by-line exchange **100**-101
linguistics 132-133, 145
linguistic turn **133**
literal language **30-31**
literal meaning 12, 41, 72, 79-80, 119
literarische Ballade/literary ballad **47**
literary
  - ballad **47**
  - communication **9**
  - criticism **3**, **10**-13
  - genres 5, **7**, 9, 14-15, 46, 106
  - history **3**, **14**-18
  - studies **2-3**
  - theory **2-3**, 14
Literatur
  - *geschichte* **14-18**
  - *kritik* **3**
  - *theorie* **2**, 123-155
  - *wissenschaft* **2**
literature
  - oral **8**, **60-61**, 63, 65, 78
  - written **8**, 60-61
litotes **37**
"Little Red Riding Hood" (Angela Carter) 82
locale **115-117**, 119
"The Locust Tree in Flowers"
    (William Carlos Williams) 44-45
Lösung (of conflict in comedy) **113**
A Long Day's Journey into Night
    (Eugene O'Neill) 120, 124-125, 230
Longfellow, Henry Wadsworth ("Nature") . . .226
"The Love Song of J. R. Prufrock"
    (Thomas Stearns Eliot) 29, 31
Lowe, Lisa 173
Lyotard, Jean-Francois 154
lyric **24**

Macbeth (William Shakespeare) 152
MacNeice, Louis ("British Museum
    Reading Room") 31
männlicher Reim **45**
Magritte, René (*La clef des songes*) 146
Maitland, Sara
    - "The Company of Wolves" 82
    - "The Wicked Stepmother's Tale" 82
The Man of Mode (George Etherege) . . .100, 109
Marx, Karl/Marxism 155-156
masculine rhyme **45**
mask 26, 110
McKay, Claude ("The White House") 49
meaning 144-145

- connotative **144**
- denotative **144**
- hermeneutic **11-13, 136-137**
- latent **139**
- manifest **139**
medium **7-10**
mehrsträngige Handlungsführung **83**
metafiction **84**
Metapher/metaphor **31-32**, 38, 41, 119
Methode/approach 2, **134**-180, 226-232
Metonymie/metonymy **32-33**
metre/*Metrum* 30, **41-46**, 53
- *Anapäst*/anapest **42**
- *Daktylus*/dactyl **42**
- *Jambus*/iamb **42**
- *Spondäus*/spondee **42**
- *Trochäus*/trochee **42**
Mexican American .173
Midsummer Night's Dream
        (William Shakespeare) 114
Miller, Arthur (*Death of a Salesman*) 229-230
Milne, A. A. (*Winnie the Pooh*) 13,18
mimesis, mimetic **4**, 6-7, 10, 73, 115
mimicry **171**
Mimik/facial expression 110
mirror stage/*Spiegelstadium* **141**
Mitleid und Furcht/pity and fear **107**
modernism/modernist 18, 23, 25, 37, **84**
Mohanti, Chandra Talpade 169
Moi, Toril 165
Monolog/monologue
        (poetry) 29
        (narrative) **73**, 76
        (drama) 99, **102-103**, 105
monologic/al **157**
Montrose, Louis 161-162
mood 7, 22, **26**
morality play **110**
Morrison, Toni
        - *Beloved* 173
motivation (character) 112-113
multicultural/ism 170, **172-174**
multimedia 9, **97**
multiple focalisation **72**
multiple strands of action 83
Mündlichkeit **8**
"My Wife is a White Russian" (Rose
        Tremain) 90

narcissism **138**
narratee **62-63**
narrating I **64**
narrative 7, **60-86**, 96, 103-104
- grand ~/master ~/metanarrative **154**, 169
narrative communication **63**
narrative report **73-74**
narrator **61-78**, 81, 85, 96, 99-100, 104-105
- autodiegetic **69-70**, 77

- covert **69**
- extradiegetic **70**
- heterodiegetic **69-70**, 74
- homodiegetic **69-70**
- intradiegetic **70**
- overt **69**
- reliable **70**, 72
- unreliable **70**, 72
"Nature" (Henry Wadsworth Longfellow) . .53-55
Nebenhandlung **114**
Nebentext **96**
neoclassical/neoclassicism **15**, 114
neutral scenic narrative **67**
New Criticism **143-145**
New Historicism **161-163**
non-realistic narrative 84
Northcote, James (*Romeo and Juliet*) 98
novel 5, **63**
        - epistolary 66
        - gothic 14
nursery rhyme **22**-23

oblique rhyme **45**
octett **48**, 54
Oedipus complex **138**, 140
offene Form (Drama) **114**
omnipresent narrator **67**
omniscient narrator **67**
"On being brought from Africa to America"
(Phillis Wheatley) 37-38, 160-161,
                174-175, 179, 231-232
O'Neill, Eugene (*Long Day's Journey
        into Night*) 120, 124-125, 230
opaque/open character/figure
        (in narrative) **86**
        (in drama) **106**
open-air theatre **116**
open ending **83**
open form (drama) **114**
opposition **147-148**
orality **8**
oral storytelling **60-61**
orature **8**
Oriental/ism **170**
Oroonoko, or the Royal Slave (Aphra Behn) . . .65
Ort (Drama) **115**
other (– self) **141**, **164-165**, 166,
                168, 170, 174
ottava rima **48**
Our Town (Thornton Wilder) 104
"Our Youth" (John Ashberry) 51-52
overt narrator **69**
oxymoron **40**

Paarreim **45**
pageant **116**
Pamela, or Virtue Rewarded
        (Samuel Richardson) 66

paradigm **146-147**, 178-179
paradox **40**
parallelism **38**
Paronomasie/pun **32**
pars pro toto (Synecdoche) **33**
pause
   (poetry) **42**
   (narrative) **77**
pentameter **42**, 46, 99
performance
- gender **167-168**
- theatre **95-102, 110-120**
persona **26**-30
personale Erzählsituation **63, 67**
personification 27, **34**
perspective/*Perspektive*
   (in narrative) 63-64, 67-68, **71-72**, 81
   (in drama) **105**
Petrarchan sonnet **8**
phallic, phallo(go)centrism 143, 165
Pilgrim's Progress (John Bunyan) 5
pity and fear/*Furcht und Mitleid* **107-108**
place
   (poetry) 26, 33
   (in stories) **79-80**
   (in drama and theatre) **108-112**
Plato 4
plot
   (narrative) 17, **56**, 73, 77-79
   (drama) **114-115**
play-within-the-play .123
pleasure and/or profit .5
Poe, Edgar Allan 6-7
   - "Annabel Lee" 47
   - "The Raven" 35-36
poetic communication **26**
poetic justice **82, 108-109**
"The Poetic Principle" (Edgar Allan Poe) 7
point-of-view 9, 65, **69**
polylogue **99**
polysyndeton **39**-40
Pope, Alexander (*An Essay on Criticism*) 25
A Portrait of the Artist as a Young Man
   (James Joyce) 68, 75, 91
positivist biographical approach **135-136**
postcolonial/ism **169**-172
postmodern **154**
Poulet, Georges 176
Pound, Ezra ("In a Station of the
   Metro") 23-24, 30, 44, 46
Preface to Lyrical Ballads
   (William Wordsworth) 25
primary text
   (in drama) **96, 117**
prolepsis **78**
prologue 98, **104-105**
properties (drama, theatre) 98, 115
proscenium stage **116**

protagonist 65, 106, 110-**112**, 114
psychoanalysis **137-143**
pun **32**

Quartett/quatrain **27, 46**, 48

race 168, **170**, 173
Raffung **77**
Rahmenerzählung **70**
"The Raven" (Edgar Allan Poe) 35-36
reader **2-6**, 8-10, 13-15, **26**, 62,
                    66-71, 76-82, 96
   - implied **62**
   - real 27, **62**
reader-response theory **175-178**
realistic narrative .84-85
reception theory **178-180**
Reim **45-46**
   - *Augenreim* **45**
   - *Binnenreim* **45**
   - *Endreim* **45**
   - *Halbreim* **45**
   - *männlicher* **45**
   - *rührender* **45**
   - *unreiner* **45**
   - *weiblicher* **45**
Reimschema **45**
   - *Kreuzreim* **46**
   - *Paarreim* **45**
   - *Schweifreim* **46**
   - *umarmender Reim* **46**
Reinigung/catharsis (effect of tragedy) **107**
reliable narrator **70**, 72
repetition
   (narrative) **22**, 23, 25, 27, 38, 43, 75, 78
repressed, return of the **138**
Requisiten/props **115**
reversal (of action in drama) 106, 108, 113
rhetorical forms (see also figurative
   language) 30-41
rhyme, ~ scheme **45-46**
   - alternate **46**
   - end **45**
   - envelope pattern **46**
   - eye- 28, **45**
   - feminine **45**
   - half- **45**
   - identical **45**
   - imperfect/impure **45**
   - internal **45**
   - masculine **45**
   - oblique **45**
   - perfect/pure **45**
   - rhyming couplet **45**
   - slant **45**
   - tail **46**
   - triple **45**
return of the repressed **138**

Rhys, Jean (*Wide Sargasso Sea*) 82
rhythm/*Rhythmus* 21-26, 30-31, **41-43**, 111
- sprung ....**.43**
Richardson, Samuel (*Pamela, or Virtue
    Rewarded*) 66
Robinson Crusoe (Daniel Defoe) 64
Roman ....**.63**
romance 5, **84-85**
romantic/ism 6, 15-17, 25, 31, 48, 108-09
Romeo and Juliet (William Shakespeare) 111
round character ....**.88**
Rückgriff ....**.78**
rührender Reim/identical rhyme ....**.45**
run-on line/*Zeilensprung* **42-43**

Said, Edward 170
Sandburg, Carl ("Chicago") 39
Satzfigur/scheme **31**, 38
Saussure, Ferdinand de **145-146**
scan/*skandieren* ....**.42**
scene
    (narrative) 63, 67, **77**
    (drama) 111, 114
Schauplatz **79, 115**
Scheme/*Satzfigur* (figures of speech) **31, 38**
The School for Scandal (Richard
    Brinsley Sheridan) 100-101
Schweifreim/tail rhyme ....**.46**
secondary text/*Nebentext* (in drama) ....**.96**
"The Second Coming" (William Butler
    Yeats) 36
selection (of paradigms) **146**, 148
self and other **141, 164-165**, 166, 168, 170
Seligmann, Kurt (*Das Ultra-Möbelstück*) 31
semiotics **145**
sentimental 5, **15**, 31
sestet/*Sextett* **48**
setting 5, 63, **80**, 115-17
Shaffer, Peter (*Black Comedy*) 115
Shakespeare, William 103
- *As You Like It* 96, 98, 108
- *Hamlet* 140
- *King Lear* 102-03, 107
- *Macbeth* 152
- *Midsummer Night's Dream* 114
- *Romeo and Juliet* 111
- "Sonnet 12" 42
- "Sonnet 20" 38
Shelley, Percy Bysshe 22, 49
- *A Defence of Poetry* 22
- "Ozymandias" 49
Sheridan, Richard Brinsley (*The School
    for Scandal*) 100-101
Shklovsky, Viktor 146-147
short story ....**.78**
Showalter, Elaine 164
showing **67**, 73, 75-76
Sidney, Sir Philip 4

sign
    (drama) **97-98**, **112**
signification, signifier/*Signifikant,
    Signifikat*/signified **145**, **150-151**
simile **31**-32
skandieren/scan ....**.42**
slant rhyme ....**.45**
Smith, Zadie (*White Teeth*) 171
social structure (of characters in drama) **81**
soliloquy **102**
sonnet/*Sonett*
    - English 8, **27**, **48-49**
    - Italian **48**
"Sonnet 12" (William Shakespeare) 42
"Sonnet 20" (William Shakespeare) 38
"Song" (John Donne) 42
"Song of Myself" (Walt Whitman) 44
sound (in poetry) 21, 25, 43-45
speaker (in poetry) **21-30**
Spivak, Gayatri Chakravorty 169, 171
Spondäus/spondee ....**.42**
spondaic, spondee ....**.42**
sprung rhythm ....**.43**
Spur (trace) **151**
stage 95-99, 104-105, 110, **115-117**
    - apron **116**
    - pageant **116**
    - picture frame **117-118**
    - proscenium 104, **116**
Standpunkt ....**.69**
Stanton, Domna C. 166
stanza 25-26, 43, **45-48**
    - ballad stanza **46**
    - couplet 8, 45-**46, 48**
    - octett **48**
    - ottava rima **48**
    - quatrain 27, **46**, 48
    - sestett **48**
    - tercet 8, **46**, 48
    - terza rima **46**
    - triplet **46**
Stanzel, Franz K. 63, 69, 73
Steigerung 113
Sterne, Laurence (*Tristram Shandy*) 77-78, 85
Stimme (see also dialogic, double-
    voiced discourse) ....**.26**
Stimmung ....**.26**
Stoker, Bram (*Dracula*) 13
story **59-86**, 113
storytelling **60-61**, 70
story time **77**
strand of action 63, **83**, 115
Straßenballade **46**
stream-of-consciousness **76**
street ballad **46**
stress (in metre) **41-42**
stretch **77**
Strophe/stanza **45**

Strophenformen
 - *Balladenstrophe* **46**
 - *Terzett* **46**
 - *Terzine* **46**
 - *Quartett* **46**
 - *Zweizeiler* **46**
structuralism **145**
structure of action **81**
structure of perspectives **81**
Struktur des Personals **111**
subaltern **171**
subconscious 67, 81, 108
subjectivity 24-25, 30, 51
sub-plot **114**
"The Sun Rising" (John Donne) 38
symbol **35-37**
symbolic order **141**
synecdoche **33**
syntax
 (schemes/*Wortfiguren*) 12, **38**, 41, 44
szenische Darstellung **77**

tail rhyme/*Schweifreim* **46**
Talking It Over (Julian Barnes) 72, 78
telling................................**67, 73**
tenor (of a metaphor) **32**
tercet/*Terzett* **46**
terza rima/*Terzine* **46**
tetrameter **42-43**, 46
textimmanente Lektüre **144**
theatre
 - anti-illusionist **110**
 - experimental **110**
 - illusionist **110**
 - non-illusionist **110**
theatrical communication **97**
third-person narrator/narrative **85**
"Three Blind Mice" **23**, 230-231
time in drama **119**
time in narrative **76-77**
 - discourse time/narrative time/
 Erzählzeit **77**
 - ellipsis **77**
 - pause **77**
 - story time/narrated time/*erzählte Zeit* ..**77**
 - stretch **77**
Tölpel **108**
tone 97, 108, **111**
To the Lighthouse (Virginia Woolf) 75-76
totum pro parte (Synecdoche) **33**
trace/*Spur* **151**
tragedy 98, **106-108**
tragic hero **107**
transcultural **172-173**
Tremain, Rose ("My Wife is a
 White Russian") 90, 228-229
trimeter **42,** 46
triple rhyme **45**

triplet **46**
Tristram Shandy (Laurence Sterne) 77-78, 85
Trochäus, trochaic, trochee **42**
trope/*Tropus* **31**, 34, 37
"The Tyger" (William Blake) 38
type (in characterisation) 81, 106, 108-109

Überbau/super-structure **155**
Über-Ich/super-ego **137**
Ulysses (James Joyce) 68, 76
uncanny/*unheimlich* **139**, 166
Uncle Sam (as an example of
 personification) 34
unconscious/subconscious **137-139**
understatement **37**
uneigentliche Sprache **30**
unheimlich **139**
unities, three 114-**115**
unreliable narrator **70,** 72
unzuverlässiger Erzähler **70,** 72

variable focalisation **72**
vehicle (of a metaphor) **32**
verborgener Erzähler/covert narrator **69**
Verdichtung **139**
verisimilitude/ *Wahrscheinlichkeit* **115**
verfremden/*defamiliarise* **147**
Vergleich **31**
Verschiebung/displacement **139**
verse **22**, 24-25, **41-44**
Versfuß/foot **42**
Versmaß/metre **41**
verse paragraphs **43-44**, 46
Victorian period **15-17**
vieldeutig/ambiguous **9**
Vierheber **42**
voice in narrative **68-69**, 75
 - in poetry 24-**26**
 - in theatre **105**
Volksballade **46**
Volpone (Ben Jonson) 109, 114
Vorausdeutung **78**
Vorderbühne **116**
Vorwissen **12**

Wahrscheinlichkeit/verisimilitude **115**
Waiting for Godot (Samuel Beckett) 102, 113
Walpole, Horace (*The Castle of Otranto*) 14
War of the Worlds (H.G. Wells) 4
Wasserstein, Wendy (*The Heidi
 Chronicles*) 120
weiblicher Reim **45**
Wells, H.G. (*War of the Worlds*) 4
werkimmanent/intrinsic 143
Wheatley, Phillis ("On being brought
 from Africa to America") **37-38**,
 160-161, 174-175, 179, 231-232
"The White House" (Claude McKay) 49

Whitman, Walt ("Song of Myself") 43-44
"The Wicked Stepmother's Tale"
  (Sara Maitland) 82
Widersacher/antagonist **112**
Wide Sargasso Sea (Jean Rhys) 82
Wilde, Oscar 40, 110, 112-113
- The Importance of Being Earnest ...112-113
Wilder, Thornton (Our Town) 104
Williams, Raymond 159
Williams, William Carlos ("The Locust
  Tree in Flowers") 44
Winnie the Pooh (A. A. Milne) 13
wit 100, **108-109**
The Woman in White (Wilkie Collins) 72
Woolf, Virginia 76, 164
- To the Lighthouse 75-76
word scenery **116**
- "I wandered lonely as a cloud"/
"Daffodils" 34-35
- "Preface to Lyrical Ballads" 25

- "She dwelt among the untrodden
  ways" 28-29
Wortspiel **32**
writerly **154**
Wyatt, Sir Thomas 48

Yeats, William Butler ("The Second
  Coming") 36-37
"The Yellow Wallpaper" (Charlotte
  Perkins Gilman) 70-71

Zäsur/caesura **42**
Zeilensprung/run-on line **42**
Zeilenstil/stichomythia **42**
Zeit
  - dehnung **77**
  - raffung **77**
zero focalisation **72**, 74
zuverlässiger Erzähler/reliable narrator ...**70**, 72
Zweizeiler/rhyming couplet **46**

Acknowledgements

Fig. 2.1, Ezra Pound. © Tullio Pericoli. Fig. 2.3, William Wordsworth by Benjamin Robert Haydon. © National Portrait Gallery, London. Fig. 2.4, T.S. Eliot. © Tullio Pericoli. Fig. 2.5, Kurt Seligmann: Das Ultra-Möbelstück (1938), © VG Bild-Kunst, Bonn 2007. Fig. 2.8, Armes Amerika. Illustration von Wieslaw Smetek in Die Zeit 34 vom 14. August 2003. Fig. 2.9, Edgar Allan Poe. © Tullio Pericoli. Fig. 2.10, William Butler Yeats. © Hulton Archive. Fig. 2.12, William Blake, "The Tyger". This item is reproduced by permission of L, RB 54039. © The Huntington Library, San Marino, California. Fig 2.13, Walt Whitman. © Hulton Archive. Fig. 3.4, James Joyce. © Tullio Pericoli. Fig. 3.9, Chinua Achebe. © Ekko von Schwichow. Fig. 3.10, Virginia Woolf. © Tullio Pericoli. Fig. 3.12, Charlotte Brontë. © The Brontë Society. Fig. 3.14, Ernest Hemingway. © Tullio Pericoli. Fig. 4.5, Samuel Beckett. © Tullio Pericoli. Fig. 4.6, William Shakespeare. © Tullio Pericoli. Fig. 4.8, King Lear 1985 Berlin. Foto: Ruth Walz. Fig. 4.10, Oscar Wilde. © Tullio Pericoli. Fig. 4.12, Benjamin Jonson by Abraham van Blyenberch. © National Portrait Gallery, London. Fig. 4.13, Peter Shaffer. © Topix. Fig. 4.14, Reconstruction of the Swan teatre, built in 1592 for about 3000 spectators, in: Richard Leacroft: The Development of the English Playhouse. Methuen Publishing Limited. Fig. 4.15 Reconstruction of the Cockpit in Court, built in 1629-30, in: Richard Leacroft: The Development of the English Playhouse. Methuen Publishing Limited. Fig. 4.16, The Empire Music Hall, Newcastle, built in 1891, in: Simon Trussler; The Cambridge Illustrated History of British Theatre. Cambridge: Cambridge University Press 1994, p. 249. Fig. 4.17, Eugene O'Neill, 1929. © Carlotta Monterey O'Neill, 1955. Fig. 5.2, Sigmund Freud. © Tullio Pericoli. Fig. 5.3, René Magritte: La clef des songes. © VG Bild-Kunst Bonn, 2007. Fig. 5.4, Karl Marx. © Tullio Pericoli. Fig. 6.1, Calvin and Hobbes © 1993 Watterson. Reprinted with permission of Universal Press Syndicate. All rights reserved. Fig. 6.2, © Sepp Buchegger. Fig. 6.3, Riassunto (1982). © Tullio Pericoli. Fig. 6.5, aus: Kurt Nagel: Erfolg durch effizientes Arbeiten, Entscheiden, Vermitteln und Lernen. München: Oldenbourg ³ 1988, p. 81.

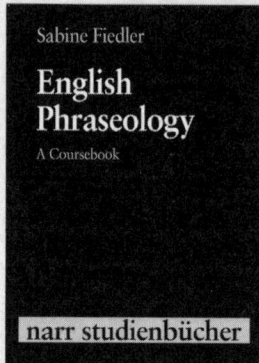

Sabine Fiedler

English Phraseology

A Coursebook

narr studienbücher
2007, 198 Seiten,
€[D] 19,90/Sfr 33,80
ISBN 978-3-8233-6338-5

This book introduces students of English to one of the most fascinating and at the same time most difficult parts of language: Phraseology. Commonly known as phrases and idioms, phraseological units are fascinating because of their colourful authenticity and the insight they provide into a language community's culture and history. Due to their frequently unpredictable meanings and their connotations these units are problematic, especially for foreign learners. The book was conceived for university classes as a coursebook with exercises, but it can also be used for self-study. It familiarizes readers with the key concepts in phraseology research and examines the behaviour and functions of phraseological units in discourse. With more than 200 examples drawn from a wide variety of written and spoken sources (including, above all, literary texts, newspapers, advertisements, comics, and films), the book illustrates the significant role that phraseology plays in the English language.

Narr Francke Attempto Verlag GmbH + Co. KG
Postfach 25 60 · D-72015 Tübingen · Fax (0 7071) 97 97-11
Internet: www.narr.de · E-Mail: info@narr.de

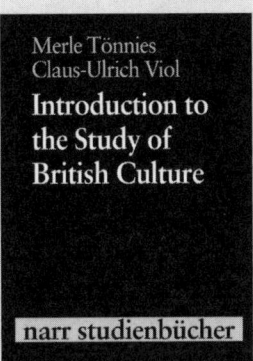

Merle Tönnies /
Claus Ulrich Viol

Introduction to the Study of British Culture

narr studienbücher
2007, IV, 314 Seiten, div. Abb.
EUR 24,90 / SFr 41,70
ISBN 978-3-8223-6126-8

This book aims at giving students a comprehensive and comprehensible overview of the main theories, methods, and fields of interest of British cultural studies. Taking the city and the university of Oxford and their manifold cultural meanings as a case study, the book covers issues of representation, identity, ethnicity, class, gender, and (new) cultural geography.

Combining the functions of a primary text reader and a conventional textbook, this innovative volume will help students to derive analytical tools from the theory excerpts and to test their own approaches to the various forms of cultural texts against these theories. Throughout, texts and images are introduced by short explanatory passages and accompanied by suggestions for a step-by-step analysis and further reading, which makes the collection suitable for BA as well as MA students.

Narr Francke Attempto Verlag GmbH + Co. KG
Postfach 2560 · D-72015 Tübingen · Fax (07071) 9797-11
Internet: www.narr.de · E-Mail: info@narr.de

UTB Anglistik

Vera Nünning (Hrsg.)

Kulturgeschichte der englischen Literatur

Von der Renaissance bis zur Gegenwart

UTB 2663 M, 2005, X, 346 Seiten, 40 Abb., € 22,90/SFr 40,10
UTB-ISBN 3-8252-2663-8

Dieses Buch stellt ein Novum in der Literaturgeschichtsschreibung dar – eine Geschichte der englischen Literatur in einem Band, die literarische Werke nicht nur beschreibt, sondern zusätzlich in ihren Wechselbeziehungen zur Kultur erörtert. Die Geschichte der englischen Literatur aus kulturwissenschaftlicher Perspektive kommt dem Orientierungsbedürfnis von Studierenden entgegen, die in Lehrplänen und Fachliteratur immer wieder mit der kulturwissenschaftlichen Neuorientierung der Literaturwissenschaft konfrontiert werden, ohne bislang die Möglichkeit zu haben, sich in kompakter Form einen Überblick über das neue Feld zu verschaffen. Um Studienanfängern die Orientierung zu erleichtern, wurde jeder Epoche eine knappe Einführung vorangestellt, in der die wichtigsten Tendenzen der Zeit skizziert, und die folgenden Kapitel in einem größeren Zusammenhang verortet werden. Diese kurzen Überblicke liefern einen Aufriss der bedeutendsten Entwicklungen der Epoche.

Preisänderungen vorbehalten

A. Francke

Narr Studienbücher

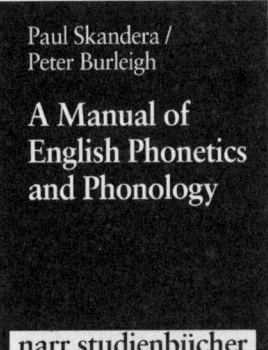

Paul Skandera /
Peter Burleigh

A Manual of
English Phonetics
and Phonology

narr studienbücher

Peter Burleigh / Paul Skandera

A Manual of
English Phonetics
and Phonology

narr studienbücher, 2005, X, 169 Seiten +
Audio CD, € 19,90/SFR 34,90
ISBN 3-8233-6125-2

A Manual of English Phonetics and Phonology is intended for students
of English language in undergraduate university courses in the German-speaking region. It is entirely self-explanatory and requires no prior
knowledge of linguistics.

The book starts with a short overview over the various branches of
linguistics and locates phonetics and phonology in this context. As the
Manual progresses, terminology and knowledge are advanced in a carefully staged manner.

It is divided into 12 lessons and exercises which can easily be managed
in a university term. Special attention is given to areas the authors have
experienced as challenging for students, such as the difference
between phonetics and phonology, inconsistencies in terminology, and
different transcription conventions.

The *Manual* combines an introduction to the theory of phonetics and
phonology with the practice of transcription. Exercises at the end of
each lesson give students the opportunity to put the theory into practice
and constitute a fully integrated course in phonetic transcription. All
spoken texts are provided on an accompanying CD.

Thus *A Manual of English Phonetics and Phonology* presents the teacher with a valuable class-ready resource, and the student with a stimulating, attainable, and insightful introduction to the study of phonetics
and phonology.

 **Narr Francke Attempto Verlag**
Postfach 2567 · D-72015 Tübingen · Fax (07071) 75288